DAILY PRAISE

DAILY PRAISE

A Daily Devotional
of
Singing Scripture and Praise Psalms

Written, Edited and Compiled by Ed Lyman

Cover Art: This painting is dedicated to my father

Edward P. Lyman, Jr.

Painted in the Renaissance Manner by *Talin* 1989

Revival Press

Worship and Praise Division
of
Destiny Image Publishers
P.O. Box 351
Shippensburg, PA 17257

ISBN 1-56043-701-4

For Worldwide Distribution
Printed in the U.S.A.

DEDICATION

Dedicated to my wife, Julie, and my daughters, Talin and Auri.

CONTENTS

FOREWORD

It has been said that "Praise is the key that unlocks the storehouse of God's blessing" — and to begin each day in the major key of praise is the unique privilege of every child of God.

To enable and encourage us in this daily practice, my good friend, Ed Lyman, has put together what he has called the "Singing Scriptures and Praise Psalms" in a single volume entitled *DAILY PRAISE*.

Featuring a verse for each day of the year, these vignettes of musical inspiration and commentary on Biblical musical themes will bring fresh meaning and added joy to your moments of meditation and praise.

DAILY PRAISE was born out of Ed's intense love for the 'music of life' and his God-given ability — developed to a masterful fine degree — to share his love for the Savior in song and spoken word with the peoples of the world. Containing fresh inspirational insight and personal experience, along with those of other "fellow pilgrims" along the way, *DAILY PRAISE* will bring to your heart and spirit a new source of rich blessing, devotion and thanksgiving from God's unlimited storehouse.

It will be a useful tool as well for Pastors, Youth Workers, Church Musicians, in providing fresh insights and personal application to scriptural truths on praise and worship.

I commend this devotional gem to you that will better enable us to "DAILY PRAISE" our wonderful Lord — to celebrate His abundant goodness — and to joyfully sing of His righteousness.

Cliff Barrows

INTRODUCTION

As you await the downbeat to join this symphony of DAILY PRAISE, think of yourself as "an instrument of ten strings."

"...Unto . . . an instrument of ten strings will I sing praises unto Thee" (Psalm 144:9).

An elderly gentleman at a midweek service offered this prayer: "Oh, Lord, we will praise Thee; we will praise Thee with an instrument of ten strings."

Those in attendance wondered what he meant, but understood as he continued to talk to the Lord. "We will praise Thee with our two eyes by looking only unto Thee. We will exalt Thee with our two ears by listening only to Thy voice. We will honor Thee with our own two hands by working in Thy service. We will honor Thee with our own two feet by walking in the way of Thy statutes. We will magnify Thee with our tongues by bearing testimony to Thy loving kindness. We will worship Thee with our hearts by loving only Thee. We thank Thee for this instrument, Lord, keep it in tune. Play upon it as Thou wilt and ring out the melodies of Thy grace! May its harmonies always express Thy glory!"

When the Apostle Paul wrote to the Romans, he said, "...Yield yourselves unto God, as those that are alive from the dead, and your members as instruments of righteousness unto God" (Romans 6:13). Then he challenged them to "...present your bodies a living sacrifice, holy, acceptable unto God." He was exhorting each believer — then and now — to praise God on his "instrument of ten strings!"

James H. Blackstone, Jr.

January

DAILY PRAISE

January 1

SINGING SCRIPTURE: **Psalm 104:33**

I will sing unto the Lord as long as I live: I will sing praise to my God while I have my being.

For a number of years I sang the leading role in the annual Arabian Nights Musicals held at the Riverside County Fair in Indio, California.

When the first strains of the haunting music wafted across the desert of Southern California, the crowds waited for the stage to come alive and transport them into the fantasy of the "Tales of the Arabian Nights."

The arc-lights pierced the darkness. The stage blazed with the splendor of ancient palaces and markets of that storybook desert empire.

I thrilled each time I stepped onto the scene and was soon caught up in the romance, intrigue, and pageantry of the musical stories.

Life is much like such a production. We all make an entrance on life's stage and soon are caught up in the problems and joys of living.

As performers and performances are judged in these musicals, the performances of life are also judged, and this judgment is done by God.

Our lives should be spent in solos and choruses of praise to God, daily.

Ed Lyman

January 2

SINGING SCRIPTURE: **Psalm 98:1**

O sing unto the Lord a new song; for he hath done marvelous things: his right hand, and his holy arm, have gotten him the victory.

On every continent I've had the privilege of leading choirs and congregations in the singing of songs of praise and witness to the love and testimony of the Lord Jesus Christ. Grand old hymns of the church, together with some of the newer songs of praise and faith, have struck a deep, responsive note in the hearts and lives of countless numbers of people. As "Bev" Shea and the Crusade choirs have blended their voices in glorifying Christ, the Spirit of God has prepared the way for the impact of the gospel message. Often, after the meetings, it has been thrilling to hear homeward-bound groups singing these songs, bringing new sounds to the streets of New York, the subways of London, buses in Germany, and the paths of Africa.

Every great moving of God's Spirit has been accompanied by the songs of the redeemed, and rightly so. Through these songs, "The Lord hath made known his salvation: his righteousness hath he openly showed" (v. 2).

I don't know how many times I've heard Billy Graham say how important it is to have the proper message presented in the music, as it is the key to the door of the heart, and through it we have seen the hand of God at work in a "marvelous" way.

As you join in singing favorite songs of praise, may you too be refreshed and blessed and drawn into an even-closer walk with Him — "speaking to yourselves in psalms and hymns and spiritual songs, singing and making melody in your heart to the Lord" (Ephesians 5:19).

Cliff Barrows

January 3

SINGING SCRIPTURE: **James 5:13**

Is any among you afflicted? let him pray. Is any merry? let him sing psalms.

Netzahuacoyotl is the antithesis of the picture-postcard Mexican village. Unpaved streets, strewn with uncollected refuse, punctuated with potholes, wend their way through the labyrinth of deprivation in this suburb on the outer fringe of Ciudad de Mexico.

Into this scene we stepped. The people were excited. In the midst of this place of poverty and crime, a tiny group of believers decided to involve themselves at significant personal sacrifice in an effort to present the gospel of Christ to their neighbors. They had prayed and worked together in spite of social and financial affliction. Anticipating, by faith, God's blessing, they rented a bull-fighting arena for their evangelistic crusade and paid the cost by selling tortillas, beans, rice, and spicy meat at the nightly gatherings.

Their spirits were merry long before the meetings began, and in happiness their songs of praise and thanksgiving were raised. "Behold, we count them happy which endure" (James 5:11).

Although an epidemic of bronchial flu and continuous traffic jams threatened to keep us from the services, night after night the sound of singing welcomed us to the arena. The message of salvation was presented. The people responded to the invitation to trust Jesus Christ as Savior. These Mexican believers were afflicted by meagre finances, undue criticism, and less than commodious circumstances, but theirs was the victory and the joy.

If you are bothered to the point of discouragement by unbelievers or legalistic, Christian critics, pray for patience. The joy that follows calls for a song of praise. That's a fact of faith.

Ed Lyman

January 4

SINGING SCRIPTURE: **Psalm 9:13,14**

Have mercy upon me, O Lord; consider my trouble which I suffer of them that hate me, thou that liftest me up from the gates of death: That I may show forth all thy praise in the gates of the daughter of Zion: I will rejoice in thy salvation.

We dream great dreams of victory for ourselves which sometimes come to nothing. Discouragement shrivels the soul. A disappointed person may try to hide his letdown, but it can dominate the mind of a Christian and rob him of joy.

Probably the greatest burden we can bear is self-will. It's the heaviest of all to carry. If everything we are and have is not wholly in His hands, we are in the position of fighting the Holy Spirit. Nothing is more wearisome than trying to live the Christian life while indulging the flesh, perhaps in a hidden area of our existence.

Coming to Christ and bearing His yoke may seem like separate steps, but they are really one. One cannot be a believer without being a disciple. Every saint is meant to be a soldier. Salvation and sanctification are inseparable. Jesus Himself wore a yoke. He invites us to share a yoke that He Himself bears — "my yoke." What is the yoke of Jesus? It is the yoke of utter surrender to the will of God. Only this yoke is bearable, the one custom-made by the hand of the Master Craftsman.

Sing in surrender today, "Lord, I accept Your yoke today; it's the one You made for me. I'm content because Your love can never shape a wrong yoke for me."

Robert P. Evans

January 5

SINGING SCRIPTURE: Habakkuk 3:19

The Lord God is my strength, and he will make my feet like hinds' feet, and he will make me to walk upon mine high places.

In talking about a watermelon seed, William Jennings Bryan said, "Under the influence of sunshine and shower, that little seed had taken off its coat and gone to work; it has gathered from somewhere two hundred thousand times its own weight, and forced that enormous weight through a tiny stem and built a watermelon. On the outside, it had put a covering of green, within that a rind of white and within that a core of red — and then it had scattered through the red, little seeds, each one capable of doing that same work over again. What architect drew the plan? Where did that little watermelon seed get its tremendous strength? Where did it find its flavoring extract and its coloring matter? How did it build a watermelon? Until you can explain a watermelon, do not be too sure you can set limits to the power of the Almighty, or tell just what He would do, or how He would do it. The most learned man in the world cannot explain a watermelon but the most ignorant man can eat a watermelon and enjoy it. God has given us the knowledge necessary to use those things, and the truth that He has revealed to us is infinitely more important for our welfare than it would be to understand the mysteries that He has seen fit to conceal from us."

The heart of a Christian sings as he thrills to the glory of God in creation. The song of the singing heart is one of praise and appreciation for the God who has so wonderfully given us of His bounty.

Ed Lyman

January 6

SINGING SCRIPTURE: **Psalm 147:7**

Sing unto the Lord with thanksgiving; sing praise upon the harp unto our God.

An elderly lady, whose age was apparent in her complexion and stance, was asked what kind of beauty aid she used. With a chuckle and the sparkle of youth in her eyes, she commented that it was probably God's brand. "I use for my lips, truth; I use for my voice, kindness; I use for my eyes, compassion; I use for my hands, charity; I use for my figure, uprightness; I use for my heart, love; I use for any who do not like me, prayer."

These aren't advertised on TV, nor will they be found on the counters of department stores. They are found in a close relationship with the Lord. When we work with "God's brand" of beauty aid, the harmonies given to us through our closeness to God remain when the discords about us seem to drown all other sound. So we can sing with thanksgiving as we journey on the way He prepares for us.

Ed Lyman

January 7

SINGING SCRIPTURE: **Hebrews 2:11,12**

For both he that sanctifieth and they who are sanctified are all of one: for which cause he is not ashamed to call them brethren, saying, I will declare thy name unto my brethren, in the midst of the church will I sing praise unto thee.

"But we see Jesus, who was made a little lower than the angels for the suffering of death, crowned with glory and honor; that he by the grace of God should taste death for every man" (Hebrews 2:9). This is the key to the relationship the believer shares not only with others of like faith, but with the Living Lord Himself. We are all one in Christ! It took the sacrificial suffering of the Savior in this supreme act of salvation to provide the only means by which man can retrieve that which he had previously irretrievably lost through rebellion and transgression. By way of suffering, Jesus Christ entered into His own glory; and by doing so, He opened the way by which we who believe can share His glory as sons of God and joint-heirs with Him.

"Looking unto Jesus the author and finisher of our faith; who for the joy that was set before him endured the cross, despising the shame, and is set down at the right hand of the throne of God" (Hebrews 12:2). The Greek word used for "author" may also be translated "pioneer." It is the description of one who is an originator, whose presence itself means benefit to everyone, but whose absence means the nonexistence of any benefits for anyone. Only because of His sacrifice on the cross is it possible for the Lord Jesus Christ to reveal God the Father to those who have trusted Him as their own personal Savior. Hebrews 2:12 is a quotation from Psalm 22, which foreshadows the crucifixion of Christ, the Son of God. It is remarkable that the Lord Himself says He will sing praise unto God, and He will do it in the midst of the church He has founded among us, His brethren.

Roy W. Gustafson

January 8

SINGING SCRIPTURE: **Exodus 15:21**

And Miriam answered them, Sing ye to the Lord, for he hath triumphed gloriously: the horse and his rider hath he thrown into the sea.

The Scriptures give many examples of God's people exalting Him and praising Him. There are also many injunctions to sing unto the Lord. Every victory, every provision, every blessing was occasion to praise Him for His goodness.

In this instance, God gave glorious national deliverance from bondage and slavery. This brought forth a tremendous volume of praise and thanksgiving.

Today God is still giving deliverance to those who put their trust in him.

Many of the great oratorical works of all time have as their central theme Christ and His redemptive work. Whether in poetry, painting, sculpture, or architecture, men and women with great gifts have often dedicated them to the praise of the Lord because of His greatness.

When we sing unto the Lord, we give witness to our faith in Him. Perhaps the unredeemed will hear and want to know what it is all about.

Norman Clayton

January 9

PRAISE PSALM: **Psalm 9:1**

I will praise thee, O Lord, with my whole heart; I will shew forth all thy marvelous works.

"I will praise." This is a conscious, volitional exercise. Living in a time-space continuum, we see life in terms of actions following causes or purposes. As we grow in the Lord, our praise becomes a natural extension of our Christian experience. God's actions too are the visible manifestation of Himself.

God doesn't just *do* salvation. He *is* salvation.

God doesn't just *give* justice. He *is* justice.

God doesn't just *send* good news. He *is* good news.

His activity is His nature.

He keeps His word because He *is* the Word. Because He kept His word to Abraham, He must keep His word to us.

In Galatians 3, we find the promise which God gave Abraham has "come on the Gentiles" through Jesus Christ. In light of this, as *believers* we should be *behavers*.

"I will praise." This activity of praise becomes song, and it follows that the nature of the believer's song is praise.

Ed Lyman

January 10

SINGING SCRIPTURE: **1 Chronicles 16:37, 39, 42**

So he left there the ark of the covenant of the Lord Asaph and his brethren, to minister before the ark continually, as everyday's work required ... and Zadok the priest, and his brethren the priests, before the tabernacle of the Lord in the high place that was at Gibeon ... And with them Heman and Jeduthun with trumpets and cymbals for those who should make a sound, and with the musical instruments of God. And the sons of Jeduthun were porters.

At this time in the history of Israel, David brought the ark of God to Jerusalem, and this divided the ancient tabernacle, which was left at Gibeon, from the ark, which was now in the city of David. Asaph, who wrote Psalms 50 and 73 through 83, ministered in music before the ark. Heman, with the priests, presented the music of thanksgiving and praise before the tabernacle. Until the Temple was later built in Jerusalem by Solomon, this presented some rearrangement of traditional worship patterns. However, here again we are clearly told of the importance of music in the total worship experience of God's people. Its purpose was neither to fill up empty space between phases of the worship service, nor was it to be merely an exercise in the production of "good" choral and instrumental presentations. The presence of musicians in the worship and praise of the Lord before the ark and in the tabernacle was to direct the diverse thoughts of the congregation toward God in thanksgiving and adoration.

The musicians prepared for the work of worship by perfecting their talents for praise and taking time to produce the kind of songs which would testify to those within earshot about the love, majesty, and salvation of God.

It has been said, "When we play football, we want to make a touchdown. When we play baseball, we want to hit a home run. When we play basketball, we want to be high-point man. But on the Lord's team we don't even want to practice!"

Ed Lyman

January 11

SINGING SCRIPTURE: **Psalm 149:1**

Praise ye the Lord. Sing unto the Lord a new song, and praise in the congregation of saints.

Many people bear testimonies to the fact that at some time or other something of a particular spiritual nature happened, which meant a great deal to them. It may have been an experience of a certain significance or a blessing in the past.

These testimonies, wonderful though they may be, are sometimes the only ones given by these people, and they may be told over and over again to the same group of church members. By such constant repetition, such experiences have become stale.

If we have a close relationship with the Lord, as all Christians should, and look constantly to His leading and direction, we should have fresh experiences and renewed blessings.

The singer of this verse was saying that we should not let our songs or praise become mechanical.

As a result of our Christian experiences, we should praise God with the vitality and joy of newfound blessings, blessings we receive daily.

This same freshness in our experiences should carry over into our fellowship with other believers in Christ.

Harold DeCou

January 12

SINGING SCRIPTURE: **1 Thessalonians 5:16**

Rejoice evermore.

This second shortest verse in God's Word interestingly has a strong relationship to the shortest verse in the Bible: "Jesus wept" (John 11:35). How can a verse which has to do with joyfulness as it may be expressed in glad songs possibly relate to the sadness of the Lord Jesus Christ? Let's take a look.

Jesus had purposely stayed away from Bethany, where his friend, Lazarus, lived and was reported to be sick. Arriving finally on the scene, Jesus is confronted with the fact that not only had Lazarus died, but his body had already been in the grave for four days. Jesus openly wept, and those present said, "Behold how he loved him."

In a very human way, the Lord of creation shared his compassion and love for His creatures. Requesting the stone covering the entrance of the tomb to be removed, Jesus prayed, "Father, I thank thee that thou hast heard me. And I knew that thou hearest me always: but because of the people which stand by I said it, that they may believe that thou hast sent me."

After this, he shouted, "Lazarus, come forth." The moans of mourning and the mumbling of lamentations ceased as the once-dead man walked out of the tomb. This is what revival is all about. It is the quickening (making alive) of what is already there. Only the living can express joy in song! The reaction to life is to rejoice evermore! Because Jesus became the Son of Man, we may become sons of God. His weeping has made us worthy to enter Heaven's gates.

Ed Lyman

January 13

PRAISE PSALM: **Psalm 22:25**

My praise shall be of thee in the great congregation: I will pay my vows before them that fear him.

In Psalm 111:10 we read, "The fear of the Lord is the beginning of wisdom." This fear is that kind of reverence for God which leads a person to obedience as a result of one's recognition of God's power as well as God's love to man.

Although we cannot prove scientifically that God exists, we would be blind indeed if we did not realize that in this world there are a great many signposts that point in the direction of God. The world is filled with signposts *to* God, but there are no signposts *away* from God that cannot be adequately explained.

The Word of God says, "The heavens declare the glory of God." The heavens do not prove God's existence, but as we look at the sky on a clear night and see the myriad of stars shedding their light upon the world, as we glory in the golden path of the harvest moon, and as we bask under the brilliance of the summer sun, our hearts naturally respond and say, "God!"

If we cannot prove the existence of God scientifically, but the signposts point definitely in the direction of God, how can we know God? That question can be answered in one word — *faith*. Such is our song of praise —inwardly and outwardly.

Paul B. Smith

January 14

SINGING SCRIPTURE: **Job 38:7**

...when the morning stars sang together, and all the sons of God shouted for joy?

A choir of stars?

Do you really believe that stars sing?

Maybe the motion-picture stars sing, but surely not the ones we see twinkling in the sky at night!

The Bible states, however, that when God created the world "the morning stars sang together."

From the time that verse was written until 1931, people have been puzzled every time they read those words. That year, the Bell Telephone Company had complaints of noise on the trans-Atlantic cable lines. Static often drowned out the voices.

Mr. Karl Jansky was asked by the company to find the cause of this difficulty. He mounted a rotating antenna on his automobile and traveled up and down the coast trying to find the cause of this noise. As he turned the antenna trying to sort out the different radio waves, he discovered that some of the noise was coming from the stars above him. He had found the singing of the stars.

Astronomers had for years looked through ordinary telescopes to find out more about the stars, but with this discovery they can explore the nature of stars by listening to them with radio telescopes. They have found that each star has its own particular voice or signal. Each is different from the other. Together they form a great and mighty choir in the heavens.

Ed Lyman

January 15

SINGING SCRIPTURE: **Zephaniah 3:14**

Sing, O daughter of Zion; shout, O Israel; be glad and rejoice with all the heart, O Israel; be glad and rejoice with all the heart, O daughter of Jerusalem.

God spoke through His prophet Zephaniah to give a message, an exhortation to His people Israel to *sing*, shout, be glad, and rejoice, for now their rebellion, haughtiness, and pride are over, and they have come in humility, trusting in the name of the Lord. The judgment was not past, and they were told they need fear no more!

God said their response should be to *sing*. This should also be the normal desire of the redeemed person, whether he is only able to chirp like a sparrow or warble like a songbird. This is the expression of true praise and thankfulness to God for all His benefits.

The importance of singing is indicated in 2 Chronicles 5. When the ark of the covenant was transferred from its temporary location to the Holy of Holies in the newly-finished temple, Solomon held a great ceremony. A male chorus dressed in finespun linen robes sang, standing on the east side of the altar. The choir was accompanied by 120 priests, who were trumpeters, while others played cymbals, lyres, and harps. The band and chorus united as one to praise and thank the Lord. Their theme was, "He is so good — so good! His lovingkindness lasts forever!"

Surely we who are redeemed, who have repented of our sins and received God's forgiveness through His Son, should voice our praise and thanksgiving with jubilant singing unto the Lord!

Merrill Dunlop

January 16

SINGING SCRIPTURE: **Psalm 147:1**

Praise ye the Lord: for it is good to sing praises unto our God; for it is pleasant; and praise is comely.

In the sprawling city of Tokyo, I had ordered my meal in the hotel dining room. As the waiter left my table, the lights dimmed somewhat and a spotlight focused upon a woman. She was dressed in a flowered silk kimono with a wide belt around her waist, her black hair piled high upon her head and held by a large comb, and her face powdered chalk-white. In her arms, she cradled a guitarlike instrument. She plucked the strings, and the resulting sound was a dissonance to my ears. Then she began to sing. The music was strange, as her voice seemed at first to be just a guttural mumble and then soared to high birdlike sounds.

As I sat there listening that evening, she continued to sing the ancient folk songs of the "Land of the Rising Sun." I became adjusted to the different harmonies and the pentatonic melodic patterns of the tunes.

Though the ears of my Western cultural experience caused me to feel somewhat uncomfortable at first, I reminded myself to listen as best I could apart from my traditional appreciation patterns. The more I heard, the more I began to realize that we often listen to music, appreciate art or poetry, and absorb spiritual truths only according to our comfortable traditions or experiences.

As we learn to praise God and listen for His leading, we begin to find beauty, reason, and appreciation for things which at first may be unappealing.

Ed Lyman

January 17

PRAISE PSALM: **Psalm 150:6**

Let every thing that hath breath praise the Lord. Praise ye the Lord.

This last verse of the Book of Psalms is a marvelous summary of the message of the book itself. Songs of praise to our Heavenly Father present a dynamic and exciting alternative — life — to the humdrum of mere existence.

Jesus said, "I am the door: by me if any man enter in, he shall be saved, and shall go in and out, and find pasture" (John 10:9).

"Let every thing that hath breath praise the Lord" for salvation. "I am the good shepherd; the good shepherd giveth his life for the sheep" (John 10:11).

Let every thing that hath breath praise the Lord" for freedom. "I am come that they might have life, and that they might have it more abundantly" (John 10:10).

Let every thing that hath breath praise the Lord" for supply. "I am the good shepherd, and know my sheep, and am known of mine" (John 10:14).

How marvelous, how wonderful!
And my song shall ever be:
How marvelous, how wonderful!
Is my Savior's love for me.

E. Barry Moore

January 18

SINGING SCRIPTURE: **1 Thessalonians 4:16, 17**

For the Lord himself shall descend from heaven with a shout, with the voice of the archangel, and with the trump of God: and the dead in Christ shall rise first: then we who are alive and remain shall be caught up together with them in the clouds, to meet the Lord in the air: and so shall we ever be with the Lord.

The trump of God brings a musical climax to life as we know it. It is also an exciting prelude to the "Hallelujah Chorus" to be sung by the redeemed as we praise the Lord God Omnipotent.

The Lord is to be "called Faithful and True, and in righteousness he doth judge" (Revelation 19:11). This is indicative of *His impartiality.*

"His eyes were as a flame of fire, and on his head were many crowns; and he had a name written, that no man knew, but he himself" (19:12). Here is the realization of *His inscrutability*; He cannot be searched or fathomed by human understanding.

Next, we find "he was clothed with a vesture dipped in blood: and his name is called The Word of God" (19:13), speaking of *His incarnation*. "In the beginning was the Word, and the Word was with God, and the Word was God.... And the Word was made flesh, and dwelt among us, (and we beheld his glory, the glory as of the only begotten of the Father), full of grace and truth" (John 1:1, 14).

We then fall in worship and adoration before *His Imperial Majesty.* "And he hath on his vesture and on his thigh a name written, KING OF KINGS, AND LORD OF LORDS" (19:16).

"And I heard, as it were the voice of a great multitude, and as the voice of many waters, and as the voice of mighty thunderings, saying, Alleluia: for the Lord God omnipotent reigneth" (Revelation 19:6).

Is the Lord presently reigning in your life?

Ed Lyman

January 19

SINGING SCRIPTURE: **2 Chronicles 20:22**

> *And when they began to sing and to praise, the Lord set ambushments against the children of Ammon, Moab, and mount Seir, which were come against Judah; and they were smitten.*

Jehoshaphat and his people exercised their faith in the Lord. The sounding of their songs of praise to God was the outward expression of their inner confidence that their victory was secure and that their dependence was upon the promise and power of Almighty God. This conviction was manifest in their music of praise. As the king and his people began to honor the Lord with their singing, God intervened on the battlefield. He set the enemy armies against each other to destroy themselves. They had lined up their troops in full battle array and success seemed certain. Judah's collapse appeared to be inevitable. Nothing could stand before this display of might, manpower, and material, but these enemies of Judah became confused and disoriented when God maneuvered behind their lines, dealing destruction and defeat.

"As goes its music, so goes a nation." The people of Judah were blessed by God as long as they looked to Him for their strength and sought to sing His praises before those around them. When the music of reverence and respect toward God began to stop in Judah and her people sought satisfaction in the worldly wealth and wisdom of paganism and idolatry, God gave them up.

William Fetler candidly warned Christians concerning their witness before the world when he said, "Only as the church fulfills her missionary obligation does she justify her existence."

Ed Lyman

January 20

SINGING SCRIPTURE: **Psalm 126:2**

Then was our mouth filled with laughter, and our tongue with singing: then said they among the heathen, the Lord hath done great things for them.

Do you know what strikes me as unusual about this verse? Look at it again. Do you notice that the mouth is not filled with singing — it's the tongue that is filled with singing? What does that say to you? It tells me that the act of singing should be intelligible and understandable. After all, what good is singing if it's not understood? And it is exactly at this point that I find I have a problem with some of today's Christian music. When the message of the song is obscured by the beat of the song, I find "caution" flags popping up in my head. The music is the vehicle upon which the message travels, and because of that, the message should move along unhindered.

Orchestral music and instrumental music are beautiful, but it is listened to for entirely another reason — not for its lyrical content. Instrumental music does not call a hearer to a place of decision, whereas music with a lyric does. Lyrics involve a person in much more than a pleasant listening experience. Christian lyrics involve a person in a narrative with the God of history. Christian lyrics call for a decision.

Secular songs make statements; gospel songs make believers.

What an awesome responsibility is ours as Christian musicians to present the gospel in song, that those who hear us will come face to face with God and say, "He has put a new song in my mouth." Lord, so be it!

Steve Musto

January 21

PRAISE PSALM: **Psalm 148 ("Creation's Praise Song")**

Praise ye the Lord. Praise ye the Lord from the heavens: praise him in the heights.
Praise ye him, all his angels; praise ye him, all his hosts.
Praise ye him, sun and moon; praise him, all ye stars of light.
Praise him, ye heavens of heavens, and ye waters that be above the heavens.
Let them praise the name of the Lord: for he commanded, and they were created.
He hath also established them for ever and ever: he hath made a decree which shall not pass.
Praise the Lord from the earth, ye dragons, and all deeps:
fire, and hail; snow, and vapor; stormy wind fulfilling his word:
mountains, and all hills; fruitful trees, and all cedars:
beasts, and all cattle; creeping things, and flying fowl:
kings of the earth, and all people; princes, and all judges of the earth;
Both young men and maidens; old men and children.
let them praise the name of the Lord: for his name alone is excellent;
his glory is above the earth and heaven.
He also exalteth the horn of his people, the praise of all his saints;
even of the children of Israel, a people near unto him.
Praise ye the Lord.

The Psalmist

January 22

SINGING SCRIPTURE: **Psalm 145:7**

They shall abundantly utter the memory of thy great goodness, and shall sing of thy righteousness.

Happy memories are among the most treasured possessions of all of us. Our school days and childhood adventures unfold through the eye of the mind like projections of motion pictures on a screen. We remember those special occasions when the whole family gathered for reunion. Memories of weddings, graduations, anniversaries, and birthdays become pages bound with love in the library of the mind.

Almost invariably, as we recount these experiences in the presence of loved ones and friends the nostalgic atmosphere which develop calls for singing together the old school songs, love songs, and fun ballads of days past.

The singing psalmist is here reminiscing about the goodness of God and the joy His people have shared as they walked in the light of God's love.

His heart is so filled with the pleasantness of these memories that he exclaims that he and his people shall constantly remind each other of the Lord's bountiful blessings, so their hearts will overflow with singing.

Our memories of salvation and blessings should cause us to sing of the righteousness of God and encourage each other to be faithful ambassadors.

Gordon L. Purdy

January 23

SINGING SCRIPTURE: **Exodus 20:18**

And all the people saw the thunderings, and the lightnings, and the noise of the trumpet, and the mountain smoking: and when the people saw it, they removed, and stood afar off.

The writer of Hebrews states that the believer no longer faces the Mountain of Sinai, which is the law, but he comes to Mount Zion, which is the gospel of Christ.

For ye are not come unto the mount that might be touched, and that burned with fire, nor unto blackness, and darkness, and tempest,
and the sound of a trumpet, and the voice of words; which voice they that heard entreated that the word should not be spoken to them any more:
(for they could not endure that which was commanded, And if so much as a beast touch the mountain, it shall be stoned, or thrust through with a dart:
and so terrible was the sight, that Moses said, I exceedingly fear and quake:)
but ye are come unto mount Zion, and unto the city of the

*living God, the heavenly Jerusalem, and to an innumerable
company of angels,
to the general assembly and church of the firstborn, which
are written in heaven, and to God the Judge of all, and to the
spirits of just men made perfect,
and to Jesus, the mediator of the new covenant, and to the
blood of sprinkling, that speaketh better things than that of
Abel (Hebrews 12:18-24).*

*Wherefore we receiving a kingdom which cannot be moved,
let us have grace, whereby we may serve God acceptably with
reverence and godly fear (Hebrews 12:28).*

Ed Lyman

January 24

SINGING SCRIPTURE: 1 Chronicles 15:27

*And David was clothed with a robe of fine linen, and all the
Levites that bare the ark, and the singers, and Chenaniah the
master of the song with the singers. David also had upon him
an ephod of linen.*

When there is a spirit of cooperation and a bond of unity among
believers, there is cause for rejoicing in song. The message of the
gospel of the Lord Jesus Christ is proclaimed and bears fruit. There
are jobs to be done and steps to follow in order for a harvest to be
produced. This is what Jesus says in John 4:37, "And herein is that
saying true, One soweth, and another reapeth."

The three-pronged program for unity used by Mao-Tse Tung
was:

1. Master your own philosophy (know what you believe).
2. Cultivate friendships in order to enlist these friends in the
cause.
3. Continue to make regular self-examinations.

If the church is sick, perhaps it would be good to make a self-
examination and ask, "Am I a source of malignancy?"

As we look unto the harvest fields, see that they are ripe, and
know the Lord of the harvest, we should strive to become "workers
together" for the honor and glory of the Savior.

Ed Lyman

January 25

SINGING SCRIPTURE: **3 John 3**

For I rejoiced greatly, when the brethren came and testified of the truth that is in thee, even as thou walkest in the truth.

Good news comes in a variety of packages. It is always an occasion for celebration, singing, and rejoicing. The Apostle John felt the song of gladness swelling in his heart when the news was brought by fellow Christians that his friend, Gaius, was continuing in the truth. With the melody of thanksgiving springing to his lips, he goes on to say, "I have no greater joy than to hear that my children walk in truth." These Christians had seen Christian love and maturity manifest in work and witness in the life of Gaius, and now John hears the enthusiastic report that the "sincere milk of the Word" has produced strong spiritual sinews and muscle.

If our hearts sing with gratitude when we see children mature mentally and physically, so we should rejoice when we see those to whom we have witnessed, for whom we have prayed, and with whom we have studied God's Word grow into discerning and dedicated believers.

The church is God's piano factory, where He is making and tuning his instruments. But Heaven is the place where every key is struck and the full anthem sweeps.

Ed Lyman

January 26

PRAISE PSALM: **Psalm 18:3**

I will call upon the name of the Lord, who is worthy to be praised: so shall I be saved from mine enemies.

This song of praise declares the truth found in both the Old and New Testaments that in the Lord and in Him only do we find salvation. In the preceding verse, David lists attributes of God which give him overwhelming personal confidence in the protective nature of the Lord: "my rock," "my fortress," "my deliverer," "my God," "my strength," "my shield," "horn (general strength and power) of my salvation," "my high tower." He sings of his personal relationship with God as emphasized by his use of the possessive pronoun "my."

S.D. Gordon tells of a Christian lady whose age began to tell on her memory. Though she had been a great Bible student, eventually all of it went from her memory save only, "I know whom I have believed, and am persuaded that he is able to keep that which I have committed unto him against that day." As her last days continued, all she could remember of this passage was, "That which I have committed unto him." On her deathbed all she could recall was "him," and she kept saying this to herself. She had lost the whole Bible but one word, but she had the whole Bible in that one word.

Are you singing praise to Him today?

Ed Lyman

January 27

SINGING SCRIPTURE: **Psalm 71:23**

My lips shall greatly rejoice when I sing unto thee; and my soul, which thou hast redeemed.

"I have a song I love to sing, since I have been redeemed." The words of this song by E.O. Excell aptly paraphrase the Psalmist's exclamation of joy. Fanny Crosby also expressed her delight in the Lord when she wrote,

I think of my blessed Redeemer,
I think of Him all the day long;
I sing for I cannot be silent;
His love is the theme of my song.

The Apostle Paul speaks of the removal of the squalor of sin forever by the redemption of the Lord Jesus Christ, and he tells of the splendor which is the believer's now. "He that spared not his own Son, but delivered him up for us all, how shall he not with him also freely give us all things?" (Romans 8:32). The redemption song is one of:

New destiny: "For Christ also hath once suffered for sins, the just for the unjust, that he might bring us to God" (1 Peter 3:18).

New deliverance: "Who gave himself for our sins, that he might deliver us from the present evil world" (Galatians 1:4).

New desire: "And that he died for all, that they which live should not henceforth live unto themselves, but unto him which died for them, and rose again" (2 Corinthians 5:15).

New dynamic: "Christ hath redeemed us from the curse of the law ... that we might receive the promise of the Spirit through faith: (Galatians 3:13, 14).

New domicile: "For God hath not appointed us to wrath, but to obtain salvation by our Lord Jesus Christ, who died for us that, whether we wake or sleep, we should live together with him" (1 Thessalonians 5:9,10).

"Then in a nobler, sweeter song, I'll sing Thy power to save!"

David E. Williams

January 28

SINGING SCRIPTURE: **Psalm 138:5**

Yea, they shall sing in the ways of the Lord: for great is the glory of the Lord.

So easily do we fall into the rut of excusing our lack of service for the Lord by assuming that the talented or privileged are the only ones who can be used as witnesses. We find a certain comfort in this feeling of inability.

One account of the many found in the Scriptures completely disintegrates our comfortable cocoon of rationalization.

While David waited to be king of Israel, many flocked to his banner over the years — everyone who was in distress, in debt, discontented.

We wonder how such a motley crowd could build anything of enduring quality. However, the exploits of these men are listed in 2 Samuel, and what accomplishments they were! Every one was a hero. Yet, at one time they were all discouraged and discontented.

Why the change?

David trusted them, encouraged them, and gave them opportunity to prove their worth. This is what God does for us. By the indwelling of the Holy Spirit, we can become victorious Christians. This possibility is before us.

Are we excusing ourselves from service, or are we exercising our opportunities to sing in all the ways of the Lord?

Ed Lyman

January 29

SINGING SCRIPTURE: **Psalm 22:26**

The meek shall eat and be satisfied: they shall praise the Lord that seek him: your heart shall live for ever.

The feeding of the meek (26) the prosperous (29) and the whole earth turning to the Lord (27) is the result of the suffering and deliverance described in this Psalm of the Messiah. In Christ's death and resurrection, we find the true song of life. Therefore:

Keep trusting the Lord. "Trust in the Lord with all thine heart; and lean not unto thine own understanding" (Proverbs 3:5).

Keep in touch with the Lord. "Continue in prayer, and watch in the same with thanksgiving" (Colossians 4:2).

Keep giving thanks to the Lord. "Giving thanks always for all things unto God and the Father in the name of our Lord Jesus Christ" (Ephesians 5:20).

Keep faithful to the Lord. "Keep that which is committed to thy trust, avoiding profane and vain babblings" (1 Timothy 6:20).

Keep in tune with the Lord. "Let the word of Christ dwell in you richly in all wisdom; teaching and admonishing one another in psalms and hymns and spiritual songs, singing with grace in your hearts to the Lord" (Colossians 3:16).

Keep on keeping on and keep looking up!

Henry Grube

January 30

SINGING SCRIPTURE: **Zechariah 2:10**

Sing and rejoice, O daughter of Zion: for, lo, I come, and I will dwell in the midst of thee, saith the Lord.

Why should Israel sing and rejoice? Because the Messiah, the Lord Jesus Christ, is soon to return to His people of old and tabernacle in their midst. The Messiah Himself alluded to this in Matthew 23:39, "For I say unto you, Ye shall not see me henceforth, till ye shall say, Blessed is he that cometh in the name of the Lord." After a long night of weeping because of their rejection of Christ and His atoning work on the Cross will dawn a new day of indescribable joy and glorious song for the cleansed remnant that survives the Great Tribulation. Then will their songs be transformed from the minor to the major chord.

The Christian has great cause to "sing and rejoice" now because Christ has come to take up permanent residence within him by virtue of His incorruptible seed. A portion of that same shekinah glory which abode in Solomon's Temple now abides in him.

The hope of the Christian is to see the King in His beauty and to dwell with Him in the New Jerusalem. What a day that will be when song and joy will superabound for the redeemed, who "shall see His face" and experience the fulfillment of His promise: "And if I go and prepare a place for you, I will come again, and receive you unto myself; that where I am, there ye may be also."

"O that will be glory for me."

Deoram Bholan

January 31

SINGING SCRIPTURE: **1 Chronicles 15:24**

And Shebaniah, and Jehoshaphat, and Nethaneel, and Amasai, and Zechariah, and Benaiah, and Eliezer, the priests, did blow with the trumpets before the ark of God: and Obed-edom and Jehiah were doorkeepers for the ark.

David had prepared a place for the ark of God in Jerusalem. Now he, the priests, Levites, and elders of Israel went to the home of Obed-edom, where the ark had been kept for the past three months, and with rejoicing and great gladness brought the ark to the city of David. The priests sounded the trumpets before the ark as the joyous procession made its way up the road to the city.

Priests held a very important position in the community of Israel. They served as intermediaries between the people and God. The function of the priest was unique from the prophet and king in that he approached God on behalf of the people to present sacrifices to atone for their sins and to pray for their forgiveness.

Jesus Christ became our High Priest and through His sacrificial atonement "hast made us unto our God kings and priest" (Revelation 5:10). In 1 Peter 2:9, we are told that we are "a chosen generation, a royal priesthood, an holy nation, a peculiar people; that ye should show forth the praises of him who hath called you out of darkness into his marvelous light."

A trumpet is in our hands! With it, we joyfully, as priests of the Lord, proclaim salvation to the world around us.

Ed Lyman

February

DAILY PRAISE

February 1

SINGING SCRIPTURE: **Isaiah 51:3**

> *For the Lord shall comfort Zion: he will comfort all her waste places; and he will make her wilderness like Eden, and her desert like the garden of the Lord; joy and gladness shall be found therein, thanksgiving, and the voice of melody.*

A desert is a place where the natural means of sustaining life are absent. Water is either very scarce or nonexistent. Vegetation is sparse, and erosion is rapid. Usually the sun burns upon the wasteland during the daylight hours, and at night the temperature drops dramatically.

Israel is a desert — barren and unfruitful. However, God tells her to trust Him and she will see the wilderness blossom into a lovely garden.

The natural man is like a spiritual desert. He is without any means of sustaining life. The Bible explains that the natural man does not understand the things of God and cannot receive them because they are spiritually discerned. Jesus said, "I am come that they might have life, and that they might have it more abundantly."

Trusting Him changes the desert of death into the garden of glory.

No wonder joy and gladness bloom in the garden of God, and thanksgiving with the voice of melody ripens in the orchard of service.

"Therefore if any man be in Christ, he is a new creature: old things are passed away; behold, all things are become new."

John Song

February 2

SINGING SCRIPTURE: **Revelation 5:9, 10**

> *And they sung a new song, saying, Thou art worthy to take the book, and to open the seals thereof: for thou wast slain, and*

*hast redeemed us to God by thy blood out of every kindred,
and tongue, and people, and nation; and hast made us unto our
God kings and priests, and we shall reign on the earth.*

Did you know that tears were shed in Heaven? Our singing
verses today climax a challenge issued in heaven: "Who is worthy to
open the book and to loose its seals?" (2). Because there are no
takers to this challenge, the fourth verses says that John wept
much. This weeping takes place in Heaven.

One of the heavenly elders quiets John in his grief, for he knows
that the Lamb, Jesus Christ, is worthy to open the seals. The four
living creatures and the twenty-four elders begin to sing a new song
of the worthiness of the Lamb to take the scroll and open it. But why
is Jesus worthy?

Because He died for our sins.

Because He redeemed us to God by His own blood.

Because He has His own family out of every kindred, tongue,
people, and nation.

Because He has made us His domain as priests representing God
to man and man to God.

Because He has promised that we would reign with Him on
earth.

God promises that He will wipe away all tears in Heaven
(Revelation 21:4). How can we help but be happy, knowing what
Jesus has done and will do for us. We, with the writer of the Book of
Revelation, sing the new song of adoration: "Blessing, and honor,
and glory, and power, be unto him that sitteth upon the throne, and
unto the Lamb for ever and ever" (Revelation 5:13).

Keith Whiticar

February 3

PRAISE PSALM: **Psalm 150:2**

*Praise him for his mighty acts: praise him according to his
excellent greatness.*

As I've flown across the country and to other parts of the world,
I've often heard the pilot tell us over the intercom system that we
would be landing on schedule at our destination. Yet, at the time of
his announcement to the passengers, our plane would be hundreds

or even thousands of miles from the landing place. It is an amazing accomplishment of our scientific age to be able to know exactly where we were and what time we would be landing at a distant airport. It was not guesswork, but a sophisticated guidance system housed in the nose of the plane that produced exact data concerning position, flight pattern, speed, and stability. Without maps, charts, and direction finders, we would constantly be losing our course. We need guidance as we wend our way through life.

However, just as we need such equipment for physical guidance, it is necessary for us to have spiritual guidance. God provides this spiritual direction. His "mighty acts" in history have attested to His leadership in a variety of circumstances. He directed Noah in the proper construction of the ark. He guided Moses and the Israelites through the wilderness.

In Psalm 48:14 we read, "For this God is our God for ever and ever: he will be our guide even unto death."

By the "excellent greatness" of God, we can be led by the Spirit of God, knowing "The steps of a good man are ordered by the Lord: and he delighteth in his way" (Psalm 37:23).

Because of His guidance, "Singing I go along life's road, Praising the Lord, Praising the Lord."

Ed Lyman

February 4

SINGING SCRIPTURE: **Nehemiah 12:27, 42**

And at the dedication of the wall of Jerusalem they sought the Levites out of their places, to bring them to Jerusalem, to keep the dedication with gladness, both with thanksgivings, and with singing, with cymbals, psalteries, and with harps.... And the singers sang loud, with Jezrahiah their overseer.

When I glanced at this passage, my first reaction was that my friend Ed Lyman had thrown me a curve." So I read it again. When I did this with the idea of finding a significant "nugget," I was immediately struck with the truth that once again we are reminded of the fact that singing is a kind of catalyst in worship. Music, properly presented with a purpose in its lyrics, has a way of bringing everything else together.

That was the obvious "gem" to be found, but then I saw something else. Why hadn't I seen it the first time I read the verses?

It wasn't so much that the singing was "loud." I've heard people singing loudly, and what they were singing was almost unintelligible. What this means is that the overseer directed the singers, and as a choir their voices were made to be heard.

Working as a team, the musicians became a choir and orchestra with purpose and praiseful presentations, just as by teamwork the people completed the wall.

It is in this way that we too are able to best communicate the truth of salvation to the world. "For we are laborers together with God" (1 Corinthians 3:9).

John DeBrine

February 5

SINGING SCRIPTURE: **2 Chronicles 13:12**

And, behold, God himself is with us for our captain, and his priests with sounding trumpets to cry alarm against you. O children of Israel, fight ye not against the Lord God of your fathers; for ye shall not prosper.

War clouds hung low. Israel had forsaken the Lord, but Judah remained faithful. "But as for us, the Lord is our God, and we have not forsaken him" (2 Chronicles 13:10).

The music of alarm gave warning to backslidden Israel that defeat was certain in a battle against the Lord's people, for the captain of Judah's army was God Himself. When the trumpets were heard, had they thought back to their own historical events, they would have turned from the battlefield.

After entering the Promised Land, Joshua came face to face with a stranger. "And it came to pass, when Joshua was by Jericho, that he lifted up his eyes and looked, and behold, there stood a man over against him with his sword drawn in his hand: and Joshua went unto him, and said unto him, Art thou for us, or for our adversaries? And he said, Nay; but as captain of the host of the Lord am I now come. And Joshua fell on his face to the earth, and did worship" (Joshua 5:13, 14). Israel should have done the same, but the musical alarm went unheeded.

Again, David sinned in numbering Israel. Pestilence killed seventy thousand men of Israel. "David lifted up his eyes, and saw the angel of the Lord stand between the earth and the heaven, having a drawn sword in his hand stretched out over Jerusalem. Then David and the elders of Israel, who were clothed in sackcloth, fell upon their faces" (1 Chronicles 21:16).

Two things are heard in this trumpet sound — this musical attention-getter — "Be not deceived; God is not mocked" (Galatians 6:7) and "If God be for us, who can be against us?" (Romans 8:31).

Ed Lyman

February 6

SINGING SCRIPTURE: **Psalm 146:10**

The Lord shall reign for ever, even thy God, O Zion, unto all generations. Praise ye the Lord.

Here is a praise song of security in the sovereignty of Almighty God.

In Psalm 31:3, David sang, "Thou art my rock and my fortress." He knew much about rocks and fortresses. During his youth in the Judean desert, he learned how animals and humans alike found caves and clefts for relief from the burning sun and the threats of predators. Dozens of his psalms speak of rocky refuges as hiding places. When he became a great warrior-king, David further appreciated the value of fortresses. He built many and besieged and destroyed others. After he captured the Zion hill in Jerusalem (2 Samuel 5:6-9, 1 Chronicles 11:6), David fortified it and made it his home. In the "City of David" he felt safe.

Francois Mitterand, president of the French Republic, said that security is the number one concern of the French people. Psychologists rank it with the longing for love and reliance as one of the greatest human needs. Even inner security eludes people. If there is no peace outside, there is even less in the heart. "I'm a civil war," said a woman recently about her turmoil of emotions and fears.

David testifies that the Lord is his rock and fortress. While every Christian has times when fears of security engulf him, such aberrations should be cyclic, not chronic. Faith can reach out to the Lord each day, saying, "Lord, everyone else may let me down, but *you* never will!" "The name of the Lord is a strong tower: the righteous runneth into it, and is safe" (Proverbs 18:10). That's enough!

Robert P. Evans

February 7

SINGING SCRIPTURE: **2 Kings 3:15**

But now bring me a minstrel. And it came to pass, when the minstrel played, that the hand of the Lord came upon him.

Elisha either had a minstrel accompanying him as he traveled across the land in his prophetic ministry or he asked for one to play from among those in attendance to the kings of Israel, Edom, and Judah. In the midst of the quandary of whether the Lord would deliver them from their enemy and the question of how to do battle against the opposing forces, the sound of music calmed the emotion-filled atmosphere, brought attention to the things of the Lord, and enabled the prophet Elisha to seek God's direction without the interruption of men with their opinions. The result of seeking the Lord's will and acting upon it was another victory wrought by God.

As the music accompanied Elisha's inquiry, the Lord showed him:

A perfect path — "As for God, his way is perfect" (2 Samuel 22:31). In a time of contradicting and confusing alternatives, the Lord says, "I am *the* way" (John 14:6).

A tested truth — "The word of the Lord is tried" (2 Samuel 22:31). In a trial of false and phony attitudes, the Lord says, "I am ... *the* truth" (John 14:6).

A proper protection — "He is a buckler to all them that trust in him" (2 Samuel 22:31).

In a testing of transient and temporary allegiances, the Lord says, "I am ... *the* life" (John 14:6).

Call for the minstrel music of God's Word to prepare you for a quiet time with the Lord, and His way will be revealed to you as it was to Elisha.

Ed Lyman

February 8

SINGING SCRIPTURE: **Jeremiah 20:13**

Sing unto the Lord, praise ye the Lord: for he hath delivered the soul of the poor from the hand of evildoers.

You only have to read the whole of Jeremiah 20 to notice that verse 13 is like a shaft of sunlight piercing a storm, one passage of praise in a dirge of doom.

Things were certainly tough for Jeremiah. Because of his fearless preaching of God's Word, he had taken a terrible battering from the religious authorities. He had been ridiculed, scorned, rejected. The Temple chief had him tortured in the stocks (v. 2); later he was to be imprisoned in a muddy cistern (38:6).

It would be nice to think that Jeremiah's reaction to this was all sweetness and light, but the Bible is more honest than that. He began to be filled with self-pity (v. 7); he was tempted to soft-pedal his message (v. 9); he got a little scared of the opposition (v. 10); he even sank into deep depression, wishing he had never been born (vv. 14-18).

The outlook was black — until Jeremiah tried the uplook! And when he did, the picture was transformed. First, he remembered the Lord's *presence* — "the Lord is with me" (v. 11), then his *power* — "as a mighty terrible one" (v. 11), then his *providence* — "Lord of hosts" (v. 12) ruling and reigning over all the circumstances of life. And all of this led him to the Lord's *praise* (v. 13) and to the tremendous statement of faith that God would vindicate him and deliver him from all his enemies.

Instead of sighing at the world, try singing to the Lord. It is a whole lot better!

John Blanchard

February 9

SINGING SCRIPTURE: **1 Chronicles 9:33**

And these are the singers, chief of the fathers of the Levites, who remaining in the chambers were free: for they were employed in that work day and night.

The Word of God stresses a very high standard of skill for the music used in public praise. We are told that "Chenaniah ... instructed about the song, because he was skillful" (1 Chronicles 15:22) and that "the number of them, with their brethren that were instructed in the songs of the Lord, even all that were cunning, was two hundred fourscore and eight" (1 Chronicles 25:7).

Music was a vital and significant facet of worship in both the Old and New Testaments. In the 40th Psalm, the Messiah is shown to be obedient unto death. Then we read His triumphant resurrection testimony, His "new song": "And he hath put a new song in my mouth, even praise unto our God: many shall see it, and fear, and shall trust in the Lord" (Psalm 40:3). This new song of joyful praise is put into the mouths of His people as they are spiritually born-again, because they have "put on the new man, which after God is created in righteousness and true holiness" (Ephesians 4:24).

Confession finds expression in the music of God's Word. David sang, "I acknowledged my sin unto thee, and mine iniquity have I not hid. I said, I will confess my transgressions unto the Lord; and thou forgavest the iniquity of my sin" (Psalm 32:5).

Comfort during times of sorrow is found in the music of God's understanding. In Psalm 27:14 this comfort is expressed with earnest exhilaration: "Wait on the Lord: be of good courage, and he shall strengthen thine heart: wait, I say, on the Lord."

Ed Lyman

February 10

SINGING SCRIPTURE: **Psalm 22:3**

But thou art holy, O thou that inhabitest the praises of Israel.

What a delightful and interesting idea that is! God abides in the songs and music of His people!

This is a cheering and challenging concept; one which can only be found in a personal commitment to living, learning, and loving in the light of the very presence of a God who cares.

God lives in our hearts.

He resides in our activities.

His presence is in our music.

We are God's home.

When visiting a home in Spanish-speaking countries, the host or hostess often greets guests with the statement, *"En su casa"* — This is your home." It is more than a welcome. It is an invitation to make yourself as comfortable as you'd be in your own living quarters. The thought is that for the Lord Jesus Christ to reside in our music, He must be comfortable with its message and with its meaning. It must be "fit" for His life-style. Our music and our lives are the dwelling-places for the abiding presence of the Holy God.

Our music, therefore, is a reflection of our relationship with the living Christ.

Ed Lyman

February 11

SINGING SCRIPTURE: **Psalm 138:1**

I will praise thee with my whole heart: before the gods will I sing praise unto thee.

Because of the Lord's gift of spiritual strength in answer to his prayer for help, David praises God in wholehearted worship. Some have interpreted "gods" to mean angels and others suggest judges. However, because of a later reference to "the kings of the earth," "gods" seems to fit. The idea conveyed is that since the kings of the earth now worship and serve their various gods, they are really bowing down to idols of wood, stone, or metal with no life. However, one day they shall worship the true God.

There is also the clear indication that David is signaling a complete dependence upon the Lord and therefore countenances no fear of worldly powers and authority. A similar statement is found in Psalm 119:46 — "I will speak of thy testimonies also before kings, and will not be ashamed." Employing the same line of reasoning, we find the Apostle Paul claiming, "For I am not ashamed of the gospel of Christ: for it is the power of God unto salvation to every one that believeth; to the Jew first, and also to the Greek" (Romans 1:16).

George Schuler wrote, "Christian, come quickly to the realization that there is no need of fear and worry, for our Lord, the Shepherd, is nearer than one's own breath — a living reality!"

Ed Lyman

February 12

SINGING SCRIPTURE: **Deuteronomy 32:44**

And Moses came and spake all the words of this song in the ears of the people, he, and Hoshea the son of Nun.

I was in the U.S. Marine Corps stationed at Quantico, Virginia, and had started making trips to New York City to sing for Jack Wyrtzen's "Word of Life" rally. Carlton Booth, the beloved and well-known tenor, was the regular soloist. Along with the Word of Life Quartet and the instrumentalists, he provided the music for the radio program. I sang for the preliminaries and the rally after the broadcast.

One Saturday night, as the rehearsals ended and times were being blocked, Carlton Booth walked to where I stood and asked if I knew the song he was to sing. I said I did, and to my surprise, he told me he wanted me to sing it on the broadcast. It was his song, his solo.

"No," he replied, "I think it's time you sang on the air. I'll lead the singing, and you sing the solo tonight."

"What will Jack and the others think of this change?" I protested.

He said he'd take care of that, and with a smile he turned, recited the plan to the instrumentalists, and then exuberantly reiterated it to Jack Wyrtzen. They looked toward me and then back to Carlton Booth. He smiled. That was that! I sang on the coast-to-coast broadcast that night, because a master musician was more interested in sharing service than in singing solo. That's what our verse for today is all about. Moses rehearsed the song of God's salvation to Joshua, and together they shared it with the people.

Carlton Booth's music was not mere lip-service in song; it was part of his life-service for the Savior. What an example!

Ed Lyman

------------------ ❀ ------------------

February 13

SINGING SCRIPTURE: **Colossians 3:16**

> *Let the word of Christ dwell in you richly in all wisdom; teaching and admonishing one another in psalms and hymns and spiritual songs, with grace in your hearts to the Lord.*

We are confronted with the great value this remarkable Christian statesman placed on music. He mentions three categories of songs: "psalms and hymns and spiritual songs." A *hymn* is a song of praise to God, Jesus Christ, and the Holy Spirit or to any one person of the Trinity. It is music of glorification and adoration. *Psalm* specifically denotes the poetic utterances from the book of Psalms set to a melodic line. *Spiritual song* includes the folk spiritual, Scripture-centered song, and gospel song. These three types, within the context of the spiritual-song category, take their lyrics from some aspect of the Scriptures.

However, all of this music, according to Paul, should be an illustration of and a witness to the specific nature of the Word of God and the true message of salvation through the Lord Jesus Christ. How can we expect to teach and admonish by means of music or any other means of witnessing unless we make the message clear and plain — "Christ receiveth sinful men"?

Ed Lyman

February 14

SINGING SCRIPTURE: **Psalm 146:1**

Praise ye the Lord. Praise the Lord, O my soul.

We praise Thee, O God: we acknowledge Thee to be the Lord. All the earth doth worship Thee, the Father everlasting. To Thee all angels cry aloud; the heavens and all the powers therein. To Thee cherubim and seraphim continually do cry: Holy, Holy, Holy, Lord God of Sabaoth. Heaven and earth are full of the majesty of Thy glory. The glorious company of the apostles praise Thee. The goodly fellowship of the prophets praise Thee. The noble army of martyrs praise Thee. The holy Church, throughout all the world, doth acknowledge Thee, the Father of an infinite majesty; Thine adorable, true, and only Son; also the Holy Spirit, the Comforter. Thou art the King of glory, O Christ. Thou art the everlasting Son of the Father. When Thou tookest upon Thee to deliver man, Thou didst humble Thyself to be born of a virgin. When Thou hadst overcome the sharpness of death, Thou didst open the kingdom of heaven to all believers. Thou sittest at the right hand of God, in the glory of the Father. We believe that Thou shalt come to be our Judge. We therefore pray Thee, help Thy servants, whom Thou hast redeemed with Thy precious blood. Make them to be numbered with Thy saints in glory everlasting. O Lord, save Thy people, and bless Thy heritage. Govern them, and lift them up forever. Day by day we magnify Thee; and we worship Thy name ever, world without end. Vouchsafe, O Lord, to keep us this day without sin. O Lord, have mercy upon us, have mercy upon us. O Lord, let Thy mercy be upon us, as our trust is in Thee. O Lord, in Thee have I trusted; let me never be confounded. Amen.

Te Deum
The Book of Common Prayer

February 15

SINGING SCRIPTURE: **Amos 8:3**

And the songs of the temple shall be howlings in that day, saith the Lord God: there shall be many dead bodies in every place; they shall cast them forth with silence.

Israel had been warned over and over by her prophets that God would judge her disobedience. Captivity is now at hand. God's judgment was already upon her. In the experiences of the past, Israel resembles a barren woman, who has been estranged from her husband. This is the picture the prophet shows us in Isaiah 54:1, where he states, "Sing, O barren, thou that didst not bear." She has produced no fruit for God during the long period in which she is indifferent to the Lord Jesus Christ. In the future, the nation will be brought down into anguish during the Tribulation, where the birth pangs of sorrow will hold her and where she will be delivered of her burden.

Then, her long confinement past and her cherished hopes realized, she will break forth into joyous song to express the overwhelming delight of her increase. She who had been thought desolate and deserted is now proven to be delightful and desirable.

The name "Hephzebah" (my delight is in her) shall be exchanged for "Beulah" (married).

The sound of singing is an appropriate substitute for lamentation and sorrow. Reunion with the heavenly Bridegroom, Jesus Christ, gives rise to the shout of gladness and the burst of sacred melody.

John L. Benson

February 16

SINGING SCRIPTURE: **Psalm 137:4**

How shall we sing the Lord's song in a strange land?

What a question! It was asked by God's people as they languished in captivity in Babylon. In asking it, they were in truth stating a desire for restoration to their former place of blessing and favor with the Lord. They were expressing need. As these captives longed for fulfillment of their needs in Jehovah, the Christian now finds completion in the Lord Jesus Christ.

Our need to be loved is met in Christ: "A new commandment I give unto you, That ye love one another; as I have loved you, that ye also love one another" (John 13:34).

Our need to belong is met in Christ: "Wherefore receive ye one another, as Christ also received us, to the glory of God" (Romans 15:7).

Our need to feel wanted is met in Christ: "For the body is not one member, but many" (1 Corinthians 12:14). There are no little people!

Our need to be given opportunity to respond to people is met in Christ: "Put on therefore, as the elect of God, holy and beloved, bowels of mercies, kindness, humbleness of mind, meekness, long-suffering; forbearing one another, and forgiving one another, if any man have a quarrel against any: even as Christ forgave you, so also do ye" (Colossians 3:12, 13).

Our need to live in open and relaxed relationship is met in Christ: "Salt is good: but if the salt have lost his saltness, wherewith will ye season it? Have salt in yourselves, and have peace one with another" (Mark 9:50).

Christians should always feel secure in the presence of God and other Christians, working and walking together in harmony.

Ed Lyman

February 17

SINGING SCRIPTURE: **2 Chronicles 29:27**

And Hezekiah commanded to offer the burnt offering upon the altar. And when the burnt offering began, the song of the Lord began also with the trumpets, and with the instruments ordained by David king of Israel.

At least from the time of David and most likely before, music was used to accompany the burnt offering and Temple worship. It is also commonly accepted that most of the Psalms were composed for such accompaniment. Hezekiah the king on this occasion has commanded the singing of "the song of the Lord." From 2 Chronicles 29:30, we readily see that this encompassed the music of David and Asaph. This was music of praise to Almighty God and was a choral confession of complete dependence upon the power and presence of God. The very name of the Lord was preserved in their music.

John Newton expressed this consecration in these words:

How sweet the name of Jesus sounds in a believer's ear!
It soothes his sorrows, heals his wounds, and drives away his fear.
It makes the wounded spirit whole, and calms the troubled breast;
'Tis manna to the hungry soul, and to the weary, rest.
Weak is the effort of my heart, and cold my warmest thought;
But when I see Thee as Thou art, I'll praise Thee as I ought.

Till then, I would Thy love proclaim with every fleeting breath;
And may the music of Thy name refresh my soul in death.

Ed Lyman

February 18

PRAISE PSALM: **Psalm 150:1**

Praise ye the Lord. Praise God in his sanctuary; praise him in the firmament of his power.

We sing God's praises, for He *dwells* in the believer: "Know ye not that ye are the temple of God, and that the Spirit of God dwelleth in you?" (1 Corinthians 3:16)

We sing God's praises, for He *walks* with the believer: "For ye are the temple of the living God; as God hath said, I will dwell in them, and walk in them; and I will be their God, and they shall be my people" (2 Corinthians 6:16).

We sing God's praises, for He *prays* for us: "Likewise the Spirit also helpeth our infirmities: for we know not what we should pray for as we ought: but the Spirit himself maketh intercession for us with groanings which cannot be uttered" (Romans 8:26).

We sing God's praises for His *provision*: "But my God shall supply all your need according to his riches in glory by Jesus Christ" (Philippians 4:19).

We sing God's praises for His *working* through us: "For it is God which worketh in you both to will and to do of his good pleasure" (Philippians 2:13).

We sing God's praises for His ruling over us: "But unto the Son he saith, Thy throne, O God, is for ever and ever: a scepter of righteousness is the scepter of thy kingdom" (Hebrews 1:8).

We sing God's praises, for He loves us: "Herein is love, not that we loved God, but that he loved us, and sent his Son to be the propitiation for our sins" (1 John 4:10).

Ed Lyman

February 19

SINGING SCRIPTURE: **Joshua 6:20**

So the people shouted when the priests blew with the trumpets; and it came to pass, when the people heard the sound of the trumpet, and the people shouted with a great shout, that the wall fell down flat, so that the people went up into the city, every man straight before him, and they took the city.

It was in the Spanish Town Prison in Jamaica on death row that I experienced a similar victory. I had played my cornet, sang, and preached the gospel in a warehouse-type building. As the men were returning to their cells, a guard asked me and my friend to stay and talk with the condemned men. This was a great surprise, for when a man is doomed to die on the gallows there, not even his wife and mother may visit him.

We agreed to do so. Crouched before me in his cell, looking more like a wild beast then a man, was a fifty-two-year-old murderer. I reached into my cornet case for the words of the song — I'd played on my cornet and finding them sang, "Now I belong to Jesus." Then I gave a brief testimony.

"I'm to die on Tuesday morning. Sir, can I be saved?" this man asked. "Indeed you can." I showed him Romans 10:13 in my Bible. "But I can't read," he said pathetically. So I read, "For whosoever shall call upon the name of the Lord shall be saved." He put his face on that dirty floor and sobbed as he called upon the name of the Lord. After a moment he turned to me and smiled through his tears. "Sing it again." "Sing what?" I asked. "What you just sang." So I sang, "Now I belong to Jesus. Jesus belongs to me." The walls of sin had fallen around the Jericho of despair.

That Tuesday morning he went gallantly to the gallows singing as he was ushered into the Lord's presence. They didn't tell me what he was singing, but I think I know: "Now I belong to Jesus!"

Roy W. Gustafson

February 20

SINGING SCRIPTURE: **Ezra 3:11**

And they sang together by course in praising and giving thanks unto the Lord; because he is good, for his mercy

*endureth for ever toward Israel. And all the people shouted
with a great shout, when they praised the Lord, because the
foundation of the house of the Lord was laid.*

This is significant singing. It is illustrative of the fact that the
ministry of God is not an outward show, but an inner glow. "For the
Lord seeth not as man seeth; for man looketh on the outward
appearance, but the Lord looketh on the heart" (1 Samuel 16:7).

Certainly it was a motley crew which had returned from
Babylonian captivity to rebuild the walls of Jerusalem and re-erect
the temple of God. Practically speaking, they didn't have the
"stuff" to do the job — except for what is found in Ezra 1:2-4.

They were acting on the *sovereignty of God* (Ezra 1:2): "Thus
saith Cyrus king of Persia, The Lord God of heaven hath given me
all the kingdoms of the earth; and he hath charged me to build him a
house at Jerusalem which is in Judah."

There was the *sending of the servants* (Ezra 1:3): "Who is there
among you of all his people? his God be with him, and let him go to
Jerusalem, which is in Judah, and build the house of the Lord God
of Israel, (he is the God), which is in Jerusalem."

There was the *sacrifice of the saints* (Ezra 1:4): "And whosoever
remaineth in any place where he sojourneth, let the men of his
place help him with silver, and with gold, and with goods, and with
beasts, besides the freewill offering for the house of God that is in
Jerusalem."

"Now therefore fear the Lord, and serve him in sincerity and in
truth" (Joshua 24:14).

Ed Lyman

February 21

SINGING SCRIPTURE: Psalm 35:18

*I will give thee thanks in the great congregation: I will praise
thee among much people.*

A young convert got up in one of our meetings and tried to
preach. He could not preach very well, but he did the best he could.
But someone stood up and said, "Young man, you cannot preach;
you ought to be ashamed of yourself." Said the young man: "So I
am, but I am not ashamed of my Lord." That is right. Do not be
ashamed of Christ — of the Man that bought us with His blood.

If Christ comes into our hearts, we are not ashamed.

I can't help thinking of the old woman who started out, when the war commenced, with a poker in her hand. When asked what she was going to do with it, she said, "I can't do much with it, but I can show what side I'm on." My friends, even if you can't do much, show to which side you belong.

I do not know anything that would wake up Chicago better than for every man and woman here who loves Him to begin to talk [and sing] about Him to their friends, and just to tell them what He has done for you. You have a circle of friends. Go and tell them of Him.

Dwight L. Moody

February 22

SINGING SCRIPTURE: **1 Corinthians 15:52**

In a moment, in the twinkling of an eye, at the last trump: for the trumpet shall sound, and the dead shall be raised incorruptible, and we shall be changed.

What music will we hear? The trumpet of God calling us to immortality! Knowing such a sound awaits those who have put their faith and trust in Jesus Christ as Lord, we are brought face to face with the truth that the "chief end of man is to glorify God and to enjoy Him forever."

God is on the throne. He reigns.

In light of that coming trumpet sound, we are to spread His glory as the waters cover the sea. This "covering" includes the glory of His power, the glory of His presence, and the glory of His purpose. Isaiah the prophet speaks of the seraphim covering their faces and feet, and with another pair of wings flying. The picture is of holy allegiance as they covered their eyes, holy dependence as they covered their feet; and with covering wings flying, they portray holy obedience. In the presence of His holiness, we should be wholly in allegiance to the Lord, wholly dependent upon Him, and wholly obedient to His Word.

Tim Zimmerman

February 23

SINGING SCRIPTURE: **Psalm 75:9**

But I will declare for ever; I will sing praises to the God of Jacob.

This song verse is a missionary challenge! In declaring and singing praises to the Lord, there is a recognition of the source of true salvation and an understanding of God's availability to dynamically alter man's mere existence.

There is the divine passion for the will of God and the work of God. There is a job for every believer. God makes only originals, not duplicates. We read about it in Ephesians 2:10, "For we are his workmanship, created in Christ Jesus unto good works, which God hath before ordained that we should walk in them." There is a plan to find, follow, and finish.

Next, there is a divine vision. "Lift up your eyes, and look on the fields; for they are white already to harvest" (John 4:35). Look and see a vast and lost world.

Finally, there is a divine mission to redeem the days of harvest and gather "fruit unto life eternal: that both he that soweth and he that reapeth may rejoice together" (John 4:36).

The harvest is the result of preparation of the soil and planting the seed — the declaration of the gospel. The singing of God's praises is like fertilizing, weeding, cultivating. Then comes the harvest and the day of rejoicing, because of the divine provision.

Ed Lyman

February 24

SINGING SCRIPTURE: **Psalm 137:2**

We hanged our harps upon the willows in the midst thereof.

The song has died. Israel's music has ended. In Isaiah 24:8, the prophet tells of God's judgment and says, "The mirth of tabrets ceaseth, the noise of them that rejoice endeth, the joy of the harp ceaseth." This is a picture of despair and disillusionment. Israel has fallen, and the joy of her melodies has utterly stopped.

What a contrast this is to the spiritual life-style of King David. He did not allow himself to languish in a lament because of unsatisfactory circumstances. Instead, he worshiped the Lord in praise and worked for the glory of God. He knew that wisdom is the implementation of Bible doctrine in daily living. This is sage advise, for as we cultivate an interest in and an understanding of the Word of God, we find that the Lord has provided His presence and His promises to dispel worry and fear.

I.S. Cutter, M.D. wrote, "The hazards of worry destroy the peace of mind and make people miserable and everyone else about them. Worry is the result of fear, and the only way to combat it is to cultivate intelligent understanding." Application of God's Word brings a new distinction, a new dimension, and a new determination to the life of a Christian. The verse for today can really be a challenge to the believer to witness in song and speak of the mercy and love of the Lord. To do this, we must bring our living into line with God's plan and purpose and put Him in the center of our activities. We should live not *under* the circumstances, but *over* circumstances. Take those harps off the willows now!

Ed Lyman

February 25

SINGING SCRIPTURE: **Psalm 81:1**

Sing aloud unto God our strength: make a joyful noise unto the God of Jacob.

In all probability this psalm was sung during the Feast of Tabernacles (Feast of In-gathering) spoken of in Leviticus 23:33-36. Asaph, one of David's chief musicians (1 Chronicles 15:19), penned this poetic song to express his assurance of God's sovereignty and the joyful confidence of knowing God's continual mercy and protection.

Asaph specified that this particular psalm should be accompanied by the *gittith*, which also complements the singing of Psalm 8 and Psalm 84. Although exact meanings are difficult to ascertain, the consensus is that this was an instrument similar to our contemporary guitar, which originated in the land of Gath (Goliath's old stomping grounds). Some commentators believe it was the name of a tune or melody, as was *altaschith* (Psalm 58) or *shushaneduth* (Psalm 60). However, opinions are more heavily weighed toward the former, that being the name of an instrument.

"Sing aloud..." Well, of course! Don't we always sing aloud?

Actually, no. Frequently I find myself singing in a very hushed, meditative way as I think about what God is doing in my life. In fact, I often sing in a way that is not "aloud" at all. It might be better described as singing to myself, even though the thoughts are directed God-ward. Asaph expressly wanted loud, recognizable sounds of worship and praise that would be understood by neighbors or co-worshippers — songs that are going to cause someone else to enter into a joyful attitude of worship with us. This is corporate worship at its best, worship into which we can wholeheartedly enter and which will present an unequivocal testimony.

Douglas E. Schoen

February 26

PRAISE PSALM: **Psalm 147:12**

Praise the Lord, O Jerusalem; praise thy God, O Zion.

If ever there was a place that should sing forth in glorious praise to the Lord, Jerusalem is that place. The first mention of this city in the Bible is in Genesis 14:18. Melchizedek, the king of peace and the priest of the Most High God, lived there. Later it became the glorious capital of Israel, and a citadel of splendor under Solomon. Throughout its history, it commanded attention. It was built, reduced to rubble, rebuilt, destroyed, and built again. It remained the focal point of Hebrew faith and the haven of Jewish hope through the centuries. It was a place steeped in prophesy, a city of destiny.

Yes, the city of Jerusalem has ample reason to burst forth in praise-song. It bears the imprint of the Messiah both in prophecy and in person. Outside its walls, God's Lamb, the Prince of Peace, was sacrificed for our sins. It was in this city where the risen Savior sent forth his disciples as ambassadors of the gospel of salvation and peace.

Jerusalem: the dwelling-place of God. In type, believers are spiritual Jerusalems, for God makes His abode in the hearts of believers. As Jerusalem is a city of prophecy, Christians are people of prophecy. By it, as we search the Scriptures, we have an understanding of the times in which we live. It confirms our faith as we see God's timetable unfolding. The panorama of God's plan develops our spiritual sensitivities, and we are enabled by God's

Spirit to keep from discouragement. God has His hand on us just as He had His purposes for Jerusalem.

Jerusalem, sing in praise! Christian, lift up your heads and sing!

Ed Lyman

February 27

SINGING SCRIPTURE: **Ezekiel 33:32**

> *And, lo, thou art unto them as a very lovely song of one that hath a pleasant voice, and can play well on an instrument: for they hear thy words, but they do them not.*

This "very lovely song" is literally "a song of love," which is a sensory sound. This was the reason for the large gathering of people. They came to listen to the prophet much as they would come to hear a hired musician sing and play for them.

They wanted a caressing of the senses and had no time for a message from God.

In Amos we read, "Woe to them that are at ease in Zion ... that chant to the sound of the viol, and invent to themselves instruments of music, like David ... they shall go captive."

The prophet's warnings went unheeded and left no impression on the listener's hearts.

The Hebrew captives were well-known among their conquerors for their musical ability. Though some had refused to sing, it may be that others did make music to entertain their captors. Perhaps the prophet saw his people gather to hear such singers and realized that they would rather be entertained for the moment than to heed his message from Jehovah.

Music, as an art, is entertaining, but we must be alert to the message God may have for us in the music we hear and sing in the church.

Ed Lyman

February 28

SINGING SCRIPTURE: **Judges 5:1-5**

Then say Deborah and Barak the son of Abinoam on that day,
saying,
Praise ye the Lord for the avenging of Israel, when the people
willingly offered themselves.
Hear, O ye kings; give ear, O ye princes;
I, even I, will sing unto the Lord;
I will sing praise to the Lord God of Israel.
Lord, when thou wentest out of Seir, when thou marchest out
of the field of Edom, the earth trembled, and the heavens
dropped, the clouds also dropped water.
The mountains melted from before the Lord, even that Sinai
from the Lord God of Israel.

This is a song of god's condescension. They were overwhelmed by the presence of the Lord, who showed Himself interested in and involved with His people.

Shortly before his death, George Schuler, the composer of *Overshadowed* and *O What a Day*, sent me a copy of a song he had just written, and condescension is the theme:

He laid His glory there,
The splendor of His throne;
And down a mystic stair,
He came to earth alone,
To clothe a sinner with immortality.
Lord Jesus, What condescension!

And when he came to Calv'ry's hill,
Our Savior crucified;
He there fulfilled His Father's will,
As for the world He died,
To clothe a sinner with immortality.
Lord Jesus, What condescension!

Ed Lyman

March

DAILY PRAISE

March 1

SINGING SCRIPTURE: **Psalm 42:5**

Why art thou cast down, O my soul? and why art thou disquieted in me? Hope thou in God: for I shall yet praise him for the help of his countenance.

It is true, if we will devote ourselves entirely to God, we must meet with contempt; but then it is because contempt is necessary to heal pride. We must renounce some sensual pleasures; but then it is because those unfit us for spiritual ones, which are infinitely better. We must renounce the love of the world; but then it is that we may be filled with the love of God: and when that has once enlarged our hearts, we shall, like Jacob when he served for his beloved Rachel, think nothing too difficult to undergo, no hardships too tedious to endure, because of the love we shall then have for our dear Redeemer. Thus easy, thus delightful will be the ways of God even in his life. But when once we throw off these bodies, and our souls are filled with all the fulness of God, O what heart can conceive, what tongue can express, with what unspeakable joy and consolation shall we then look back on our past sincere and hearty services! Shall we then repent that we have done too much; or rather do you not think we shall be ashamed that we did no more; and blush that we were so backward to give up all to God, when He intended hereafter to give us Himself?

Let me therefore, to conclude, exhort you my brethren, to have always before you the unspeakable happiness of enjoying God ... in whose presence there is fulness of joy, and at whose right hand there are pleasures for evermore.

George Whitefield

March 2

SINGING SCRIPTURE: **Isaiah 24:8**

The mirth of the tabrets ceaseth, the noise of them that rejoice endeth, the joy of the harp ceaseth.

"Stop the music!" That's the prophet's exclamation. Once again we are introduced to his prediction of judgment. Intolerable sin has left God no recourse but to bring destruction upon all who are unrepentant. Music turns to silence. Rejoicing ends.

Prophecy was given by the Lord to change the hearts of people in the present. Prophecy does for us from the perspective of time what the voyage to the moon did for the astronauts in space. It should change my attitude about *things, myself,* and *others.*

Someone said, "We sing about the 'Sweet Bye and Bye,' but we are living in the nasty now!" However, Jesus said, "But lay up for yourselves treasures in heaven." Peter tells us that if we look at what is to come, we'll be properly prepared for today. People, not things, are important.

Next, my attitude toward myself should change. Instead of jumping from one disaster to the next, I must apply Romans 8:28 to my life. "And we know that all things work together for good to them that love God, to them who are called according to his purpose." I know whose I am, why I am here, and where I am going.

Then I am to have a different attitude about others. I am to be aware of the future of the lost and mindful of my opportunities to witness and not envious of the success of the wicked since their prosperity is only for this present season (Psalm 73).

Prophecy should therefore encourage us to extol the salvation of the Lord by speech, service, and song.

Ed Lyman

March 3

SINGING SCRIPTURE: **Psalm 135:3**

Praise the Lord; for the Lord is good: sing praises unto his name; for it is pleasant.

One evening, as I walked down a snow-packed street in northern Saskatchewan on my way to sing in an evangelistic crusade service, the 40-degree-below-zero cold seemed to freeze the joints of my bones. I could think of nothing else but the cold as my breath made a cloud before my eyes.

As I approached the meeting-place, I heard the sound of singing as the choir rehearsed its music for the evening. The cold remained. The chilling wind still whipped my cheeks. My toes and fingers tingled, but I found myself humming along as they sang.

Through the discomfort, the pleasant song of praise to God changed my attitude.

God tells us that we will have distress and tribulation, even as I was greatly annoyed by the comfort-shattering temperatures of that northern climate. However, we can have peace within if we have set our affections on things above and not on the constant harassment of the world, the flesh, and Satan.

In the midst of life's frustrations and the helplessness we feel, we can praise the Lord for his so great salvation and sing thanksgiving songs for his multiplied blessings.

The pleasantness of God's presence can change our attitudes and give a melody when things are darkest.

Ed Lyman

March 4

SINGING SCRIPTURE: 2 Chronicles 5:13

It came even to pass, as the trumpeters and singers were as one, to make one sound to be heard in praising and thanking the Lord; and when they lifted up their voice with the trumpets and cymbals and instruments of music, and praised the Lord, saying, For he is good; for his mercy endureth for ever: that then the house was filled with a cloud, even the house of the Lord.

March 4th is our wedding anniversary. As we knelt at the altar on the day of our marriage, I slipped a brand new band on Julie's finger. The significance of being "as one" was manifest in the act as we committed ourselves to each other. Inscribed on the inside of her wedding ring is Psalm 34:3 — "Oh magnify the Lord with me, and let us exalt his name together."

In a true sense we entered that sanctuary as two people, but we left the little white country church as one, united in one holy bond. Our vows to each other before the gathered congregation held the same significance of oneness which was revealed at the dedication of the Temple. The "singers were as one" making the "one sound to be heard in praising and thanking the Lord."

Although we are often separated by many hundreds of miles, Julie and I are together "as one" in our desire to see Christ honored and lives changed by the gospel. Neither of us can sit on the sidelines. We are both involved by our oneness in marriage and our oneness in Christ.

The blending of individual tones — each Christian putting himself and his gifts in tune with God's will — raises one harmonious chorus of triumphant testimony in the midst of a watching, wondering world, and the "glory of the Lord" is revealed.

Ed Lyman

March 5

SINGING SCRIPTURE: **Daniel 3:5, 6**

...that at what time ye hear the sound of the coronet, flute, harp, sackbut, psaltery, dulcimer, and all kinds of music, ye fall down and worship the golden image that Nebuchadnezzar the king hath set up; and whoso falleth not down and worshipeth shall the same hour be cast into the midst of a burning fiery furnace.

Ancient Babylon has been described as a "golden, music-loving city." But when King Nebuchadnezzar's orchestra struck up this particular tune, it was no concert. "Turn or burn" was the message: either fall down and worship the king's gold-plated idol, or be roasted to death (v. 6). Matthew Henry once wrote, "There is nothing so bad which the careless world will not be drawn to by a concert of music, or driven to by a fiery furnace" — and it is hardly surprising that as soon as the band struck up, all the people fell down (vs. 7).

But not quite *all*. Three expatriate Jews, recently appointed to civic leadership (2:49), flatly refused to join in the wholesale idolatry. They were immediately arrested (vs. 12) and brought before the king (vs. 13). Perhaps as confused as he was angry, the king tried a slightly more subtle approach. Surely they could stretch their consciences and obey his edict? After all, who could possibly withstand his power?

Their reply was clear, concise, and clinching: "our God whom we serve is able" (v. 17). And as we know from the end of the story, their courage was wholly justified, and they walked out of the fire not only unshaken, but unsinged (v. 27).

The whole incident is a vindication of *faith in God* (see Hebrews 11:36). No Christian can expect an easy passage in this world. In fact, he has been promised "persecution" (2 Timothy 3:12). There never yet was an unscarred saint. But neither devil nor idol, man nor beast, pain nor pressure, life nor death can separate the Christian from his heavenly Father's watchful eye, open ear, tender heart, and powerful arm.

John Blanchard

March 6

PRAISE PSALM: **Psalm 22:22**

I will declare thy name unto my brethren: in the midst of the congregation will I praise thee.

Psalms 22, 23, and 24 make up a trilogy of triumph. In Psalm 22, the *Good Shepherd* gives His life for His sheep. It is known as the Cross Psalm. The *Great Shepherd* in Psalm 23 takes care of His sheep. This is the Crook Psalm. Finally, the Crown Psalm represents the *Chief Shepherd*, who appears as King of Glory to reward His sheep.

At verse 22 in Psalm 22, the emphasis changes from crucifixion of Christ to the resurrection of the Redeemer. It finds fulfillment in John 20:17 when Jesus says to Mary, "Go to my brethren, and say unto them, I ascend unto my Father, and your Father; and to my God, and your God." Such a song of declaration sets our souls at liberty, and we find life and reality in the living Christ. This same song of freedom should be on the lips of every believer in consequence of the resurrection of the Lord Jesus Christ, and our Christian growth should be characterized by:

Grace orientation — going the second mile.
Relaxed mental attitude — not jealous or worrisome.
Abiding inner happiness — stability in a storm.
Capacity for love in all categories — not just talking, but walking.
Everyday mastery over the details of living — Christ in command.

Jesus carried the cross that we may claim the crown of life.

Ralph Norwood

March 7

SINGING SCRIPTURE: **Ephesians 5:19**

Speaking to yourselves in psalms and hymns and spiritual songs, singing and making melody in your heart to the Lord;

I have always been grateful to the Lord for placing me in a Christian home, where it was natural for us to sing hymns and spiritual songs. Regularly when we gathered around the table for a meal, we not only had someone say a blessing, but we sang a hymn.

On Sunday evenings, after three or four services in God's House, the whole family would gather in the den and close the day singing hymns, accompanied by my father with his harp-guitar. With that background, I have always been blessed by church music, especially in group singing, where one feels the depth of spiritual commitment, love, and joy of others who blend their voices in harmony.

A special blessing of Christian fellowship was experienced by my wife and me when we were worshiping with a small congregation of Chinese believers in Lotung on the island of Taiwan. Although we couldn't sing in Chinese with them, the tunes were all familiar. And as we sang the words we knew in English, a thrill of joy surged up in our hearts as we realized that we were truly in the same family of God with these Chinese Christians, redeemed by the same precious blood, and renewed by the same indwelling Holy Spirit. Truly the singing of "psalms and hymns and spiritual songs" can play on the strings of the heart, making melody unto the Lord.

James H. Blackstone, Jr.

March 8

SINGING SCRIPTURE: **Nehemiah 12:28, 29**

> *And the sons of the singers gathered themselves together, both out of the plain round about Jerusalem, and from the villages of Netophathi; also from the house of Gilgal, and out of the fields of Geba and Azmaveth: for the singers had builded them villages round about Jerusalem.*

It seemed as if they were coming from everywhere. It was time to dedicate the wall of Jerusalem. None should be left out. Israel was going to communicate with God in worship and with the people surrounding Jerusalem that the Lord Jehovah is truly God.

There is a strong lesson found here for the believer today. Our prayer should be for *opportunities* to communicate — "praying also for us, that God would open unto us a door of utterance, to speak the mystery of Christ, for which I am also in bonds" (Colossians 4:3) — and for the *ability* to communicate the message effectively — "that I may make it manifest, as I ought to speak" (Colossians 4:4).

We are to *reach out in love* — "put on love, which is the bond of perfectness" (Colossians 3:14); *relax in peace* — "let the peace of God rule in your hearts" (3:15); *rejoice in thankfulness* — "be ye thankful" (3:15).

The gathering of the singers is a practical picture of the principles which we find in Colossians. The Lord prepared an opportunity for witness, and those who were prepared by education and experience became involved. Colossians 4:5 puts it very clearly: we are to *"Walk in wisdom"* for the *work of witness* — "Let your speech [song, or sermon] be always with grace, seasoned with salt, that ye may know how ye ought to answer every man" (Colossians 4:6).

Ed Lyman

March 9

SINGING SCRIPTURE: **Isaiah 49:13**

Sing, O heavens; and be joyful, O earth; and break forth into singing, O mountains: for the Lord hath comforted his people, and will have mercy upon his afflicted.

As we crossed a muddy stream in a dugout canoe in the interior of Haiti one warm evening at dusk and began the trek across the desert section, we could hear singing in the distance.

It seemed as if the earth itself were making melody. However, as we neared a clearing with some thatched-roof huts standing as sentinels on the alert, the singing grew louder and we could make shapes and shadows of people standing together under a brush arbor.

They were singing in the Creole language, "Everything's All Right in My Father's House."

Here were Christians in the midst of abject poverty singing a song of safety and assurance.

When our souls are right with God, we have a better attitude toward family, friends, and neighbors.

There is music of hope in the midst of despair, praise in the time of trouble, and thanksgiving when discouragement is upon us.

Ed Lyman

March 10

SINGING SCRIPTURE: **Psalm 43:5**

Why art thou cast down, O my soul? And why art thou disquieted within me? Hope in God: for I shall yet praise him, who is the health of my countenance, and my God.

In the Forty-second Psalm we read this same verse two times, and now it is repeated once more. However, as David said in Psalm 31:7, "Thou hast known my soul in adversities." Certainly he had had a lot of these, especially while carrying out guerrilla warfare against King Saul. He and his band were hunted men, constantly moving, hitting the enemy and then fading back into the hills. But worse than military adversities were the treacheries of David's own heart. David's great sins regarding Uriah and Bathsheba included lying, deceit, adultery, and murder. His deep cry for forgiveness in Psalm 51 may echo that. He could say later, "The Lord is nigh unto them that are of a broken heart" (Psalm 34:18), and "He brought me up also out of a horrible pit, out of the miry clay, and set my feet upon a rock, and established my goings. And he hath put a new song in my mouth" (Psalm 40:2, 3).

Most of our adversities result from our own sins or those of others. Some have no apparent causes we can identify. For them we need the profound walk with God reflected in David's thought, "You've known me when I was on the bottom." Suffering is faith's graduate school. When we have feared for our own health, we can pray better with the sick. After we've looked at a dear, dead face of someone we've loved and lost, we can better comfort the bereaved. The One who knows our souls in adversities stays very close at such times. Thank You, Lord, that You're always there.

Robert P. Evans

March 11

SINGING SCRIPTURE: 1 Samuel 2:1-4 ("Hannah's Song")

And Hannah prayed, and said,
My heart rejoiceth in the Lord, mine horn (strength) is
exalted in the Lord; my mouth is enlarged over mine enemies;
because I rejoice in my salvation.
There is none holy as the Lord: for there is none besides thee:
neither is there any rock like our God.
Talk no more so exceeding proudly; let not arrogancy come
out of your mouth: for the Lord is a God of knowledge, and by
him actions are weighed.
The bows of the mighty men are broken, and they that
stumbled are girded with strength.

Hannah knew the joy of walking where the Lord led. In Psalm 27, David prayed, "Teach me Thy way, O Lord, and lead me in a plain (level) path." Can you pray that and mean it or do you try to teach the Lord your way and hope He will lead you in it?

The story is told of an old Scottish woman, who went about selling goods from house to house. Whenever she came to a crossroad, she tossed a stick into the air and took the way to which it pointed. One day, she tossed the stick into the air several times before moving on and when she was questioned about this, she replied, "The road to the right looked so dreary, I kept tossing the stick until it landed pointing to the left, which seemed a more pleasant way."

I wonder how often we go to God for guidance in this same fashion? If God's way seems rough, we prefer to choose a smoother one, forgetting He sees the end as well as the beginning. It's only as we seek to know His will and follow His way that we find our steps plainly directed and experience peace and blessing.

John Fletcher

March 12

SINGING SCRIPTURE: **1 Chronicles 15:16**

And David spake to the chief of the Levites to appoint their brethren to be the singers with instruments of music, psalteries and harps and cymbals, sounding, by lifting up the voice with joy.

As with one voice, all of the singers and instrumentalists were to present music of praise to reflect the joy found in faithfully following the Lord. Walking in the way of the Lord brings joy! "Thou wilt show me the path of life: in thy presence is fulness of joy; at thy right hand there are pleasures for evermore" (Psalm 16:11). The joy of the Lord is the emphasis of this music verse:

It is the *joy of believing* — Whom having not seen, ye love; in whom, though now ye see him not, yet believing, ye rejoice with joy unspeakable and full of glory" (1 Peter 1:8).

It is the *joy of fulfillment* — "These things I speak in the world, that they might have my joy fulfilled in themselves" (John 17:13).

It is the *joy of asking* — "Hitherto have ye asked nothing in my name: ask, and ye shall receive, that your joy may be full" (John 16:24).

It is the *joy of obedience* — "If ye know these things, happy are ye if ye do them" (John 13:17).

It is the *joy of abiding* — "These things have I spoken unto you, that my joy might remain in you, and that your joy might be full" (John 15:11).

It is the *joy of testifying* — "that I might finish my course with joy, and the ministry, which I have received of the Lord Jesus, to testify the gospel of the grace of God" (Acts 20:24).

Ed Lyman

March 13

SINGING SCRIPTURE: 2 Chronicles 5:12

Also the Levites who were the singers, all of them of Asaph, of Heman, of Jeduthun, with their sons and their brethren, being arrayed in white linen, having cymbals and psalteries and harps, stood at the east end of the altar, and with them a hundred and twenty priests sounding with trumpets.

Solomon built the Temple and dedicated it to God, and the Lord accepted his act of worship and prayer of consecration. "And when all the children of Israel saw how the fire came down, and the glory of the Lord upon the house, they bowed themselves with their faces to the ground upon the pavement, and worshiped, and praised the Lord, saying, For he is good; for his mercy endureth for ever" (2 Chronicles 7:3).

Often we are reminded that the believer is God's by creation and by redemption. However, there is another way in which we are the Lord's. This is by dedication to Him and voluntarily becoming His disciples. This is the same commitment made so long ago in Jerusalem. We often sing, "Take my life and let it be, Consecrated, Lord, to thee." It is one thing to sing those words, but quite another thing to mean them.

That song, sung from the heart, commits us to believe Christ's teaching. "If ye continue in my word, then ye are my disciples" (John 8:31).

Such a consecration is also a commitment to love the people of God — "A new commandment I give unto you, That ye love one another; as I have loved you, that ye also love one another" (John 13:34).

The music that great, festive day presented the people of Israel in sacrifice to the Lord to be bearers of His Word. "This too is our song of commitment, to bear fruit — "I am the vine, ye are the branches.

He that abideth in me, and I in him, the same bringeth forth much fruit; for without me ye can do nothing" (John 15:5).

Ed Lyman

March 14

PRAISE PSALM: **Psalm 149:9**

... to execute upon them the judgment written: this honor have all his saints. Praise ye the Lord.

Just as God's people, Israel, were to be diligent in their warfare against God's enemies, we are expected as believers in the Lord Jesus Christ to work and witness for Him in our daily confrontation with the world around us. The nation of Israel was to be prepared with powerful weapons in hand to defend their land, punish those who brought pagan practices into their community, contain the aggression of the heathen rulers surrounding them, and, as our text states, "execute upon them the judgment written" by the Lord. As it was a privilege for Israel to act on behalf of the Lord, we are also made the sentinels of the Lord to defend the faith, servants of the Lord to do His bidding, and soldiers of the Lord to march into the conflict of carnal command posts with the banner of the Good News of salvation.

"For though we walk in the flesh, we do not war after the flesh: (for the weapons of our warfare are not carnal, but mighty through God to the pulling down of strongholds;) casting down imaginations, and every high thing that exalteth itself against the knowledge of God, and bringing into captivity every thought to the obedience of Christ" (2 Corinthians 10:3-5).

It is an honor to serve the Lord with gladness and thanksgiving, coming before his presence with singing, for our strength is "in the Lord, and in the power of his might" (Ephesians 6:10).

Ed Lyman

March 15

SINGING SCRIPTURE: **Isaiah 51:11**

Therefore the redeemed of the Lord shall return, and come with singing unto Zion; and everlasting joy shall be upon their head; they shall obtain gladness and joy; and sorrow and mourning shall flee away.

In Isaiah 35:1, 2 the prophet Isaiah describes the joyful flourishing of Christ's millennial kingdom. The desert will blossom "as the rose," bringing "joy and singing." Instead of a waste place, arid and bleak, the Lord will display His glory, His majesty, His beauty everywhere. His restoration and divine excellence will prevail, and as we see in today's Scripture, the redeemed shall obtain "gladness and joy."

So it is for every person who has been set free from the desert and wilderness of sin. Without God, this sin-cursed world is a barren and parched place. There is nothing to sustain divine life — nothing to insure spiritual health — nothing to promote the soul's eternal welfare.

But what a transformation takes place when the good news of the gospel brings us to God. All things become new! The "fruits of the Spirit" spring up. Desertlike existence suddenly blossoms with life.

The focus of this experience is joy and singing! There's no song so joyous as the song of the redeemed. Beauty blooms and melody rings in every step of this new way of life.

If your life has known this transformation, then let songs of joy flow through you.

John C. Hallett

❋

March 16

SINGING SCRIPTURE: **Psalm 119:54**

Thy statutes have been my songs in the house of my pilgrimage.

Much is said about the "call" of God to some kind of distinct, Christian service. A man is often heard to say, "I was called to the pastoral ministry," but what constitutes this "call?"

Is it a dramatic intervention by God into a person's life, a "thunderbolt" experience, or is it something else?

Though there are instances of such unique calling, God calls every Christian to His service, and He does this within the context of a person's talent and ability.

The Lord tells us in Ephesians that Christians "are his workmanship, created in Christ Jesus unto good works, which God hath before ordained that we should walk in them."

God has prepared us and has also prepared the way for us to go. Our "calling" is to trust and obey.

So, "we are his *poem*; his song created in Christ Jesus unto good works." In order to be useful, a poem must have direction and a song must be in tune.

Are you?

Ed Lyman

March 17

SINGING SCRIPTURE: **Psalm 138:2**

I will worship toward thy holy temple, and praise thy name for thy lovingkindness and for thy truth; for thou hast magnified thy word above all thy name.

In remembering God's goodness, God's direction, God's protection, we must be cognizant that the past provision of God is just a prelude to what He has planned for His children for the future. He continually magnifies His Word above all that we already know about Him. As a result, singing becomes a wellspring of thanksgiving and commitment bursting forth from the heart of the believer.

"My heart shall sing, when I pause to remember" is the first line of a song I've often sung. It reminds me that from Singapore to Saskatchewan, India to Ireland, Korea to Kitchener, I've seen it happen. When the Word of God is presented in clarity of content and in purity of purpose — by song or sermon — response is forthcoming. Without question or qualm, I have found that songs of praise form on the lips of both those who have honestly and openly confessed and professed Christ as Savior, and those who have been blessed by seeing loved ones and others come to know the Lord they themselves love. Color of skin, differences in language, contrasts in culture all disappear as the Word of God forms a bond of fellowship and praise among believers. "What a fellowship, what a joy divine,

Leaning on the Everlasting Arms!'' The spirit is refreshed; the thirst of the soul is quenched. Truly, "my heart shall sing.''

E. Barry Moore

March 18

SINGING SCRIPTURE: **Psalm 77:6**

I call to remembrance my song in the night: I commune with mine own heart: and my spirit made diligent search.

God speeds the thoughts of His servant to those past, bright experiences which were like a "song.'' The sweet memories of those times set his spirit to searching, and as a result he is brought to the conclusion that all of his dark, foreboding thoughts about the Lord's departure forever from him are just nightmares of his soul. They are altogether false and untrue, not to be believed.

The purposes of the Lord had changed, but not His heart.

As he thinks about the songs of praise and thanksgiving he once sang in the long hours of the night, he realizes the source of his forlorn condition is not Jehovah, but his own weakness and lack of faith.

The young preacher Timothy is told by the Apostle Paul to "call to remembrance the unfeigned faith that is in thee.''

The creeping in of disbelief and doubt works distress into our lives.

The "song in the night'' suggests special memories when our hearts were cheerful and trustful even during times of distress.

Often we refuse to be comforted when "I will trust'' would enable us to "not be afraid.''

The Lord will command his lovingkindness, and in the night his song shall be with me.

Ed Lyman

March 19

SINGING SCRIPTURE: **1 Corinthians 14:26**

How is it then, brethren? when ye come together, every one of you hath a psalm, hath a doctrine, hath a tongue, hath a revelation, hath an interpretation. Let all things be done unto edifying.

The last sentence, "Let all things be done unto edifying," as Ron Blue says, deals a blow to "super-saturated solutions of slush," which picture God as a kindly, white-bearded grandfather smiling down on both naughty and nice children. Our ministries must have purpose!

The word "psalms" is a title derived from the Greek *psalmos* and denotes a poem sung to accompaniment by musical instruments. Though in the context of the Hebrew-Christian community the word did refer basically to the Psalms of the Old Testament, there is no reason to believe that new music would not fall into this terminology also.

The title in Hebrew as *Sepher Tehillim*, which means "Book of Praises."

Therefore, if "all things" in our ministry should have purpose and edification, we must accept the challenge of putting our talents and gifts in proper perspective. We should not allow incorrect concepts and spurious interpretations in music, Christian education, missions, and other areas of outreach and ministry than we allow to be preached from the pulpit. We are to "sing with the spirit" and "sing with the understanding also."

Ed Lyman

March 20

SINGING SCRIPTURE: **Joel 2:15**

Blow the trumpet in Zion, sanctify a fast, call a solemn assembly.

We think of the trumpet mainly as a musical instrument used in bands, orchestras, or combos. However, in the Bible the trumpet had many other uses.

God, through Moses, gave the command to make silver trumpets for the purposes of calling the assembly or sounding the alarm.

At the conquest of Jericho, the Lord spoke through Joshua that seven priests should bear seven trumpets or ram's horns before the ark of the covenant as they encompassed the city. Then, after marching around the city seven times on the seventh day, a long trumpet blast was sounded, the people shouted, and instantly the walls fell down flat.

Likewise, Gideon and his men blew trumpets, broke their pitchers, held their lamps in their hands, and the enemy was routed.

The trumpet was also used in Temple worship according to the directions God gave David: "And when the burnt offering began, the song of the Lord began also with the trumpets" (2 Chronicles 29:27).

Best of all, every born-again believer should be awaiting the trumpet announcement when "the Lord himself shall descend from heaven with a shout, with the voice of the archangel, and with the trump of God: and the dead in Christ shall rise first: then we which are alive and remain shall be caught up together with them in the clouds, to meet the Lord in the air: and so shall we ever be with the Lord" (1 Thessalonians 4:16-18).

Hallelujah! What comfort we should take in these words!

Merrill Dunlop

March 21

SINGING SCRIPTURE: **Psalm 22:23**

Ye that fear the Lord, praise him; all ye the seed of Jacob, glorify him; and fear him, all ye the seed of Israel.

Revival is a quickening or making alive of what is already there. This is a song of revival. Its use of the term "fear the Lord" is an expression often read in the Old Testament which has to do with reverential trust. Within the context of the term "fear the Lord" is also the idea of the hatred of evildoing. It is almost as if David were singing:

Revive us again;
Fill each heart with Thy love;
May each soul be rekindled
With fire from above.

Often the life of the Christian is dulled by the tedious trippings of the world around him, and his vision is blurred by the mundane chores of the routine of life. However, David's song of revival is a challenge to each of us who trust the Lord to praise and glorify Him who is our quickening. In John 11, after Jesus had commanded the stone to be removed from Lazarus' tomb and called Lazarus to come forth from the dead, He said, "Loose him, and let him go." Once we are loosed from false ideas, false religion, and false faith by the power of Jesus Christ, we are free to be a witness for the resurrected Savior.

Ed Lyman

March 22

SINGING SCRIPTURE: **Judges 6:34**

But the Spirit of the Lord came upon Gideon, and he blew a trumpet; and Abiezer was gathered after him.

Once again the trumpet calls Israel to battle. The music strikes a familiar chord in the hearts of God's children, and they assemble to wield the sword of the Lord against those who would put Israel in bondage. However, this does not happen until something significant takes place in the life of Gideon.

The enemy arrayed itself against Israel, and adversity appeared to position itself for a frontal attack. "But the Spirit of the Lord came upon Gideon," and the whole scene was changed. The Holy Spirit literally clothed Himself with Gideon, taking complete possession of him. As the garment of the Holy Spirit, Gideon became the instrument by which God delivered His people.

This same Holy Spirit who made the difference in the life of Gideon makes the difference also in our lives as believers in the Lord Jesus Christ. His indwelling presence empowers us to successfully live the Christian life, to sound the trumpet of testimony in presenting the love and salvation of Christ, and to pray purposefully.

As the believer lives in obedience to the will of God, a special harmony results from the music of the Holy Spirit's ministry. No longer the victim of outside influences, the Christian is victor over these circumstances.

"Ye are of God, little children, and have overcome them: because greater is he that is in you, than he that is in the world" (1 John 4:4).

Ed Lyman

March 23

SINGING SCRIPTURE: **1 Kings 4:29, 32**

And God gave Solomon wisdom and understanding exceeding much, and largeness of heart, even as the sand that is on the seashore...
And he spake three thousand proverbs: and his songs were a thousand and five.

I read "JOIN US FOR MUSIC ON YOUR MIND — DISCO TONIGHT" on the marquee of the hotel where I was staying in Southern California. That evening, returning from a concert, I entered the lobby and was assaulted by the sheer volume of the sounds which blasted from the ballroom. It prevented any verbal communication other than shouting. Thinking processes were short-circuited as the magnitude of the tones and the thump of the beat drowned out all else. This was not a hearing and understanding of music; it was the feeling of sound. It was not music for the mind. It was rhythm for the body, and that only if the ears could stand it.

Solomon, however, had music on his mind. His was a creative provision of proverbs and song which have lasted through the centuries to inspire, edify, and bless the hearts of millions. The splendor of his golden courts has faded along with the wealth of his kingdom and the magnificence of his palace, just as the rhythmic cacophony that California night finally faded into the stillness of the desert air. Yet, the wisdom of his words and the truth of his psalms live today and still affect the lives and destinies of men.

"For God hath not given us the spirit of fear; but of power, and of love, and of a sound mind" (2 Timothy 1:7).

Ed Lyman

March 24

SINGING SCRIPTURE: 1 Samuel 13:3

And Jonathan smote the garrison of the Philistines that was in Geba, and the Philistines heard of it. And Saul blew the trumpet throughout all the land, saying, Let the Hebrews hear.

Saul's son, Jonathan, was a man of character and had clear awareness of the will of God. When his father was reluctant to move into the battle, which the Lord had promised would be a victory for Israel, Jonathan believed God and took it upon himself to prove the word of the Lord to be dependable.

At Hopetown, our school and conference center for handicapped children and young people, we have learned by marvelous experiences that God is concerned with our predicaments and that His Word is truth. As music — the sound of the trumpet — was a witness to Israel that the Lord had triumphed over their foes and a challenge to join in the battle for complete victory, so music has shown us some wonderful things in our ministry.

A young child, unable to walk and confined to a wheelchair, who cannot speak and has never been taught that Jesus loves her, hears the gospel message and asks the Lord Jesus to come into her heart. The next time the children join in a time of song, this little child rings a bell with excitement: "Jesus loves me, this I know!" That bell-song is her testimony that she is a child of God, having overcome the problem of deformity and vocal incapacity through the love of Christ. But that song on her little bell is also a challenge to all of us to touch the lives of others through song and testimony. "Give of your best to the Master.... Join in the battle for truth."

Winfield F. Ruelke

March 25

PRAISE PSALM: **Psalm 118:28**

Thou art my God, and I will praise thee: thou art my God, I will exalt thee.

O Lord our Lord, how excellent is thy name in all the earth! who hast set thy glory above the heavens.

Out of the mouth of babes and sucklings hast thou ordained strength because of thine enemies, that thou mightest still the enemy and the avenger.

When I consider thy heavens, the work of thy fingers, the moon and the stars, which thou hast ordained;

What is man, that thou art mindful of him? And the son of man, that thou visitest him?

For thou hast made him a little lower than the angels, and hast crowned him with glory and honor.

Thou madest him to have dominion over the works of thy hands; thou hast put all things under his feet:

All sheep and oxen, yea, and the beasts of the field;

The fowl of the air, and the fish of the sea, and whatsoever passeth through the paths of the seas.

O Lord, our Lord, how excellent is thy name in all the earth!

David,
Psalm 8

March 26

SINGING SCRIPTURE: **Psalm 118:14**

The Lord is my strength and song, and is become my salvation.

Sometimes we are prone to forget that we are just as dependent upon God in our good times of health and happiness as we are in times of distress and anxiety.

Often when we are feeling on top of the world and things seem to be rolling along just the way we want, there is a tendency to take our eyes off the Lord and become confident in our own strength and ability.

Our only true source of strength ultimately rests in the Lord.

He provides the daily physical need for everyone. In the realm of spiritual things, God also gives peace as a direct result of his presence. Instead of the wail and moan of helplessness, "Christ rejuvenates the spirit with the confidence of sins forgiven. He gives a new song of faith and hope. Fellowship with Jesus Christ promises salvation for the soul. It leads to strength for weakness. It puts a song in the heart.

God provides salvation for eternity, but he also cares for our every need in this earthy life.

Ed Lyman

March 27

SINGING SCRIPTURE: **Jeremiah 33:11**

...The voice of joy, and the voice of gladness, the voice of the bridegroom, and the voice of the bride, the voice of them that shall say, Praise the Lord of hosts: for the Lord is good; for his mercy endureth for ever: and of them that shall bring the sacrifice of praise into the house of the Lord. For I will cause to return the captivity of the land, as at the first, saith the Lord.

Before we were saved, we were obsessed with one desire; there was no question about pleasing God. We lived for ourselves. After one comes to Christ, his basic interest in life should be to please Christ. If this interest is not there, his relationship to the Lord is doubtful. The true believer will long to obey God, and even though he fails on occasion, he will confess to the Lord and continue to move forward in his Christian experience. When he disobeys, he is made aware of it by the indwelling Holy Spirit; but the moment he confesses to the Lord in sincerity, he is back in fellowship.

It is important to understand that though the believer still has the old nature, there is no compulsion to yield to the weaknesses of the flesh. He can be victorious through continuous dependence on the Lord. He should take time daily to meditate on the Scriptures as he commits his way to the Lord.

J. Allen Blair

March 28

PRAISE PSALM: **Psalm 149:6**

Let the high praises of God be in their mouth, and a two-edged sword in their hand.

Here is a joyful, singing band of believers equipped to defend the faith and ready to declare the glorious truth of God's Word. What a picture! With such a weapon in hand, they have ample reason to raise their songs on high. Though the two-edged sword is a weapon used by soldiers to correct disorders, control rebellion, and conduct warfare against enemies, there is a strong allusion to other two-edged swords found in the Bible.

One is the two-edged sword of the Savior. John, the disciple whom Jesus loved as a young man, is given a vision of the Risen Christ in Revelation 1:16 and he describes what he sees: "And he had in his right hand seven stars: and out of his mouth went a sharp two-edged sword: and his countenance was as the sun shineth in its strength." This weapon which Jesus wields is also the weapon we are to use in our spiritual warfare. The writer of Hebrews describes it: "For the word of God is quick, and powerful, and sharper than any two-edged sword, piercing even to the dividing asunder of soul and spirit, and of joints and marrow, and is a discerner of the thoughts and intents of the heart" (Hebrews 4:12).

No wonder we should sing, "And now, O King Eternal, we lift our battle song."

"Wherefore, take unto you the whole armor of God, that ye may be able to withstand in the evil day, and having done all, to stand.... And take the helmet of salvation, and the sword of the Spirit, which is the word of God" (Ephesians 6:13, 17).

Ed Lyman

March 29

SINGING SCRIPTURE: **Isaiah 42:10**

*Sing unto the Lord a new song, and his praise from the end of
the earth, ye that go down to the sea, and all that is therein: the
isles, and the inhabitants thereof.*

The challenge is given to be witnesses for the Lord and to carry
the message of new life and praise around the world.

The Apostle Paul told us we are ambassadors for Christ. Those
who went down to the sea were sailors, and they would carry these
praises with them to the islands and nations they would visit on
their voyages.

No man who has found hope and abundant life through his
relationship with Jesus Christ can become an island unto himself.
He must share his new freedom and joy with those with whom he
comes in contact.

Most of us have stood on the shore of a lake and had the
interesting experience of listening to the sounds coming from
people and activities from the far shore or a boat on the other side of
the lake. The sound carries, and often it reaches us after the voices
or activities producing the sound have stopped. If there is singing,
the song is often ended while the melody lingers upon the ears.

In our daily activities and associations with people, our witnessing
may end, but the memory lingers and may cause someone to find
the Lord.

Ed Lyman

March 30

SINGING SCRIPTURE: **Psalm 89:1**

*I will sing of the mercies of the Lord for ever: with my mouth
will I make known thy faithfulness to all generations.*

When I consider the words "sing of the mercies of the Lord" and
"make known thy faithfulness", I remember Mama. One of the
many things I learned from her was that we really don't grow old
from living — it is only as we lose interest in living that we grow old!
Until the last few weeks of her almost ninety-four years, she was
alert and always refreshing to talk with. Then, quite suddenly, it
seemed that she felt her time was complete, and the Lord called her
to Himself.

While she was with us, her advice was never outdated. It was always to the point, well thought out, and usually sprinkled with verses or thoughts from Scripture. When she held court, she programmed everything, and if you introduced a new subject, she would acknowledge your input, but suggest that "we" would get back to it as soon as "we" had discussed whatever her present thought was. If you had elected to hold your breath while waiting to get back to your thought, you might have found your complexion turning to a "cool blue." However, when the conversation ended, you had learned to "sing of the mercies of the Lord" because His faithfulness had been made known. Yes, I am reminded of a loving, praying mother who spent many hours in prayer for a now very thankful son.

John M. Johansen

March 31

SINGING SCRIPTURE: **I Corinthians 14:15**

I will pray with the spirit, and I will pray with the understanding also:
I will sing with the spirit, and I will sing with the understanding also.

Given here, with direct simplicity, are guidelines for praying and singing in a Christian assembly or church.

First mentioned is the necessity of singing with the spirit. For years, I have listened to countless vocal presentations in church services, rallies, and evangelistic crusades. Often the singing has left me spiritually unedified even though I was desirous of spiritual blessing. On some of these occasions, the personnel involved have exhibited a high degree of musical ability.

Not infrequently, glittering performances have resulted in garbled words, which were apparently considered to be secondary in importance and consequently were quite meaningless. One such rendition caused an observant Christian to remark, "What that singing needs is a broken heart before the Lord." Paradoxically, I have witnessed mediocre presentations which have lifted me to spiritual heights.

Understanding is the second ingredient. This is a two-way street. The performer must understand the message of the song and then so present it as to be clearly understood by his audience. Musical excellence must go hand in hand with spiritual understanding. This can be highly rewarding and honoring to the Lord.

Merrill Dunlop

April

DAILY PRAISE

April 1

SINGING SCRIPTURE: **Job 30:31**

My harp also is turned into mourning, and my organ into the voice of them that weep.

Job was at the apparent limit of endurance. He had once been great, but now was brought low. His music was nothing but discord, and his songs had turned to lamenting.

Have you ever had the feeling that you were looking up at the bottom of the barrel? Have you ever had the overwhelming urge to quit? I'm sure you have. It is a condition common to all men at some time or other. Even Moses found himself in the "quit quagmire" as he endeavored to perform his duties as leader of Israel and to help his stumbling people. He was weary in well-doing. "And the people murmured against Moses, saying, What shall we drink? And he cried unto the Lord; and the Lord showed him a tree, which when he had cast into the waters, the waters were made sweet. There he made for them a statute and an ordinance, and there he proved them" (Exodus 15:24, 25).

When we have been gnawed on by people and put down by critical personalities and cankerlike prejudices, we become dejected and ready to throw in the towel.

This is just the time when we really need the help of the Lord to prevent us from doing damage to our testimonies and hurting people around us.

We must make every effort to concentrate on the fact that God's ways are not always easily followed in a world of godlessness. Doing the Lord's will demands grit and gumption. Stiffen your backbone, trust the Lord, and tune up a song of praise.

Ed Lyman

April 2

SINGING SCRIPTURE: **Psalm 44:8**

In God we boast all the day long, and praise thy name for ever. Selah.

Irked by the inactivity of the upper room, Peter said to his companions, "I go a-fishing," only to toil all night without a catch. Indeed, in the morning they were so busily engaged with their empty nets and boats that they lost the very sight of Jesus; not even the miracle of the drought of fish made any impression upon them, except to make them think they were lucky. Finally John, sensing the situation, said, "Peter, it is the Lord!" Many are so occupied in and with the Lord's service and work (this important movement and that necessary project — so labeled) that they fail to recognize the Lord Himself. To sit and rest awhile and place one's self in meditative communion with Him is of more importance than to be busily engrossed in Christian activity. After Paul's striking conversion, did he not go into Arabia for three years? Was it to work? No! He came apart to learn of Jesus whom he had been persecuting.

Dr. Vance Havner pens it this way: "If we do not come apart to pray, we will soon fall apart in experience."

"Prayer-craft is mightier than air-craft!" says an English clergyman.

The one who is at the hub of a wheel is not called upon to exert himself to hold on as does the one who is at the circumference of the fast-revolving wheel. The farther away one is from the hub toward the place of the grind, the noise, the mud, the more difficult it is to hold on so as to keep from being whirled off. Stay on key with Him.

George S. Schuler

April 3

SINGING SCRIPTURE: 1 Samuel 16:16

Let our Lord now command thy servants, which are before thee, to seek out a man, who is a cunning player on a harp: and it shall come to pass, when the evil spirit from God is upon thee, that he shall play with his hand, and thou shalt be well.

Suddenly the world of Saul was crumbling around him. One day, as a boy looking for his father's donkeys he was turned into another man with a new heart, having the Spirit of God within, and anointed king of Israel. How vividly he recalled that day Samuel gathered all Israel together to announce their new king, but he was too embarrassed and self-conscious to appear and hid himself from the activities. After he was found, he remembered the thrill when he stood before the people and heard, "God save the king."

Later, defeating the Ammonites, his soul rejoiced with pride as the nation united under his leadership. But then the conflict with the Philistines and Amalekites turned all the glory and joy to despair. He was rejected by God as king and was left troubled with an evil spirit. Depressed, confused, and empty, Saul listened to the melody skillfully played on the harp by David, and he was refreshed. The ministry of this music mended his broken spirit, expelled the evil influence, and made Saul emotionally well.

As believers gifted with skills, gifts, and abilities in musical disciplines, are we seeking to entertain the ears only, or are we to seek to edify the soul? In other words, is your music a profession or a ministry?

Robert and RoseMarie Lehmann

April 4

SINGING SCRIPTURE: **Psalm 108:3**

I will praise thee, O Lord, among the people: and I will sing praises unto thee among the nations.

"I simply argue that the cross be raised again at the center of the marketplace as well as on the steeple of the church. I am recovering the claim that Jesus was not crucified in a cathedral between two candles, but on a cross between two thieves; on the town garbage heap; at a crossroad so cosmopolitan that they had to write his title in Hebrew and in Latin and in Greek ... at the kind of place where cynics talk smut, and thieves curse, and soldiers gamble. Because that is where he died. And that is what he died about. And that is where churchmen ought to be, and what churchmen should be about."

In saying that, George McLeod summed up the meaning of the cross, the commission, and the Christian commitment.

We are to be living stones in the foundation of the house of the Lord, which He is building for Himself in a pagan world. If what we are doing is not counting for the Lord, it is not counting. David said, "Neither will I offer burnt offerings unto the Lord my God of that which doth cost me nothing."

Ed Lyman

April 5

SINGING SCRIPTURE: **Psalm 33:1**

Rejoice in the Lord, O ye righteous: for praise is comely for the upright.

A little boy came in from the barnyard and said, "Mom, that old donkey must be a wonderful Christian."

"Why?" asked the startled mother.

The boy replied, "He has such a long face."

Our music should reflect the radiant joy of a rejoicing soul. A song of praise is "comely for the upright," and our rejoicing takes on a new character as we delight in the Word of God. The process of applying the Scripture to the routine of living brings about a personal relationship with the Lord Jesus Christ, unique to Christianity.

Greek philosophy said, "Be moderate; know thyself."

Roman philosophy said, "Be strong; order thyself."

Confucianism said, "Be superior; correct thyself."

Buddhism says, "Be disillusioned; annihilate thyself."

Hinduism says, "Be separated; merge thyself."

Islam says, "Be submissive; bend thyself."

Materialism says, "Be industrious; enjoy thyself."

Modern dilettantism says, "Be broad; cultivate thyself."

Christianity is different from all religions and philosophies. It says, "Be Christ-like; give thyself."

Ed Lyman

April 6

SINGING SCRIPTURE: **Ezekiel 27:25**

The ships of Tarshish did sing of thee in thy market: and thou wast replenished, and made very glorious in the midst of the seas.

Few passages reveal more clearly the fact that God and man do not always think the same way (Isaiah 55:8).

Humanly speaking, Tyre was the epitome of success. This chief city of Phoenicia was a prosperous seaport and center of commerce. Isaiah says of it: "whose merchants were princes, whose traders were the honored of the earth." Speedy Phoenician ships plowed the seas of the ancient world. Commercial routes were established from Tyre to Western Asia, Egypt, Greece, Spain, Britain, and even to India. Men readily and eagerly sing the praises of a city like Tyre.

This city symbolizes the world's concept of greatness, even as prophetic Babylon will in the future (Revelation 17 and 18). Today the world acclaims men and nations that achieve this position in life. Be successful and self-sufficient and men will sing your praises.

Tyre was also deeply religious, but the object of its devotion was Baal, Ashtoreth, and many lesser deities. Their worship encouraged cruelty, corruption and immorality. It was this, along with its arrogance, that led to its destruction.

Tyre is a grim reminder to all of us that ultimately it doesn't matter if men sing our praises. What really counts is what God thinks about us. The Lord Jesus underlined this when He said: "For what shall it profit a man, if he shall gain the whole world, and lose his own soul?"

John A. Beerley

April 7

SINGING SCRIPTURE: 1 Kings 10:12

And the king made of the almug trees pillars for the house of the Lord, and for the king's house, harps also and psalteries for singers: there came no such almug trees, nor were seen unto this day.

Almug wood was known for its weight, its hardness, and its fine grain, as well as its beautiful color. It was a very rare wood in the Middle East, basically found in India and Ceylon. Solomon's use of this valuable wood was not an exercise in extravagance, but an example of the excellence he insisted upon for those furnishings and adornments used to honor the Lord. Such wood might be expected to be used in pillars, posts, and furniture in the Temple, because its beauty and durability would enhance the appearance and construction of the sanctuary. However, though willow branches might have been more accessible and easily carved for the musical instruments which would accompany the singing of praise in the worship services, again Solomon chose the best to be carved and fashioned for the presentation of praise to the Lord. Such preference on the part of Solomon reminds us of the responsibility spoken of in the song, "Give of your best to the Master."

Is it any wonder the Queen of Sheba exclaimed, "Blessed be the Lord thy God, which delighteth in thee, to set thee on the throne of Israel: because the Lord loved Israel for ever, therefore made he thee king, to do judgment and justice."

Jesus said, "Let your light so shine before men, that they may see your good works, and glorify your Father which is in heaven."

Ed Lyman

April 8

SINGING SCRIPTURE: **Psalm 113:9**

He maketh the barren woman to keep house, and to be a joyful mother of children. Praise ye the Lord.

What is so distinctive about our God? That question is answered by the 113th Psalm.

He is *distinct* because *His nature*, as it is revealed throughout the Word of God by His name, encourages His followers to praise Him in grateful song. The form in which the verbs are found suggests *worthy* to be praised, *worthy* to be blessed. By praising Him in joyful song, we acknowledge who He is.

He is *distinct* because of *His exaltation* — the Highest. Nothing and no one is over Him.

Yet, He is *distinct* because of *His compassion*. He draws Himself close to the helpless and needy in order to deliver them from their fears and inadequacies, to satisfy their longings, and to transform their sorry state of helplessness and despair into consciousness of His provision.

The song of praise to our worthy Lord echoes the truth that God "redeemeth thy life from destruction; who crowneth thee with lovingkindness and tender mercies; who satisfieth thy mouth with good things; so that thy youth is renewed like the eagle's" (Psalm 103:4, 5).

Ed Lyman

April 9

SINGING SCRIPTURE: **1 Samuel 16:17**

And Saul said unto his servants, Provide me now a man that can play well, and bring him to me.

Saul was troubled in spirit and sought comfort. His servants suggested music. But notice, it was not just anybody playing and singing any kind of music. It was to be a person who "can play well." Too often, skill is the neglected ingredient in Christian music and its performance.

Today there is a fresh barrage of new Christian music, some of which is good and effective. How do we evaluate all of this new music? Is it necessarily good or necessarily bad simply because it is new?

Three basic questions help to evaluate all church music and penetrate to the very heart of the issues involved. They are:

1. Is the message Biblically sound and theologically accurate?

2. Are the lyrics poetic and aesthetically appropriate to the message?

3. Does the music fittingly underscore and adequately enhance the lyrics?

Put very simply, is the song Biblical, is it poetic, and is it musical?

The musician who came to Saul was none other than David, whose well-played music and carefully chosen lyrics doubtlessly reminded Saul of the Source of his position and power and the wages of sin.

Don Wyrtzen

April 10

SINGING SCRIPTURE: **Psalm 106:47**

Save us, O Lord our God, and gather us from among the heathen, to give thanks unto thy holy name, and to triumph in thy praise.

We find a counterpart to this Psalm in Romans 12:12, where Paul states, "rejoicing in hope; patient in tribulation; continuing instant in prayer." Even in the midst of tribulation, we are to rejoice. Our joy is not based on outward circumstances, but on the inward relationship we have to our Lord. Wuest says it is rejoicing in the sphere of hope. This is not a "I hope things will turn out all right" type of hope, but a positive knowledge that we shall utterly be delivered from our trials and until then God will take care of us. This brings joy to our lives, music to our hearts, and a song to our lips.

Peter tells us to rejoice in that we are partakers in Christ's sufferings. We are never to suffer for wrongdoing, but only for our witness for Christ.

James tells us to count it all joy when trials and temptations come into our lives for as we respond properly to them, we are maturing and are being made complete in Christ.

Had Paul and Silas not rejoiced and sung in jail, they probably would not have led the Philippian jailer to Christ. The next time you have a trial (which will probably be soon), rejoice and watch God's maturing process in your life.

Paul Crosson

April 11

SINGING SCRIPTURE: **Psalm 106:12**

Then believed they his words; they sang his praise.

In this Psalm, we are reminded of the marvelous deliverance of the Israelites as they left Egypt and crossed the Red Sea on dry ground. God provided a highway of safety through the waters of adversity of His people, while using these same waters to destroy their enemies. As a result of this provision, the people believed the Lord's words and were full of praise. Immediately a song of deliverance was sung. However, this experience was soon forgotten, and their tongues were again dragging on the desert sands. The song was forgotten as moans of despair sprang from dry throats.

If we are trusting in continual "bigger and better" experiences — miracles and wonders — to keep our spiritual batteries charged, we are missing the meaning of faith and trust in Jesus Christ. Reminding ourselves of whose we are and whom we serve brings a praiseful song to our lips in recognition that our relationship to the Lord is dependent upon His finished work on Calvary and not on ecstatic and emotional feelings. So sang Israel for the fact of God's presence.

The face of the Christian singing along life's road smiles in God's service.

Ed Lyman

April 12

SINGING SCRIPTURE: **1 Corinthians 13:1**

Though I speak with the tongues of men and of angels, and have not charity, I am become as sounding brass, or a tinkling cymbal.

It could very well be that in some areas of our lives we should stop praying and start believing. Some people are still walking around the walls of Jericho. They have never given the shout for the walls to fall. Learning from the Word of God means learning triumph.

Jesus Christ removed His robes of deity and took upon Himself the rags of poverty in order that we might don the garments of righteousness as sons of God. No wonder Paul puts double emphasis upon rejoicing: "Rejoice in the Lord always: and again I say, Rejoice" (Philippians 4:4). It is almost as if he tells us to rejoice in our newfound relationship to the Son of God and then says, "Did you hear me? Listen again! Rejoice!" Our song of praise should be one continual adoration, because the gospel of the Lord Jesus Christ is not just "the way in," it is also "the way on."

These things have I written unto you that believe on the name of the Son of God; that ye may know that ye have eternal life, and that ye may believe on the name of the Son of God" (1 John 5:13).

What a song of rejoicing we can sing as we put belief into shoe-leather faith.

Ed Lyman

April 13

SINGING SCRIPTURE: **Psalm 89:15**

Blessed is the people that know the joyful sound: they shall walk, O Lord, in the light of thy countenance.

In April 1979 I went back to Mainland China to see my family. We had not seen each other since 1949 when I left as a refugee.

During the train trip I had a sleeping berth — so different from thirty years ago when I came out of China hanging on the narrow steps outside the train. I couldn't sleep during this trip home because I was too excited.

Eagerly I ran up the stairs. My mother was waiting for me at the kitchen door. We both broke down and cried as I took her in my arms. Then she prayed right there, thanking the Lord for bringing her son back and for guiding and using me as His servant. This had been my mother's prayer all those years. My father had been placed under house arrest in 1958. As a minister, he could not have food coupons and there was no job for him. Due to inadequate food intake, he died of a heart condition.

Then we had a family prayer meeting and Bible study together. I sang for Mother; we sang many of the old, old songs which my parents taught me. My mother took a little handwritten piece of paper from her pocket and told me this was her only Bible. I gave her a large-print Bible. She hugged it to her heart and said it was the most precious gift I'd bought her. For three days we shared, talked, and worshiped together.

"Blessed is the people that know the joyful sound."

Paul Chang

April 14

SINGING SCRIPTURE: **Psalm 30:9**

What profit is there in my blood, when I go down to the pit? Shall the dust praise thee? Shall it declare thy truth?

This whole Psalm deals with the experience of facing death as a result of a very serious illness and then finding deliverance from the "pit" by the hand of the Lord. Such a marvelous and marked recovery produces a jubilant thanksgiving, and there is cause to reflect upon the nature of God's lovingkindness and the character of His mercy. This is a kind of musical memorial to the personal concern God has for His children. As a result of the time of suffering, there is a drawing closer to the Lord and an acute awareness of the fact that man's breath is in the hands of God alone.

Before the sickness, the Psalmist speaks of a boastful attitude toward his own self-sufficiency. However, the onslaught of illness brings a quick end to pride as a complete dependence upon his Maker is recognized. After crying out for help and healing, he is delivered by the mercy of the God of creation.

The lesson of this particular verse is one of changing lamentation to a song of praise. Being concerned only with self-pride and self-purpose brings no praise to the Lord. When a life is lived with these goals uppermost, nothing is left behind for God's glory. "Shall the dust praise thee?" However, a life presented to the Lord produces a lasting song, a memorial of testimony and praise.

Ed Lyman

April 15

SINGING SCRIPTURE: **Hosea 8:1**

Set the trumpet to thy mouth. He shall come like as an eagle against the house of the Lord, because they have transgressed my covenant, and trespassed against my law.

The music of the trumpet is a clarion call marking a time of judgment against God's people, Israel. They had refused to repent of their sin and turn to the Lord.

Pride had consumed them. Their music was a discord of self-assurance. They called themselves God's people, but they wanted Him to stand aside while they "did their own thing." They had opted for partial sanctification. "Ephraim ... hath mixed himself among the people; Ephraim is a cake not turned" (7:8). They had become unpalatable. You might say they were "half-baked"!

"And the pride of Israel testifieth to his face: and they do not return to the Lord their God, nor seek him for all this" (7:10).

The sound of the trumpet breaks into the myopic melodies of "me-ism" and is a startling and poignant reminder that they had:

No heart for the Lord — "Ephraim also is like a silly dove without heart" (7:11a).

No homing instinct for God — "they call to Egypt, they go to Assyria" (7:11b).

No honorable direction — "for they have fled from me" (7:13).

Like Israel preening in pride, the Christian caught up in himself is a "deceitful bow" (7:16) — insincere, not on the mark.

The significance of the trumpet sound is that we are called to look up. In so doing, we see the face of the Lord. It may be necessary as we look at the Lord and then see ourselves that we join the song of repentance: "Come, and let us return unto the Lord: for he hath torn, and he will heal us; he hath smitten, and he will bind us up ... he will raise us up, and we shall live in his sight" (6:1, 2).

Ed Lyman

April 16

SINGING SCRIPTURE: **1 Samuel 16:18**

Then answered one of the servants, and said, Behold, I have seen a son of Jesse the Bethlehemite, that is cunning in playing, and a mighty valiant man, and a man of war, and prudent in matters, and a comely person, and the Lord is with him.

The ideal Christian musician — is he the singer with the silky voice, the Hollywood appearance, the show-biz delivery of tunes and monologue — or the one who is demure, meek, unostentatious, concerned with focusing attention on the Lord in a self-depreciatory way? Some prefer the dynamic and charismatic. Others want musicians to speak only when spoken to. Perhaps David's presentation can give us a clue since Saul was looking for the best person to provide musical therapy for his troubled spirit.

David was brave and not shy about facing confrontation. He knew when to speak and when to keep quiet. He had a relaxed presence. Sounds to me like the All-American (or I should say All-Hebrew) boy. But what was the first thing mentioned about him?

He was "skillful in playing"!

Why was this the first quality? Did Saul need a warrior? No! A counselor? Orator? No! He wanted a musician, someone who could play well. There is a great lesson in this. Christian musicians should take more time to develop their skills. This goes for those in other pursuits also. Courage, wisdom, speaking ability, pleasing appearance, etc. are all important in their ways; yet, they are secondary to being skilled at whatever is to be done in Christ's name.

The ideal Christian musician? First thing — skillful in playing — "and the Lord is with him."

Douglas E. Schoen

April 17

SINGING SCRIPTURE: **Psalm 106:1**

Praise ye the Lord. O give thanks unto the Lord; for he is good: for his mercy endureth for ever.

The meeting in South Caicos, West Indies, had already begun when I recognized a very familiar song. It was a chorus I had taught on another island some five hundred miles away. The tune was slightly different, but the words were the same. It was a song about God's forgiveness of sin. Someone had attended a meeting on that other island, liked the song, and brought it with him on his visit to South Caicos. Music spreads like wildfire; therefore, we should make use of this vital art in the evangelization of children.

One of the easiest ways of memorizing anything is by setting it to music. Children have fantastic memories. When they sing a good chorus, they are planting a Biblical truth in their fertile minds which will remain with them for the rest of their lives. The child's great imagination helps him visualize and feel the message of the song. A Bible verse put to music is an easy way for a child (and most others) to memorize a portion of Scripture. Every time we sing of the crucifixion and resurrection, we are reminded again of the meaning of these important Bible truths.

Praising the Lord and giving thanks to Him through song is a potent reminder to a child that the Lord is good and "his mercy endureth for ever." This is the musical meaning of "Train up a child in the way he should go," and then as he grows older he'll not escape the message of the song and the Scripture.

Bill Salisbury

April 18

SINGING SCRIPTURE: **2 Chronicles 35:25**

And Jeremiah lamented for Josiah: and all the singing men and the singing women spake of Josiah in their lamentations to this day, and made them an ordinance in Israel: and, behold, they are written in the lamentations.

Songs lamenting the death of Josiah, the king, were sung. He had honored the Lord and done those things which were right in the eyes of God.

Again, we are cognizant of the many facets of musical involvement in the lives and religious activities of Israel. Throughout the Scriptures we find songs composed and sung upon important occasions. Moses made a song after the passage through the sea to thank God for the deliverance of Israel. David composed numerous songs for many occasions. Jeremiah wrote his Lamentations, a special song in which he deplores calamity befalling Jerusalem. Deborah and Barak sang a triumphant hymn after the defeat of Sisera. The Song of Solomon and the 45th Psalm are wedding songs and are considered by many to be allegorical. Hannah, the mother of Samuel, and Hezekiah returned thanks to God in song for special favors from the Lord. Other thanksgiving songs are sung by Mary (Jesus' mother), Zacharias, and Simeon.

It is a blessing much overlooked, this comforter called music.

Ed Lyman

April 19

SINGING SCRIPTURE: **Job 29:13**

> *The blessing of him that was ready to perish came upon me;*
> *and I caused the widow's heart to sing for joy.*

What a marvelous statement on the part of the patriarch Job! Here Job is in the midst of the most awful trial of his life. There had come upon him a set of circumstances that would make many a spiritual person even in our time fall into deep depression. Many, in these circumstances, would have lifted a fist in resentment against God and pressed upon the Lord the question, "Why do these things happen to me?" Job's situation is a demonstration of the fact that the realities of life are not produced by external circumstances but inner attitudes.

Notice Job's inner attitude of rejoicing. He speaks, even in the midst of his untoward moments, of the blessing of God coming upon his life. Indeed, the Bible tells us that true riches come in the form of divine blessing, certainly not in the coin of the realm. The result was that his heart sang for joy, and he was able to impart that kind of joy which produced song even in the heart of the widow.

The lesson is clear. The greatest desolations of life — widowhood, financial reversals, absence of physical health — can still be a time in which the heart sings for joy because of the blessing of God. Surely every one of us should pursue such an understanding of God's wonderful working on our behalf, so that our hearts too share that song of joy.

Dave Breese

April 20

SINGING SCRIPTURE: **Psalm 147:20**

> *He hath not dealt so with any nation: and as for his judgments,*
> *they have not know them. Praise ye the Lord.*

God's people have been privileged as recipients of His very presence. The Lord has personally chosen them. How much and often they ought to lift their songs of praise to Him!

We who know Him are in possession of His Word: the written Word of God and the Word of God in person. How much more ought we then to praise the Lord!

"And the Word was made flesh, and dwelt among us, (and we beheld his glory, the glory as of the only begotten of the Father), full of grace and truth" (John 1:14).

David himself presents an apt commentary in Psalm 19:7-14: "The law of the Lord is perfect, converting the soul: the testimony of the Lord is sure, making wise the simple. The statutes of the Lord are right, rejoicing the heart: the commandment of the Lord is pure, enlightening the eyes. The fear of the Lord is clean, enduring for ever: the judgments of the Lord are true and righteous altogether. More to be desired are they than gold, yea, than much fine gold: sweeter also than honey and the honeycomb. Moreover by them is thy servant warned: and in keeping of them there is great reward. Who can understand his errors? Cleanse thou me from secret faults. Keep back thy servant also from presumptuous sins; let them not have dominion over me: then shall I be upright, and I shall be innocent from the great transgression. Let the words of my mouth, and the meditation of my heart, be acceptable in thy sight, O Lord, my strength, and my redeemer."

Ed Lyman

April 21

SINGING SCRIPTURE: **Psalm 105:2**

Sing unto him, sing psalms unto him: talk ye of all his wondrous works.

There is music all around us.

Life and love and music are bound into a wondrous symphonic poem. They are inseparable, like the lyrics, melody, and rhythm of a lilting song.

Vincent Youmans wrote, "Without a song, the day would never end." Music had its creation in the hallowed halls of Heaven when the morning stars sang together. It has been blessing man throughout the eons of time. Songs can fill the vacuum of lost love and burst forth into the flowering joy of living. God Himself will enjoy the songs of salvation and adoration sung by the redeemed of all ages: the lovesong of God. Life overflows with melody, but let us lay aside the chorus of the commonplace and take up the matchless song of redemption in Jesus Christ.

Surely Christ has put a new song in our hearts, a matchless melody on our lips, and has broken sin's bondage with the song of a soul set free.

Since we have been set at liberty, let us join in raising the song of freedom found in the salvation of our Lord Jesus Christ.

Ed Lyman

April 22

SINGING SCRIPTURE: **Jeremiah 31:7**

For thus saith the Lord; Sing with gladness for Jacob, and shout among the chief of the nations: publish ye, praise ye, and say, O Lord, save thy people, the remnant of Israel.

Here we have a command of God given by the prophet Jeremiah — often called the weeping prophet — that we are to "sing with gladness." A proper relationship to God can hardly be expressed by mere words and by the causal responses of the average personality. Not at all! The blessings of God are best expressed, as we see in this Scripture, in glad song. The song of Israel and the song of the church should therefore be not the troublesome duty of a mumbling Christian, but rather the glad expression of a heart that has been released from the fearful power of sin and is enjoying the blessing of God.

This passage also tells us that we are called upon both to sing and also to publish. We can rejoice therefore that talented people have been raised up in our midst with the ability to sing not only for themselves, but to write the notes and the words that can set the Christian world to singing. While the test of time is the final revelation, nevertheless it appears that in our time, some of the finest Christian music is being written and sung by glad responsive hearts. We can rejoice that such music is available to us from those who have committed both to sing the praises of God and to duplicate with today's remarkable media those praises which set our hearts to singing as well. The blessing of God was the song of Israel in that day. May the joy of the Lord be our song today.

Dave Breese

April 23

SINGING SCRIPTURE: **1 Corinthians 14:8**

For if the trumpet give an uncertain sound, who shall prepare himself to the battle?

It is quite obvious even to the most casual observer of military affairs that in the days when the charge was sounded by trumpets on the battlefield, troops could not properly respond unless the trumpet call was clear. The playing of the wrong call could change the whole course of the conflict, or the blowing of wrong notes could confuse soldiers along the line and the carefully planned timing of the operation could be drastically upset.

The "sound" we present in our witnessing should not be a vague presentation of religion, but a positive call to the Lord Jesus Christ.

Jesus: his human name. This name saves us; it means "God, our salvation."

Christ: his official name. "Messiah"; this speaks of His administration, His Kingdom.

Lord: his title. He is to be both Lord and Christ.

His full name: the Lord Jesus Christ.

Ed Lyman

April 24

SINGING SCRIPTURE: **Psalm 5:11**

> *But let all those that put their trust in thee rejoice: let them ever shout for joy, because thou defendest them: let them also that love thy name be joyful in thee.*

David described the believer in Psalm 1:3, saying, "He shall be like a tree planted by the rivers of water, that bringeth forth his fruit in his season; his leaf also shall not wither; and whatsoever he doeth shall prosper." In certain areas in Palestine, there are underground waterways running in various directions. Above, on the dry ground, is vegetation which draws on these underground waterways for life and sustenance. This is similar to the way it is when one is in Christ. He has hidden resources that others know nothing about. He has a peace that cannot be understood by the world. He can praise the Lord with no fear that he'll ever be without the presence of the Lord, no matter where he finds himself.

Hundreds of thousands of empty lives need God's presence and peace. More and more, the unsaved are recognizing their total inability to find rest for either body or soul. Millions of dollars are being spent annually on drugs and alcohol in an attempt to experience release from anxiety. This is man's way, but it is totally insufficient. There is a way that seems right unto man, but it is not

God's way. Man's way leads to insecurity and fear. How different is God's way as described by the prophet Isaiah: "Thou wilt keep him in perfect peace, whose mind is stayed on thee" (Isaiah 26:3).

J. Allen Blair

April 25

SINGING SCRIPTURE: **Psalm 34:1**

> *I will bless the Lord at all times: his praise shall continually be in my mouth.*

If we are to have, so to speak, a song of praise in our mouths continually, it is important that we undertake a systematic and progressive study of the Word of God. If we are to be thoroughly furnished unto every good work, we must acquaint ourselves with all Scripture, which "is given by inspiration of God, and is profitable for doctrine, for reproof, for correction, for instruction in righteousness: that the man of God may be perfect, thoroughly furnished...." The thought is not that we are to master the Scriptures' contents so much as that we must allow the Word of God to grasp us. As it masters us, we are gripped by the living hand of the living God, kept by His grace, and in communion with Him who is the author, object, and source of all Scripture.

It is not mere intellectual appreciation or apprehension of the contents of the revelation of the Bible, mere knowledge. It must rather be an entering into the thoughts of God in a lowly spirit of obedience and faith.

Timothy, Paul's son in the ministry, had known the Holy Scriptures from his childhood, and they were able to make him "wise unto salvation through faith which is in Christ Jesus." Such awareness of the ministry of the Word of God puts us in the mood and climate of praiseful song.

Ed Lyman

April 26

SINGING SCRIPTURE: **1 Samuel 21:11**

> *And the servants of Achish said unto him, Is not this David the king of the land? did not they sing one to another of him in dances, saying, Saul hath slain his thousands, and David his ten thousands.*

The songs which had been sung about David had carried a message even beyond the borders of Israel. David's fame and position were known to "outsiders" because the songs about him had spread abroad.

His reputation was actually carried on wings of song.

There are a number of meanings for the term word of God.

It can mean a divine utterance. God actually spoke to various people at particular times, as we read in the Scriptures.

Secondly, Jesus Christ is the living Word, the Word made flesh.

Next, it is true that the Bible is the Word of God: "All Scripture is given by inspiration of God."

There is also the Word of God which is preached by ministers, pastors, evangelists, Bible teachers, and Sunday school teachers.

However, there is another truth involved as we recognize that our lives, as Christians, are in a real sense epistles, luminaries to the world around us. We are also the word of God in that we are instruments God uses to present Himself to the lost.

Ed Lyman

April 27

SINGING SCRIPTURE: **Isaiah 54:1**

Sing, O barren, thou that didst not bear; break forth into singing, and cry aloud, thou that didst not travail with child: for more are the children of the desolate than the children of the married wife, saith the Lord.

There are many references to barren women in the Bible. Among them are the names of Sarah, Rachel, Hannah, and Elizabeth. The latter two did "break forth into singing" after they were healed of barrenness.

Hannah's prophetic song mentions that the "barren hath born seven" (1 Samuel 2:5). Seven is the number of completion and typifies the fullness of fruit the Lord expects His saints to produce — the nine-fold fruit of the Spirit (Galatians 5:22, 23).

The barren woman typifies the soul that is sterile until vivified by the divine life of Christ. The miracle of regeneration enables the soul to rejoice in singing. A singing heart is like fertile soil from which the fruit of the Spirit will emerge. Our Lord desires that we bring forth "more fruit" and "much fruit" (John 15:2, 5).

In the life a Christian, graces should flourish (2 Peter 1:5-8). If these virtues abound in us, we shall neither be barren nor unfruitful in the knowledge of the Lord.

Deoram Bholan

April 28

SINGING SCRIPTURE: **Psalm 48:10**

According to thy name, O God, so is thy praise unto the ends of the earth: thy right hand is full of righteousness.

When a fungus growth developed on the leander tree, an effort was made to destroy it through importation of another biological growth that would accomplish this purpose. However, unbeknown to the Bermuda government at that time, although this growth would help the leander, it also destroyed all of the Bermuda cedars. Following this blight, there was the necessity of finding a quick-growing tree that would give some green to the island. The cassarina was chosen.

After leaving the island for a number of years and then returning for my first visit, the cassarina caught my attention. It was not its height and color, but the sound produced when the wind whistled through its branches. What a beautiful listening experience! Multiply that sound with a forest of cassarina trees and you can imagine what is produced.

If creation can produce such beautiful sounds with the wind passing through some branches, try to fathom what will happen when the Master Himself allows inanimate objects to sound forth praise to Him. Truly He is deserving of our praise. Commit yourself today to blend your voice with all of the redeemed in worship of the Lord Jesus Christ.

Ted and Pat Cowen

April 29

SINGING SCRIPTURE: **1 Samuel 18:6**

And it came to pass as they came, when David was returned from the slaughter of the Philistine, that the women came out of all cities of Israel, singing and dancing, to meet king Saul, with tabrets, with joy, and with instruments of music.

There is victory for Israel. The triumphs of King Saul are sung, but when compared to those of David, Saul is reminded of his failures and shortcomings. He becomes angered and suspicious of David. The song touches the personal experience of Saul's life, and it takes on special meaning.

Much music comes from personal experience. The composer puts his thoughts and emotions into his music and many who hear the composition are able to identify with it because they have also experienced the same. There is a point of reference which sparks the memory. In Exodus 15 we find the Israelites remembering God's leading, protection, and deliverance in a song, and we also remember incidents we associate with a song.

So often this is told of a child who goes week after week to Sunday school, where he hears many of the familiar gospel songs. As he grows older, he may reject the church and then after more years of being away from the sanctuary of God's house somehow finds his way back. Upon hearing some of the same songs, those lessons and truths he had forgotten return. A point of reference — music of the past — becomes a catalyst to convict, confirm, and challenge. His mind and heart are directed upward in praise and adoration.

Mark Moore

April 30

SINGING SCRIPTURE: **Hosea 5:8, 9**

Blow ye the cornet in Gibeah, and the trumpet in Ramah; cry aloud at Bethaven, after thee, O Benjamin. Ephraim shall be desolate in the day of rebuke: among the tribes of Israel have I made known that which shall surely be.

Dr. Ralph Keiper says we will sing one of two songs in Heaven: "Crown Him with Many Crowns" or "Have I Come Empty-handed?"

The song of rejoicing comes as we "press toward the mark for the prize of the high calling of God in Christ Jesus ... holding forth the word of life; that I may rejoice in the day of Christ, that I have not run in vain, neither labored in vain" (Philippians 3:14; 2:16).

Ed Lyman

May

DAILY PRAISE

May 1

SINGING SCRIPTURE: **Psalm 149:3**

> *Let them praise his name in the dance: let them sing praises unto him with the timbrel and harp.*

While rereading the Psalms, as I rested on the shore at Lake Pleasant, high in the New York Adirondacks, I noted the word "praise" is used more frequently than most words.

The Hebrew title for the Psalms is *Tehilim*, which means "praises" or "hymns." A common thread traced through the entire book is that an inherent characteristic of the Christian is the desire to worship and glorify God in song and praise.

Great is the Lord and worthy of our praise (48). As we read in the Psalms, we are often admonished to praise God with the harp and the ten-stringed lyre. The harp is a musical instrument, having many strings of graded lengths, stretched across an open triangular frame and played by plucking these strings. If we would emulate the strings by individually being spread across the trinitarian frame, orchestrated by the Maestro Himself, what wonderful music and worthy praise we could share one with another. Joining with the Psalmist, "the music of the strings makes you glad" (45), we would "clap [your] hands all you nations; shout to God with cries of joy" (47) and together "sing of your love, for you are my fortress, my refuge in times of trouble" (59).

"With singing lips my mouth will praise you because you are my help. I will sing in the shadow of your wings" (63).

John M. Johansen

---------------- ❀ ----------------

May 2

SINGING SCRIPTURE: **Psalm 35:28**

> *And my tongue shall speak of thy righteousness and of thy praise all the day long.*

This Psalm is a cry of distress. It probably had its origin during the time David was being hunted by Saul. At the king's court David had many enemies, who constantly sought occasion to drive thorns into the relationship between Saul and David, agitating the jealousy of the king. Saul's instability of character was a fertile field for hatred and ingratitude to flourish. David's purpose in this Psalm is not to show malice toward Saul. He had proven this by sparing the king's life. Instead, he is making a plea for God's intervention. The Psalm can easily be divided into three sections, each ending in a song of thanksgiving and praise for expected deliverance.

Being able to face life's trials with a melody of praise upon our lips, while we are still in the dark about the course which the Lord has charted, indicates a peace and rest which is completely foreign to worldly thinking.

In the first section, David prays for deliverance from physical harm. In anticipation of God's protection, he rejoices in song (v. 9, 10). Next he prays for deliverance from unjust criticism and testimony against him. Expecting such, he sings in praise of the Lord's rescue (v. 18). Finally, as we come to our verse (28), David has prayed for a change of the hearts of his enemies. He has a clear conscience and appeals to the righteousness of God. He closes this section with a ringing, singing coda of confidence that the Lord does all things well. This is the confidence we can and should have in Him.

Ed Lyman

May 3

SINGING SCRIPTURE: **Psalm 149:4, 5**

For the Lord taketh pleasure in his people: he will beautify the meek with salvation.
Let the saints be joyful in glory: let them sing aloud upon their beds.

The Psalmist exhorts the saints to be "joyful" and to "sing aloud upon their beds." We do not normally associate night time and beds with an occasion to sing. However, Job speaks of God his maker "who giveth songs in the night" (Job 35:10).

Night can be a time of fear and dread, when trouble and adversity are present. But the true child of God can see even the darkest night hours transformed into victory by lifting his voice in a praise-filled song "upon his bed." Trust God for your song in the night.

Suffering is also associated with being *in* bed. This exhortation from the Psalmist is also a message for the time of sickness. Sing to God's glory when sleep won't come! The highest kind of praise often comes out of a body wracked with pain. Praise the Lord in the midst of illness; "let them sing aloud upon their beds"!

Commune with God upon your bed. Sometimes to be on a bed means the necessity of being alone, in seclusion. In such a case, sing His praise aloud! There's a special lift available from heaven when you exercise this form of worship. As you "draw nigh to God" by this means, "he will draw nigh to you"!

John C. Hallett

May 4

SINGING SCRIPTURE: **Isaiah 38:20**

> *The Lord was ready to save me, therefore, we will sing my songs to the stringed instruments all the days of our life in the house of the Lord.*

As we drove down the tree-lined Plaza de la Revolucion in Mexico City on our way to the National Museum, which is a fascinating architectural masterpiece, we passed a crowd which had gathered near the steps of the Art Gallery. The traffic slowed somewhat, and we heard a trumpet playing a familiar gospel song. Soon we heard the happy sound of young voices singing. I said to my friend Pablo, who was driving, "Let's stop and see who these people are."

So, with horn blowing and our arms waving signals to other drivers, we threaded our way to a parking place. We walked to the steps as the music continued and saw someone we knew directing a group of shining-faced young people in song.

These fellows and girls were traveling through Central America on a concert tour, and during some sight-seeing in this Aztec country, they had stopped for lunch, a rest, and to sing. People had soon gathered around for an impromptu concert.

They recognized me as we talked and requested a song. So I sang in Spanish, *"Que Bella Historia"* which is translated, "What a Beautiful Story," and is our gospel song, "Down from His Glory."

I became aware once again that the most beautiful story ever known is that of Jesus, who left his throne in heaven to die for people of every race, every nation, every social stratum, and every tongue. Though there was a language barrier, we had fellowship because we are all one in Christ and can join in a great family choir to sing the songs of redemption. Those, who do not know the Savior, cannot sing these songs until they too fall at the feet of Jesus Christ the Lord.

                                                                    Ed Lyman

May 5

SINGING SCRIPTURE: **Romans 15:9**

> *And that the Gentiles might glorify God for his mercy; as it is written, For this cause I will confess to thee among the Gentiles, and sing unto thy name.*

In the church, God has given various gifts to His people. He has chosen to do His work by means of human hands. Our responsibility is to give ourselves wholeheartedly to the work to which we have been called. Too often we confine our gifts to the fishbowl instead of getting out into the pond of the world. God uses us in reaching out as we put ourselves at His disposal. The result of our confessional song will bring honor to Him.

A belittling painter sneered that violin-making was an uncreative craft and looked down his nose at the work of Stradivarius, the maker of the beautiful violins which are now almost beyond price. To this painter the craftsman replied, "'Tis God gives skill, but not without men's hands. He could not make Antonio Stradivarius' violins without Antonio.''

                                                                    Ed Lyman

May 6

PRAISE PSALM: **Psalm 104:35**

> *Let the sinners be consumed out of the earth, and let the wicked be no more. Bless thou the Lord, O My soul. Praise ye the Lord.*

This is a song of sinners in bondage and of saints in liberty. In Psalm 31:5 David acknowledges God's redemption and says, "Thou hast redeemed me."

The biggest lie of Satan is that we will lose our liberty when God "enslaves" us as His disciples. Satan told Adam and Eve in the garden that they would lose out if they kept God's prohibition to avoid the fruit of the tree of life. "It's sure that you won't die," said the deceiver. Then he promised them they would be emancipated by eating it. "Your eyes will be opened and you'll be like God."

When David says, "You have redeemed me," he is looking forward to the Cross, where Christ died for him. Paul, in Romans 4:6, 7, quotes David's words in Psalm 32:1 — "Blessed are they whose iniquities are forgiven, and whose sins are covered." Paul shows that both Abraham and David believed God for righteousness and were fully justified *before* the Cross through the death and resurrection of Christ, just like those who live *after* Calvary.

A redeemed person is the only free person in the universe. Everyone else is enthralled in sin. David was "blessed" because he was free from the *penalty* of sin. We can join him in this joyful freedom. It also includes deliverance from the *practice* of sin. That's the promise in Romans 6:14. Is there any freedom like obeying the Lord? Within the wide circle of His permissive freedom we find our true selves.

Robert P. Evans

May 7

SINGING SCRIPTURE: Ezra 2:65

> *... besides their servants and their maids, of whom there seven thousand three hundred thirty and seven: and there were among them two hundred singing men and singing women.*

Ezra is listing the returned captives to Jerusalem. He has told the numbers of family members and the names of the heads of family groups. The whole congregation of returning Israel together was 42,380. Then Ezra tells that servants accompanied the returnees, and among them were singing men and women.

We are reminded in a very practical way how important music is in the life of people and especially how valued it is in our worship. It cannot be emphasized too much that if music has such a strong

influence in our lives, we must make it meaningful in our worship
and evangelistic efforts.

> *No friend like music when the last word's spoken*
> *And every pleading is a plea in vain.*
> *No friend like music when the heart is broken,*
> *To mend its wing and give it flight again.*

Ed Lyman

May 8

SINGING SCRIPTURE: Psalm 67:4

*O let the nations be glad and sing for joy; for thou shalt judge
the people righteously, and govern the nations upon earth.
Selah.*

First impressions often carry strange conclusions. How can the
nations rejoice knowing they are to be judged? Judgment is
normally accompanied by fear and trembling, but here gladness
and a joyful song are the norm. Why?

The Psalmist states who the judge is, how He will judge the
nations, and what the result will be. These three irrevocable facts
give rise to the sound of nations, who should be glad and sing for joy.

I have lived long enough to recognize the inability of nations or of
men to judge each other correctly, or even impartially. Our text
says that God is the Judge. Is there anything more fearful, yet
comforting, than the knowledge that our ways will be evaluated by
the all-knowing God who loves us?

Nations are people, and God will judge them righteously. Acts
10:34 clearly states that God is no respecter of persons. The nations
that honor Him will be known by Him. Just as righteousness exalts
a nation, so God in His righteous judgment will fulfill His promise
and bless those who follow His Word.

The finale is yet to come when the Lord Himself will not only
judge but govern the nations. No longer will the blind lead the
blind. No longer will Satan's deception be the fashion of the day. No
longer will sin motivate man's activity. Instead, Jesus Christ will be
the Lord of lords and the King of kings — the government shall be
upon His shoulders.

Keith Whiticar

May 9

SINGING SCRIPTURE: **Psalm 101:1**

I will sing of mercy and judgment: unto thee O Lord, will I sing.

Music has always been the handmaiden of Christianity.

On that wintry evening when Jesus Christ was born, the massed choirs of Heaven joined their voices over the hills of Bethlehem singing, "Glory to God in the highest."

At the Last Supper, Jesus and His disciples raised their voices in a hymn of praise before going out to the Garden of Gethsemane.

Paul and Silas sang exuberantly while chained in a dungeon cell. It has been said that God appreciated their singing so much that he climaxed their music with such a powerful "Amen" it tore down the prison doors.

Pagan religions have their chants and dirges, but Christianity alone of the world's religions philosophies, and ethical systems has come down through the ages as a nightingale singing on its way.

The first impulse of the soul which has been born from above is to burst into songs of praise.

Ed Lyman

May 10

PRAISE PSALM: **Psalm 42:4**

When I remember these things, I pour out my soul in me: for I had gone with the multitude, I went with them to the house of God, with the voice of joy and praise, with a multitude that kept holyday.

The writer of this song-poem evidently lived in the northern part of Israel and was constantly being teased and mocked by enemies who felt no desire for the things of the Lord. As we read the first words of this verse, "When I remember these things," we are immediately drawn to ask, "What things?" He then tells us about the joy of remembering his participation in the great festival of worship and praise. At the time of his writing, being buffeted by the taunts of others, he hopes to again add his own voice in a great chorus of rejoicing, and he bursts forth in praiseful song to tell of his desire for the Lord. He allays his dependency through trust in the presence and provision of Almighty God. "My soul thirsteth for God, for the living God" (v. 2) is a magnificent expression of complete dependence upon the faithfulness of the God who loves us and gave His only Son for us.

In the midst of gross darkness, God gives gracious light which will show His great glory. How then can we neglect the given responsibility to share the message of love?

"As the hart panteth after the water brooks, so panteth my soul after thee, O God" (v. 1).

Jesus said, "Blessed are they which do hunger and thirst after righteousness: for they shall be filled" (Matthew 5:6).

Ed Lyman

May 11

SINGING SCRIPTURE: 2 Samuel 6:5

And David and all the house of Israel played before the Lord on all manner of instruments made of fir wood, even on harps, and on psalteries, and on timbrels, and on cornets, and on cymbals.

Few verses are translated in as many different ways as this. The RSV says David and his men were "making merry before the Lord." One modern-language Bible renders it as "dancing before the Lord," and *The Living Bible* paraphrases their actions as "joyously waving branches of juniper trees and playing every sort of musical instrument." I would not be at all surprised if the real picture did not include all of these happening simultaneously! Although a study of Biblical history reveals David's lack of care in following God's instruction about moving the ark (Numbers 4:15) and the resulting retribution, nevertheless his joy at the prospect of returning the ark to Jerusalem was quite obvious.

David's approach to doing the things of God is an example to us — "with all his might." No halfhearted singing or playing or dancing satisfied David and his men. Some preachers or commentators might hastily add that his actions should have been tempered with a bit of discretion, and this has merit. However, in this day it seems that so much of our praise is tempered with so much discretion it becomes wishy-washy — lacking in joy, devoid of exuberance, afraid of being called "fanatic" or extreme. Perhaps we need a little of David's zeal — being excited in the Lord, so full of enthusiasm that we are unhindered by the reactions of spectators and critics. Maybe then the real excitement of praising God would become obvious to those who watch us.

Douglas E. Schoen

May 12

SINGING SCRIPTURE: **Psalm 23 (The Shepherd's Psalm)**

The Lord is my shepherd; I shall not want.
He maketh me to lie down in green pastures: he leadeth me beside the still waters.
He restoreth my soul; he leadeth me in the paths of righteousness for his name's sake.
Yea though I walk through the valley of the shadow of death, I will fear no evil: for thou art with me; thy rod and thy staff they comfort me. Thou preparest a table before me in the presence of mine enemies: thou anointest my head with oil; my cup runneth over. Surely goodness and mercy shall follow me all the days of my life; and I will dwell in the house of the Lord for ever.

This is a psalm of relationship and it gives us a picture of our overall participation in the presence of the Lord.

Walking with Christ (Luke 24:15) is the proper relationship.

Talking with Christ (Luke 9:30) is the proper fellowship.

Listening to Christ (Luke 10:39) is the proper communication or instruction.

Abiding in Christ (John 1:39) is the real joy of living.

Living with Christ (John 1:39) is true oneness.

Waiting upon Christ (Acts 4:31) is lasting refreshment. God always does something special!

Watching for Christ (Acts 8:40) is joyful expectancy.

(Billy) Kim, Chan Huan

May 13

SINGING SCRIPTURE: **Deuteronomy 31:21**

And it shall come to pass, when many evils and troubles are befallen them, that this song shall testify against them as a witness; for it shall not be forgotten out of the mouths of their seed: for I know their imagination which they go about, even now, before I have brought them into the land which I sware.

God told His people through Moses, by means of a song, which way to look: "And he said unto them, Set your hearts unto all the words which I testify among you this day, which ye shall command your children to observe to do, all the words of this law. For it is not a vain thing for you; because it is your life: and through this thing ye shall prolong your days in the land, whither ye go over Jordan to possess it" (Deuteronomy 32:46, 47).

There was a pattern which they were to follow, and it is just as timely today.

If you wish to be miserable and upset, look within (Psalm 77:1-9).

If you wish to be distracted and on the wrong road through life, look around (Psalm 73:1-5).

If you wish to be happy and content, look up (Psalm 73:16-28).

Israel constantly strove to try to be what they were not and not to be what they were. Our lives often mirror those same attitudes when, as the song says, we should endeavor "only to be what He wants me to be, every moment of every day."

Reaching up, we praise the God of our salvation. Reaching out, we engage others by the outworking of our righteousness. Then God reaches down to orchestrate our lives.

Ed Lyman

May 14

SINGING SCRIPTURE: **Psalm 145:21**

My mouth shall speak the praise of the Lord: and let all flesh bless his holy name for ever and ever.

Throughout the Scriptures, the names of God are demonstrably associated with some particular or specific need of His people. This is illustrative of the fact that every need man may have finds its source of fulfillment in God. Therefore, we find provision and blessing only in Him.

The act of grateful homage to the Lord in word and song is the outcome of the realization that God has designed man to find his complete satisfaction in God and in Him alone. God abides with us, and not only *with* us, but *in* us! "What! know ye not that your body is the temple of the Holy Spirit which is *in you*, which ye have of God, and ye are not your own? For ye are bought with a price: therefore glorify God in your body, and in your spirit, which are God's" (1 Corinthians 6:19, 20).

As believers, we have become children of light, no longer groping in darkness for safety and security. We have become partakers of the light which shines forth from the power of the resurrection of the Lord Jesus Christ. We are to walk in this light. We are to worship in this light. We are to witness in this light. Paul reminds us in 2 Corinthians 6:14 that light has no communion, no partnership with darkness. In the 16th verse he says the temple of God can have no agreement with idols, because we "are the temple of the living God; as God hath said, I will dwell in them, and walk in them; and I will be their God, and they shall be my people."

The music of my mouth today should be songs of praise to the Lord, who dwells within.

Ed Lyman

May 15

SINGING SCRIPTURE: Isaiah 55:12

> *For ye shall go out with joy, and be led forth with peace: the mountains and the hills shall break forth before you into singing, and all the trees of the field shall clap their hands.*

The whole of creation breaks into singing. It does so because there is an understanding of the holiness of God. The understanding of who He is brings reverence and salvation.

The genius of the Reformation was its ability to give the common people the Word of God in their own language. It was not until the fifteenth century that printing of books began in Europe. Before this time books were rare; only the affluent and elite could own them. Now everyone could potentially own his own Bible. People began interacting with the Word on an intensely personal level.

Erasmus wrote in 1516,

> *I utterly disagree with those who do not want the Holy Scriptures to be read by the uneducated in their own language.... I hope the farmer may sing snatches of Scripture at his plough, that the weaver may hum bits of Scripture to the tune of his shuttle, that the traveller may lighten the weariness of his journey with stories from Scripture.*

One of Martin Luther's major achievements was his translation of the Bible into German. Latourette says, "He endeavored to make the apostles and prophets speak to the Germans as though they had been natives of the country." What Luther did with the Scriptures, he practiced also with his songs so that all could understand.

Believer, sing with understanding!

Don Wyrtzen

------------------------------ ❈ ------------------------------

May 16

SINGING SCRIPTURE: **Acts 16:25**

And at midnight Paul and Silas prayed, and sang praises unto God: and the prisoners heard them.

Somewhere along the line all religious music, other than hymns and psalms, has been termed "gospel music." However, the nature of the word "gospel" makes the gospel song very specific.

The Apostle Paul wrote in I Corinthians 15, "Moreover, brethren, I declare unto you the gospel ... by which also ye are saved ... how that Christ died for our sins according to the Scriptures; and that he was buried, and that he rose again the third day according to the Scriptures." Religion is man's quest for God, but the Christian gospel is God's quest for man.

As we seek to present the claims of Christ to a lost world or to a Christian congregation, we should try to use that music, as Paul has said, which best conveys the truths of God to the listening ears and hearts of the people.

Ed Lyman

------------------------------ ❈ ------------------------------

May 17

SINGING SCRIPTURE: **Psalm 100:2**

Serve the Lord with gladness: come before his presence with singing.

This passage of Scripture is interesting because it tells us what our attitude should be as we follow Jesus Christ. We are to serve with joy and happiness.

His blessing and presence should be expected. As we continue to read, we find that if we have come into a personal relationship with Christ, we are His people and we are also the sheep of His pasture. As sheep, we follow the Shepherd.

We are admonished to enter His gates with thanksgiving and His courts with praise. When sheep are brought through the gates and into the Temple court, they are ready for sacrifice. We are told in this Psalm to sacrifice ourselves gladly with a song in our hearts for the service of our Lord and Shepherd.

When the sheep follow the shepherd, they follow because of trust. We should follow the Good Shepherd through love and trust, not through fear or for personal reward.

As our eyes focus more on Christ and less on ourselves, we are able to come before His presence with singing.

Ed Lyman

May 18

SINGING SCRIPTURE: **Jeremiah 31:12**

Therefore they shall come and sing in the height of Zion, and shall flow together to the goodness of the Lord, for wheat, and for wine, and for oil, and for the young of the flock and of the herd: and their soul shall be as a watered garden; and they shall not sorrow any more at all.

John Newton wrote so beautifully the concept expressed in this verse when he penned "Amazing Grace."

In Jeremiah 30 and 31, we see in effect the prophet's own version of this song. Israel is in grievous suffering brought on by its sin and rebellion. This divine judgment brings the nation to repentance and brings restoration to their land. The climax is this marvelous tribute to God's sovereign grace: "They shall come and sing in the height of Zion...."

The New Testament continues this concept with Paul's paean of praise to God's grace (Romans 9-11), underlining Israel's future restoration to the land. Israel will one day be saved (Zechariah 12:10; 13:7-9).

In the light of what God will one day do for Israel, think of His infinite grace toward us. Grace has been defined as God bestowing on us that which we can never merit or deserve. Paul expressed it so well: "For by grace are ye saved through faith...." "For the grace of God that bringeth salvation hath appeared to all men..." (Titus 2:11).

Thus, the Word becomes flesh. Jesus Christ comes as the Savior of all who believe on Him.

Today let us praise Him with hearts of love:

Amazing grace,
how sweet the sound, that saved a wretch like me!
I once was lost,
but now am found;
was blind, but now I see.

John A. Beerley

May 19

SINGING SCRIPTURE: **Psalm 117:1, 2**

O praise the Lord, all ye nations; praise him, all ye people. For his merciful kindness is great toward us: and the truth of the Lord endureth for ever. Praise ye the Lord.

This is a doxology of praise for the comprehensiveness of God's overall concern for man. It includes all nations in its directive to praise the Lord. Paul refers to this in Romans 15:9, 10 as he shows Jewish and Gentile believers that they are one in Christ: "and that the Gentiles might glorify God for his mercy; as it is written, For this cause I will confess to thee among the Gentiles, and sing unto thy name. And again he saith, Rejoice, ye Gentiles, with his people."

The privileged place Israel knew in God's presence is precisely where the Lord would now have all of the people of the world. The salvation he provided for the Jew is the same salvation he makes available to all people.

Israel was chosen by God to witness that there is one God (Deuteronomy 6:4), to show the blessing of serving God (Deuteronomy 33:29), to carry the oracles of God as writers, preservers, and transmitters of the Bible (Romans 3:1), and to be the channel through which the Messiah would come (Matthew 1 and Galatians 4:4).

"Make a joyful noise unto the Lord, all ye lands. Serve the Lord with gladness: come before his presence with singing. Know ye that the Lord he is God: it is he that hath made us, and not we ourselves; we are his people, and the sheep of his pasture. Enter into his gates with thanksgiving, and into his courts with praise: be thankful unto him, and bless his name. For the Lord is good; his mercy is everlasting, and his truth endureth to all generations" (Psalm 100).

Ed Lyman

May 20
SINGING SCRIPTURE: **Psalm 7:17**

I will praise the Lord according to his righteousness: and will sing praise to the name of the Lord most high.

This is a musical expression of faith in action. "The just shall live by faith" — and being saved by faith is just the beginning. This initial step must be followed by a life of constant acts of faith. It is surprising where these little "faithlettes" turn up. A very vivid "faithlette" occurred in the preparation of one of our song sermons. At first this was just a thought running through my mind and as ideas began to jell, I put them on paper for consideration. Music, singers, scenery, staging, preaching — all came up for possible use. Underneath lay these questions: "Why are we doing this? What are we trying to say?" It was like a conductor's score. Each instrument, though unique in itself, joins with the others to form a great work that comes alive under the touch of a master's hand. That's where the "faithlette" comes into existence. We tried to do everything we could to make it a "success," but there were so many variables. What should I do? I simply bowed my head once more and prayed, "Lord, I commit this work into Your hands for Your glory. You are the Master. Please make it a work of spiritual art. I believe in faith that You will take it and make it a blessing."

When the program was over, it was evident that the Lord had done just that. All came together under His hand, the Master's hand, and what a blessing! From a program typed on a piece of paper, it had become audible reality and a spiritual blessing. "Thank you, Lord, for being so good to us." Have you been putting your "faithlettes" into action?

David E. Williams

May 21
SINGING SCRIPTURE: **Judges 5:12**

Awake, awake, Deborah; awake, awake, utter a song: arise, Barak, and lead thy captivity captive.

Here is a call to awake and sing the songs of triumph and victory. Deborah, one of the judges of Israel during the time before the coronation of kings, was called upon to deliver her people from the hands of the enemy.

They were to go to battle with a song of certain victory on their lips because the Lord, Jehovah, had already promised their success.

After the surrender of General Robert E. Lee to the Federal troops, a group of Confederate Army officers was listening to some Northern officers sing their battle songs and patriotic marching choruses. The singing was applauded with great enthusiasm by the Southerners. When the music had ended, one of the Confederate officers expressed his appreciation and in a voice shaking with emotion said, "Gentlemen, if we had had your songs, we'd have licked you out of your boots."

Here is a challenge to Christians everywhere. If God is for us, who can be against us? We shall be triumphant because Christ has already conquered sin, death, and the grave. Let us therefore press the battle with a sure song of victory in our hearts and praise upon our lips.

Ed Lyman

May 22

SINGING SCRIPTURE **Psalm 150:3**

Praise him with the sound of the trumpet: praise him with the psaltery and harp.

The song of self-praise is always sung as a solo!

Bragging brings disunity to the fellowship of believers and is contrary to the Biblical truth that each of us has a particular part to play in the ministering functions of the body.

We only appreciate the "sacredness" of an instrumental piece if we know the lyrics or if the music is known as part of the sacred repertoire over the years, such as Bach's chorales or the various Masses of the masters. Therefore, the instrumentalist in witness and worship by means of music has a unique responsibility to prepare his presentations to meet the needs of those for whom he is playing. If his music is not printed in a program of some sort, explained by himself or another before he plays, or fits into the associations I just mentioned, it could be just an exercise in his playing expertise.

Therefore, it is evident that if there are no word associations for the instrumental pieces played, the music may be musically mute. Those who are not "speaking" their praise to the Lord but are playing upon instruments as part of the total ministry must recognize that we are all parts of the body of Christ. We then use our abilities to move the body into the place where the tongue can say what we want the Lord and the world to know. As the "one body" becomes a "whole body," we praise the Lord in "spirit and in truth."

Talin Lyman

May 23

SINGING SCRIPTURE: **Psalm 42:11**

Why art thou cast down, O my soul? And why are thou disquieted within me? Hope thou in God: for I shall yet praise him, who is the health of my countenance, and my God.

The old preacher stood to preach. He read his text: "Thy brought to Jesus all sick people that were taken with divers diseases."

The preacher then began to explain, "Now the doctors can scrutinize you, analyze you, and sometimes cure your ills, but when you have divers diseases, then only the Lord can cure. And brethren, there is a regular epidemic of divers diseases among us!

"Some dive for the door after Bible school is over.

"Some dive for the television set during the evening services.

"Some dive into a bag of excuses about work that needs to be done for Jesus.

"Others dive for the car and take a trip over the weekend, forsake the assembling and teaching assignments.

"Then a few dive into a flurry of fault-finding every time the church takes on a work program. Yes, brethren, it takes the Lord and love of the church to cure divers diseases. You are in a bad way, brethren."

If we would ask the Lord to remove our "divers diseases," our song of praise would sound forth on pitch and in harmony.

Ed Lyman

May 24

SINGING SCRIPTURE: **Isaiah 35:10**

And the ransomed of the Lord shall return, and come to Zion with songs and everlasting joy upon their heads: they shall obtain joy and gladness, and sorrow and sighing shall flee away.

When the Lord Jesus Christ returns, great wonders shall be wrought. The redeemed of the Lord shall walk in the way of God's commandments, and this way shall bring everlasting joy.

Here is Good News.

God opens a door of escape from their captivity. Those who by faith have been made citizens of Zion, the city of the living God, will enter with rejoicing. They who mourn shall be blessed and comforted.

When God's people returned from Babylon to Jerusalem, they came with weeping; but believers shall enter heaven singing a new song which no man can learn.

Their joy shall be proclaimed to the glory of God.

Our joyful prospects of eternal life and the hope of Heaven should swallow the sorrows, discouragements, and even the fleeting joys of this present life.

Ed Lyman

May 25

SINGING SCRIPTURE: Song of Solomon 2:12

The flowers appear on the earth; the time of the singing of birds is come, and the voice of the turtle is heard in our land.

Spring in Virginia is beautiful. The dogwood and azalea, amidst other flowering shrubs, shout for attention as they become a great symphony of praise to the Creator.

"The flowers appear" is the Creation movement with an added chorale from Psalm 19, "The heavens declare the glory of God; and the firmament showeth his handiwork." This theme is played again and again to put man's mind on the fact that we *do* have a Creator.

The second movement is Redemption as "the time of singing is come" and a crescendo builds at the announcement that God's Son was "sent forth in the fullness of time." Established before the worlds began, the redemption theme is heard throughout the symphony, becoming particularly exciting as the angels sing at the birth of a baby. Job adds a counter-melody from early creation as "morning stars sang together." Isaiah's voice sings an obbligato, asking the heavens to sing and the mountains to break forth into song.

"And the voice of the turtle-[dove] is heard in our land." God has chosen the human instrument to carry His message, and this movement is Salvation. The Holy Spirit places us into the hands of God, the Master Musician. Just as the call of the Lord is in the "music" of creation and redemption, so it is produced by God through the believer.

The climax of the symphony comes as the instruments and Creator become one. "Praise ye the Lord" (Psalm 150).

James E. Emery

May 26

SINGING SCRIPTURE: **Psalm 145:10**

And thy works shall praise thee, O Lord; and thy saints shall bless thee.

For a sinner to become a saint, it takes the saving grace of the Lord Jesus Christ and the creative power of God. "Therefore if any man be in Christ, he is a new creature: old things are passed away: behold, all things are become new" (2 Corinthians 5:17). This work is certainly cause for songs of praise!

However, saints may sometimes be unsaintly. It takes attendance to the desires of God for a saint to bring blessing to the Lord.

As saints, we are to be strong: "that he would grant you according to the riches of his glory, to be strengthened with might by his Spirit in the inner man" (Ephesians 3:16).

As saints, we are to be stable: "that ye, being rooted and grounded in love ..." (Ephesians 3:17).

As saints, we are to be scholarly: "able to comprehend with all saints what is the breadth, and length, and depth, and height; and to know the love of Christ, which passeth knowledge" (Ephesians 3:18, 19).

As saints, we are to be successful: "that ye might be filled with all the fulness of God" (Ephesians 3:19). This is success from God's standpoint, not man's.

As saints, we are to be saintly: "that ye put off concerning the former conversation (manner of life) the old man ... and that ye put on the new man" (Ephesians 4:22, 24).

As saints, we are to be spiritual: "And be not drunk with wine, wherein is excess, but be filled with the Spirit" (Ephesians 5:18).

Ed Lyman

May 27

SINGING SCRIPTURE: **2 Samuel 22:1**

And David spake unto the Lord the words of this song in the day that the Lord had delivered him out of the hand of all his enemies, and out of the hand of Saul: and he said,

The Lord is my rock, and my fortress, and my deliverer;
the God of my rock; in him will I trust: he is my shield, and the horn of my salvation, my high tower, and my refuge, my savior; thou savest me from violence.
I will call on the Lord, who is worthy to be praised: so shall I be saved from mine enemies.
When the waves of death compassed me, the floods of ungodly men made me afraid;
the sorrows of hell compassed me about; the snares of death prevented me;
in my distress I called upon the Lord, and cried to my God: and he did hear my voice out of his temple, and my cry did enter into his ears.

Ed Lyman

May 28

SINGING SCRIPTURE: **Psalm 98:6**

With trumpets and sound of cornet make a joyful noise before the Lord, the King.

This is a thrilling directive on the part of the Psalmist. He is inviting all creation to praise God. The sound of the instruments of brass wakes the world to the presence of the Lord, and this bright fanfare of musical expectancy brings a new attitude and outlook.

But remember, a song that can be heard on the outside must first be on the inside.

Ed Lyman

May 29

SINGING SCRIPTURE: 1 Corinthians 14:7

And even things without life giving sound, whether pipe or harp, except they give a distinction in the sounds, how shall it be known what is piped or harped?

Using an analogy of uncertain sounding instruments and unclear tones, the Apostle Paul relates in musical terms the necessity for clear presentation of Biblical truth.

Children who are reared in an atmosphere of hypocrisy soon catch on, and as soon as they come of age they will want to leave that kind of home. When they do, they will also say good-bye to its church and its God.

It is better to live much and teach little than to teach much and live little. It is better still to both live much and teach much.

It is true that mistakes can still be made even as individuals in an orchestra can "flub." But if instruments are tuned correctly, a missed beat or a misplayed note doesn't mean the instrument or musicians cannot get back to the score.

"Let your light so shine before men [your children], that they may see your good works, and glorify your father which is in heaven" (Matthew 5:16).

Paul B. Smith

May 30

SINGING SCRIPTURE: Numbers 31:6

And Moses sent them to the war, a thousand of every tribe, them and Phinehas, the son of Eleazar the priest, to the war, with the holy instruments, and the trumpets to blow in his hand.

During the time of war, each tribe did its part in providing soldiers for the conflict. These troops assembled in one place for the battle. Trumpets were used for various assemblies in the Israelite camp, but during such times of national danger, these particular trumpets were used to sound the alarm. The special trumpet sound on these occasions can be likened to the horn on a modern naval vessel which calls the men to battle stations. The trumpet blasts were distinguished from other trumpet calls which summoned the people to other gatherings. It was an alarm signal and tradition says it consisted of a succession of short blasts.

The priests blew these trumpets as representatives of Yahweh. This was symbolic of God's place of leadership and control over all of the affairs of His people. "And if ye go to war in your land against the enemy that oppresseth you, then ye shall blow an alarm with the trumpets; and ye shall be remembered before the Lord your God, and ye shall be saved from your enemies" (Numbers 10:9).

The music of the alarm trumpets is heard clearly in Paul's command to "Put on the whole armor of God, that ye may be able to stand against the wiles of the devil" (Ephesians 6:11). The Christian is not on a playground but a battle ground and must heed the trumpet sound which calls him to enter the conflict.

Ed Lyman

May 31

SINGING SCRIPTURE: **Psalm 45:17**

I will make thy name to be remembered in all generations: therefore shall thy people praise thee for ever and ever.

How many gods have been worshipped down through the ages? What were their names? The number is unknown, and the names have been lost, forgotten, or buried in books of ancient lore and legend. However, in Malachi 1:11 we read of a name which will be remembered. "For, from the rising of the sun even unto the going down of the same, my name shall be great among the Gentiles; and in every place incense shall be offered unto my name, and a pure offering: for my name shall be great among the heathen, saith the Lord of hosts." Remembrance of the Lord's name evokes an experiential song of praise because of the marvelous manifestations of His presence. Our song of remembrance brings memories of:

"How excellent is *thy name* in all the earth" (Psalm 8:1).

"How great is *thy goodness*, which thou hast laid up for them that fear thee" (Psalm 31:19).

"How precious is *thy loving-kindness*" (Psalm 36:7).

"How amiable are *thy tabernacles*" (Psalm 84:1).

"How sweet are *thy words* unto my taste" (Psalm 119:103).

"How precious also are *thy thoughts* unto me" (Psalm 139:17).

The Apostle Paul wrote to Timothy, "Wherefore I put thee in remembrance, that thou stir up the gift of God, which is in thee" (2 Timothy 1:6). Whatever our gifts of song, service, sacrifice, speech, they should be used to bring the name of the Lord Jesus Christ to remembrance.

Ed Lyman

June

DAILY PRAISE

June 1

SINGING SCRIPTURE: **Isaiah 14:7**

The whole earth is at rest, and is quiet: they break forth into singing.

This verse brings to mind Sundays in our country many years ago, before cars, radio, movies, TV, and the like occupied our days of leisure. These were the Sundays when the normal, expected thing was: Sunday we go to church. The chores were kept to a minimum, whether on the farm or in town, and the earth was at rest and quiet.

My reverie takes me back to the sound of the old classic hymns with their clear messages of salvation, victory in our daily lives, the Lord's return, sung in the quiet of those afternoons. How can I forget, "Jesus Paid It All," "For God So Loved the World", and "Amazing Grace."

While the earth was at rest and quiet, those were the sounds we would hear. Loved ones were singing their thanks and praise to God, lifting their voices in worship to the One they knew was concerned about every facet of their lives.

Today it is nice to return to that place of rest and quiet, there to break forth into singing. "Music, when soft voices die, vibrates in the memory."

Lynette Trout

June 2

SINGING SCRIPTURE: **Psalm 98:4**

Make a joyful noise unto the Lord, all the earth: make a loud noise, and rejoice, and sing praise.

Many times during the months of my training in the United States Marine Corps Officers Candidate School, we found ourselves far from our camp after a whole day of maneuvers. No one looked forward to the long walk ahead. There were always some who griped, and others who lagged behind the rest of the platoon. We would make slow progress along the way, and tempers flared occasionally when someone stepped on another marine's tired foot or a rifle butt swung against a knee or elbow.

After a time of this mob movement, an officer would shout, "Attention! Fall in line! Forward march!"

What a change took place as the cadence began, "One, two, three, four, one, two, three, four!"

Stooped shoulders straightened. Spirits lifted. Tired feet quickened their pace.

Soon we would be singing marching songs as miles passed beneath the soles of our combat boots and we rapidly advanced to our base.

A meandering mob, by means of a coordinated effort and a spirited song, became a purposeful platoon of marching marines.

With purpose, planning, and a song of praise in the heart, a Christian who is a wandering worrier can become a worthwhile witness.

Ed Lyman

June 3

PRAISE PSALM: **Psalm 145:4**

One generation shall praise thy works to another, and shall declare thy mighty acts.

Those who have come to know the Lord Jesus Christ as their own personal Savior are bound to tell others about Him. What are we showing and what are we telling? In our deeds and in our declarations, are we seen as sharing servants and heard as sacred songs by the world around us, or are we selfish and silent in our witness?

The essence of praising God's "works to another" is found in Romans 1:13-16 — "Now I would not have you ignorant, brethren, that oftentimes I purposed to come unto you (but was let [prevented] hitherto,) that I might have some fruit among you also, even as among other Gentiles. I am debtor both to the Greeks, and to the barbarians; both to the wise, and to the unwise. So, as much as in me is, I am ready to preach the gospel to you that are at Rome also. For I am not ashamed of the gospel of Christ; for it is the power of God unto salvation to everyone that believeth; to the Jew first, and also to the Greek.''

Paul's *objective* was to go to those people in order to have some fruit — converts to Christianity — among them. He considered his witnessing not an option, but an *obligation* — he was a debtor to those who knew not Christ. "I am ready to preach," he said, "at Rome also." This presented itself as an *opportunity* he was ready to accept. When Paul pronounces that he is "not ashamed," he presents his *obsession* with the marvelous gospel of grace, which saves to the uttermost.

Ed Lyman

June 4

SINGING SCRIPTURE: **Amos 8:10**

And I will turn your feasts into mourning, and all your songs into lamentation; and I will bring up sackcloth upon your loins, and baldness upon every head; and I will make it as the mourning for an only son, and the end thereof as a bitter day.

Amos has compared Israel to a basket of fruit in summer which will soon perish. Captivity was impending and the Lord had told the prophet,
"The end is come upon my people of Israel," because they had refused to follow His leadership. They had fumbled the greatest opportunity any people ever had. No wonder the Lord said He would turn their songs into lamentations.

In the New Testament, Paul puts the warning of Amos into the context of personal responsibility. Whether we face the lament of a lost life or the song of a saved soul depends upon our response to the issues of this verse: "For the wages of sin is death; but the gift of God is eternal life through Jesus Christ our Lord."

Life's greatest *reality* is "sin."
Life's greatest *certainty* is, "the wages of sin is death."
Life's greatest *offer* is the "gift of God."
Life's greatest *issues* are "death" or "life."
Life's greatest *choice* is "wages" or "gift."
Life's greatest *medium* is "through Jesus Christ our Lord."

Ed Lyman

June 5

SINGING SCRIPTURE: **Isaiah 12:5**

Sing unto the Lord; for he hath done excellent things: this is known in all the earth.

This passage grows out of earlier descriptions of fascinating imagery. The preceding chapter speaks of the "shoot from the root of Jesse," and the context indicates a vivid prophetic description of Jesus Christ in His future return as King of kings and Lord of lords. This chapter also contains the portrayal of the well-known "Peaceable Kingdom," and both passages have been set to music from Renaissance times to the present day.

The meaningful culmination is Isaiah 12:5, for it is a command for exultant self-expression to the glory of God and for sincere gratitude for personal salvation in Christ. It is to be shown and shared with others without respect to persons in the choice of personal witness.

From verse 5 it is apparent that the act of praising God is part of a basic spiritual law. Allowing Christ to work through our personal life is a natural outgrowth of the Christian experience. Indeed, it is central to it! It is intended for our own benefit and becomes the basic spiritual light to others.

Stephen Cushman

June 6

PRAISE PSALM: **Psalm 145:3**

Great is the Lord, and greatly to be praised; and his greatness is unsearchable.

O sing unto the Lord a new song; sing unto the Lord all the earth.

Sing unto the Lord, bless his name; show forth his salvation from day to day.

Declare his glory among the nations, his wonders among his peoples.

For the Lord is great, and greatly to be praised; he is to be feared above all gods.

His greatness includes His salvation, His glory, His wonders.

The formula for a spiritually successful musical ministry and witness of any kind is:

MOTIVATION + ABILITY + OPPORTUNITY = ACHIEVEMENT

Motivation is at the heart of every achievement in life. Our *motivation*, which reflects His greatness, is found in His love: "For the love of Christ constraineth us" (2 Corinthians 5:14). In 1 Corinthians 12:4, Paul speaks of our various *abilities*: "Now there are diversities of gifts, but the same Spirit." The Holy Spirit bestows gifts upon us all for service unto the Lord Jesus Christ. Jesus Himself presents the *opportunity*: "Behold, I say unto you, Lift up your eyes, and look on the fields; for they are white already to harvest" (John 4:35b).

As we apply this formula to our work for the Lord, the promise is realized: "Delight thyself also in the Lord; and he shall give thee the desires of thine heart. Commit thy way unto the Lord; trust also in him, and he shall bring it to pass" (Psalm 37:4, 5).

Ed Lyman

June 7

SINGING SCRIPTURE: **Psalm 95:2**

Let us come before his presence with thanksgiving, and make a joyful noise unto him with psalms.

Here is a definite and enthusiastic appeal to those who love the Lord to take time to be in His presence to thank Him and praise Him for Himself.

You may be saying that you just cannot find time or you may even be in some specialized ministry for the Lord and you cannot spare the time to just wait upon Him. If that's the way you think, just consider Susanna Wesley. She was busy too with nineteen children. Those were the days too when they did not have schools and she had to teach them herself. She couldn't shop for clothes, but had to make them for everyone in the family. She also had to provide and prepare the daily food.

Yet, every day from one o'clock until two, Susanna Wesley went into her bedroom, closed the door, and on her knees spent time alone with God. No one interrupted her during that hour. Everyone knew what she was doing. No wonder she gave the world John and Charles Wesley, whose messages and hymns have touched the hearts of millions for the Lord. Susanna Wesley knew what it meant to get alone with God.

Ed Lyman

June 8

SINGING SCRIPTURE: **2 Samuel 23:1-5 (David's last song)**

Now these be the last words of David. David the son of Jesse said, and the man who was raised up on high, the anointed of the God of Jacob, and the sweet psalmist of Israel, said,

The Spirit of the Lord spake by me, and his word was in my tongue.
The God of Israel said, the Rock of Israel spake to me, He that ruleth over men must be just, ruling in the fear of God.
And he shall be as the light of the morning, when the sun riseth, even a morning without clouds; as the tender grass springing out of the earth by clear shining after the rain.
Although my house be not so with God; yet he hath made with me an everlasting covenant, ordered in all things, and sure: for this is all my salvation, and all my desire, although he made it not to grow.

Ed Lyman

June 9

SINGING SCRIPTURE: **Luke 24:44**

And he said unto them, These are the words which I spoke unto you, while I was yet with you, that all things must be fulfilled, which were written in the law of Moses, and in the prophets, and in the psalms, concerning me.

This chapter of the Gospel of Luke could be called the "Opening Chapter." In it, the risen Savior meets two disciples on their way home to the town of Emmaus. As they walk, the discussion is concerned with the events, which have just taken place in Jerusalem, and the disciples are sad because the One, whom they had thought was the Messiah, had been crucified. In the conversation, Jesus makes a positive presentation and "beginning at Moses, and all the prophets, he expounded unto them in all the scriptures, the things concerning himself" (24:27).

There is a definite sequence to the revelation Jesus gives.

First, He *opens the Scriptures* (24:32). Next, he *opens their eyes* (24:31).

When the disciples discover His identity, they immediately return to Jerusalem to tell the others that the Christ is risen. Even as they are sharing this marvelous news, Jesus appears and after showing Himself to them in all of the Scriptures — this time —using the Psalms, the songs of prophecy, praise, and salvation — He *opens their understanding.* As living songs, our lives reflect the pattern of opening the Scriptures, opening the eyes, and opening the understanding as we allow the Holy Spirit to use us.

Ed Lyman

June 10

PRAISE PSALM: **Psalm 49:16-18**

Be not thou afraid when one is made rich, when the glory of his house is increased;
For when he dieth he shall carry nothing away: his glory shall not descend after him.
Though while he lived he blessed his soul: and men will praise thee, when thou doest well to thyself.

The verse immediately preceding this passage of Scripture is one of the clearest verses hinting of immortality in the Old Testament. "But God will redeem my soul from the power of the grave: for he shall receive me." However, in contrast to this hope and security, which is the prospect for those who have their trust in the Lord, there is little praise for the man whose life consists of calculated and continual accumulation of riches, whose selfishness provides for no awareness of the needs of others and no room for God.

The life of that person who examines himself to determine just where the Lord wants him becomes one of upright purposefulness and, as others see his "good works," they catch a glimpse of the Lord. Our walk should witness to our love for God. It should be a continual song of service to Him.

In 2 Timothy 4:13, the elderly apostle tells his son in the ministry,

"The cloke I left at Troas with Carpus, when thou comest, bring with thee, and the books, but especially the parchments." These three things illustrate the steps we need to take in preparation for our song of service. The cloke indicates the physical need for warmth or comfort. As believers, we must be aware of the needs of others in the physical realm and be ready to give a cup of cold water in the name of Jesus. The books signify a mental aspect of service in which we must keep mentally alert to questions of others and aware of the Biblical truths. Then, the parchments are illustrative of the spiritual dimension; allowing the Holy Spirit to guide as we step in the light of God's Word with a song in our hearts.

Ed Lyman

June 11

SINGING SCRIPTURE: Isaiah 35:6

Then shall the lame man leap as an hart, and the tongue of the dumb sing: for in the wilderness shall waters break out and streams in the desert.

Jamaica is truly an emerald rising from the azure waters of the romantic Caribbean, like a crown in a majestic setting. The blue hills are clothed in robes of growing bananas. Fields of sugar cane are caressed by the gentle breezes and groves of orange trees cast their fragrances across the valleys.

A two-hour drive from the historic pirate port of Kingston, nestled in the cool country of the interior, is a place of silence, but a place of singing.

Many times I have watched the children in this home sing, but I have never heard their voices. This is a Christian school for the deaf.

The children have been taught to express the music in their hearts by moving their hands. Their fingers sing the lyrics. It is a communication with our Heavenly Father, which cannot be destroyed by deafness. Every time I have watched them "sing", I have been reminded that the Christian has a song within his heart, which should find its expression in some outward sign. The deaf people call their language "signing."

Are we, who are capable of hearing and singing, any less responsible to "sign" our faith in Jesus Christ for the world to see?

Ed Lyman

June 12

SINGING SCRIPTURE: **Psalm 13:6**

I will sing unto the Lord, because he hath dealt bountifully with me.

One of the characteristics of a song is that it can remain with you as a kind of haunting refrain. I remember times, when I was a young man and I would be talking with my father about things that "used to be" or people that "once were", and he would say something — perhaps a word or even a phrase — which would remind me of a favorite song. Often, throughout the rest of that day, I'd find myself almost unconsciously singing lines from that tune. It remained with me.

Songs are good reminders. They bring to our memories situations from the past, special people, or specific places. We can hear an old tune and right away our minds go back to certain events.

When I hear certain hymns, I am reminded of such things as the first time I ever heard it, someone singing it for some occasion, or how it first spoke to my own heart. "Saved, "Saved" is such a song. The night I received Jesus Christ as my Savior, that hymn was sung and it is always a reminder of that decisive moment in my life.

Hymns can remind us of special times when the Lord has "dealt bountifully" with us and the more we are in tune with Him, the more His spiritual sonnets will speak to our hearts. So, if God is giving you a blessing today, seal it with an appropriate hymn. Then, the next time you hear or sing that particular song of praise, it will be a wonderful reminder of that choice bountiful blessing and its presence will remain as a memento of God's abiding fellowship.

Uncle Bill Salisbury

June 13

SINGING SCRIPTURE: **Numbers 21:17**

Then Israel sang this song, Spring up, O well; sing ye unto it.

The people of Israel were coming closer to the Promised Land and in verse 10 of this chapter it says, they "set forward." On our way to heaven, we should be active in the work of the Lord.

At Beer, which signifies a "well" or "fountain," God wonderfully supplied His people. Up to this time, they had been discontented and complaining in their demands for water and God was displeased even as He supplied their needs. However, in the 16th verse, we find that here God gave it to them in love. The Lord gave them the water even before they prayed and they received it with thanksgiving and gladness.

They sang this song in praise to God's glory and to encourage each other.

The "well" is very much a figure of the Holy Spirit coming forth for our comfort. Jesus said, "He that believeth on me, as the Scripture hath said, out of his belly shall flow rivers of living water."

Before this, names were given to the places where strife and murmuring took place in order to perpetuate the remembrance of receiving water. Now, they remembered with a song of praise!

God had promised them water, but they had to open the wells to receive it.

The Lord's blessings must be expected as we make use of the means within our grasp and power, but the power, itself, is always from God.

Ed Lyman

June 14

PRAISE PSALM: **Psalm 145:2**

Every day will I bless thee, and I will praise thy name forever and ever.

Every day blessing can and will be the result of a daily encounter with the Word of God, because the Bible has the answer to what God wants us to know for the present. The music of praise permeates the life of the believer as he opens his mind to the presence and purposes of God as found in His Word. So, practice the study of the Scriptures daily — and here's a way to keep the daily meditation of God's Word fresh. Instead of starting at Genesis 1 and reading straight through the Bible, try this method for reading the whole Bible in a year:

Monday	Read Genesis through Deuteronomy	The Books of the Law
Tuesday	Read Joshua through Esther	The Books of History
Wednesday	Read Job through Song of Solomon	The Books of Poetry

Thursday	Read Isaiah through Malachi	The Books of Prophecy
Friday	Read Matthew through John	The Gospels
Saturday	Read Acts through Revelation	The Epistles

Reading consistently every day the perspective of God's Word will infiltrate the thinking processes and affect the daily walk of the believer. As the mind is motivated by the message of God's provision and promises, the witness of the Christian takes on added dimension in his daily activities and relationships.

Ed Lyman

June 15

SINGING SCRIPTURE: Isaiah 44:23

Sing, O ye heavens; for the Lord hath done it: shout, ye lower parts of the earth: break forth into singing, ye mountains, O forest, and every tree therein: for the Lord hath redeemed Jacob, and glorified himself in Israel.

As he considers the mighty work of God in accomplishing the redemption of Israel, the prophet with his great eloquence calls upon all of nature to join in a song and shout of praise. "The Lord hath done it," he declares. Yet, he is talking of the future redemption of the captives in Babylon and the cities of the north, where they would be scattered a hundred years after his death. Nearly fifty thousand returned to Jerusalem to rebuild the Temple under the edict of Cyrus (Ezra 2:64, 65), but was that an event worthy of calling upon all nature to sing the praise of God? Only if we think of it as part of the necessary preparation for the coming of the One Who would accomplish the redemption of Israel through His death upon the Cross. There the Lord Jesus cried, "It is finished." There the great work of atonement was accomplished and the sins of His people could be blotted out as a thick cloud. There the Savior truly set the captives free to escape from their bondage and to live in the city "whose Builder and Maker is God." So, even as Isaiah prophesies of God's redeeming work in forgiving Israel and restoring them to their homeland, he foretells a greater act of redemption, that of Jesus upon the Cross, and calls upon the heavens, the lower parts of earth, and the earth to join in singing of God's GLORY!

James H. Blackstone, Jr.

June 16

SINGING SCRIPTURE: **Psalm 95:1**

O come, let us sing unto the Lord; let us make a joyful noise to the rock of our salvation.

This Psalm is known as the "Invitation Psalm" because of its fervent invitation to praise, to listen to the voice of the Lord, and to believe.

We are first told that the praise is to be given to the Lord, Jehovah, the "Rock of our Salvation." The word "rock" reminds us of God's interest in us and his concern for our needs.

God is "as the shadow of a great rock in a weary land" and this signifies shade for those who love Him.

He is strength for the faint: "Thou hast set my feet upon a rock."

He is home for "the inhabitants of the rock."

He is the defense for the weak: "Thou art my Rock and my Fortress."

The praise called for is to be hearty and emphatic. Loudness was regarded by the ancients to indicate an earnest heart. As it invited Israel to praise, so this Psalm invites the Christian to worship in spirit and in truth.

Ed Lyman

June 17

PRAISE PSALM: **Psalm 50:23**

Whoso offereth praise glorifieth me: and to him that ordereth his conversation aright will I shew the salvation of God.

Even in members of the body of Christ, whose excellent characters are clearly seen, there are often "dead flies" in the ointment of the apothecary (Ecclesiastes 10:1). However, everything excellent is blended in perfection and harmony in the Lord Jesus Christ. He is the "altogether lovely" of Song of Solomon 5:16. We, who have seen the salvation of God and come to know His Son, Jesus Christ, as our personal Savior, ought through the indwelling presence of the Holy Spirit seek to be altogether pleasing to Him. As we walk with God, we learn the kindness and courtesy of love. It is often said that we do not glorify God so much by what we do in life but by what we are. As we walk with the Lord, we gain a certain rightness of character, which gives us a ready grace to handle the circumstances of life.

God says, "I dwell in the high and holy place, with him also that is of a contrite and humble spirit" (Isaiah 57:15).

Whatever our service, when God is with us, living and controlling our lives, He makes our service honorable.

The song of the Christian life is a song of praise to the glory of God.

Ed Lyman

June 18

SINGING SCRIPTURE: **Psalm 98:5**

Sing unto the Lord with the harp; with the harp, and the voice of a psalm.

Music displays the recesses of the heart. As go the people, so go their songs.

We find noisy, tumultuous, multitudinous, discordant sounds eked out by men, who have forsaken the Lord and are without a song. Ezekiel 26:13 offers such an example as God says to Tyre, "And I will cause the noise of thy songs to cease; and the sound of thy harps shall be no more heard." God's judgment upon sin was forthcoming; harmony, melody, and rhythm, the basic properties of beautiful music, instead of melding together, were clashing in such proportion, that it is now "noise." As God was about to pour out His fury upon sin, even the "noise" ceased and there was no joy. There was nothing to sing about. The gloom of doom left little room for making melody.

In the heart of the Christian today, there is a time for joy. There is a time for singing. There is time for hearts and harps to blend in harmonious tones and tunes to the God of all creation. Faith in the Son has produced hope in the heart. Life eternal constitutes reason for exercising praise to Him in every form — instrumentally and vocally.

Ted and Pat Cowen

June 19

SINGING SCRIPTURE: **Exodus 32:18**

And he said, It is not the voice of them that shout for mastery, neither is it the voice of them that cry for being overcome: but the noise of them that sing do I hear.

Joshua hears the noise of the people as he descends the mountain with Moses after God has given the Ten Commandments. It isn't the sound of men winning a battle and it isn't the lament of the defeated. Instead, he calls it the noise of "them that sing."

Joshua is referring to the sound of the singing. It is not the melodious music of rejoicing and praising God; instead, it is a carnal composition, which reverts to the idolatrous existence in Egypt. The people have taken unto themselves idols of the calf gods of the land from which God delivered them.

It is an interesting phenomenon that when we begin ebbing from the Lord's fellowship and the truth of His Word, our music is sure to reflect our slipping.

I've heard it said that the best way to determine the spiritual condition of a church is to take the temperature of the congregation with the thermometer of a song. Israel's backsliding proved this to be true.

Ed Lyman

June 20

SINGING SCRIPTURE: **Isaiah 35:1, 2**

The wilderness and the solitary place shall be glad for them; and the desert shall rejoice, and blossom like the rose. It shall blossom abundantly, and rejoice even with joy and singing; the glory of Lebanon shall be given unto it, the excellency of Carmel and Sharon; they shall see the glory of the Lord, and the excellency of our God.

The Lord is coming! He is coming to take His people home. The desert of mere existence is to undergo a fantastic transformation. The blossoming of the crocus produces a carpet of fragrance and beauty. As in the coming of spring, there is a freshness in the atmosphere and a new dimension to living.

The Lord is coming! The biting winds of adversity and the scorching sun of dehydration and depression are diverted by the "glory of Lebanon" — the great shade trees, which form a protective barrier against the onslaught of destructive circumstances.

The Lord is coming! His presence creates an oasis of calm and serenity in the midst of storm. His glory and excellency are seen and rejoicing is the order of the day "even with joy and singing." It is a time to "Strengthen the weak hands, and confirm the feeble knees. Say to those who are of a fearful heart, Be strong, fear not; behold your God will come with vengeance, even God, with a recompense; he will come and save you" (vs. 3, 4).

The Lord is coming! "And to you who are troubled, rest with us, when the Lord Jesus shall be revealed from heaven with his mighty angels, In flaming fire taking vengeance on them that know not God, and that obey not the gospel of our Lord Jesus Christ" (2 Thessalonians 1:7, 8).

The Lord is coming! "Rejoice evermore" (1 Thessalonians 5:16).

Ed Lyman

June 21

SINGING SCRIPTURE: **Revelation 15:3**

And they sang the song of Moses the servant of God, and the song of the Lamb, saying, Great and marvelous are thy works, Lord God Almighty; just and true are thy ways, thou King of saints.

When the Lord Jesus returns for his blood-bought saints, the dead in Christ shall rise and we, which are alive, will be caught up with them to meet the Lord in the air. What a day of joyful shouting and singing there will be! Surely this is something for all believers to anticipate.

First of all, we will see Jesus. Now we see Him through the eyes of faith, but then we shall behold Him with the eyes of our new creation.

Second, we will then see our loved ones gone before.

Third, we will be experiencing our new, resurrected bodies.

Fourth, we will at that time realize that Jesus has clothed us with immortality.

What shouting of joy will fill the air.

Indeed, we will join in the singing of that new song of the Lamb. Jesus will be leading His redeemed bride heavenward to the Father's house. As this enormous company of singing and shouting approaches the gates of heaven, the gate keeper hears the Lord Jesus say, "Lift up your heads, O ye gates; be ye lifted up that the Lord may enter in with his bride." The gate keeper asks, "Who is the Lord?" I can then envision the great company of the redeemed singing, "He is the Lord of Hosts. He is the King of Glory!"

Then the gates will open as a grand Hallelujah Chorus rings through the courts of heaven.

George Schuler

❋

June 22

PRAISE PSALM: **Psalm 142:7**

Bring my soul out of prison, that I may praise thy name. The righteous shall compass me about; for thou shalt deal bountifully with me.

The "prison" is not presented as a jail, but it is used in this verse in the sense of being a restriction of movement and a rejection. However, this is a song of assurance in the midst of human frailty and overpowering by the enemy. God can be depended upon to deliver, restore freedom, bring a song of gladness, and reinstate the fellowship of the righteous. "Bountifully" has the marvelous meaning of completeness. The thought is expressed that the Lord completely meets the needs of His own. Once again, we are reminded of the truth, which pervades all Scripture. This manifests itself again here. The Lord's promise is to supply all of our needs NOT necessarily all of our wants. How often we have learned as hindsight that some of the things for which we have prayed and which God withheld were actually selfishly "wanted" and would have been destructive to our witness or Christian service.

To request release from the bondage of self-serving desires and worldly pursuits should be the believer's prayer. Continued contamination puts us behind the bars of banality and blight. No purposeful praise is forthcoming and we meet with constant struggles in the inner man. When we rise to the occasion, turn our peer pressure and prideful personalities over to the Lord, we are compassed about by His righteousness and He completely cares for us.

Ed Lyman

June 23

SINGING SCRIPTURE: **1 Chronicles 6:31, 32 and 1 Chronicles 23:30**

And these are they whom David set over the service of song in the house of the Lord, after that the ark had rest. And they ministered before the dwelling place of the tabernacle of the congregation with singing, until Solomon had built the house of the Lord in Jerusalem: and they waited on their office according to their order.
And to stand every morning to thank and praise the Lord, and likewise at even.

In the very early years of my Christian life I commenced observing what I have called the "Morning Watch." Every morning, day in and day out, I get alone with God. I would not dream of going to my office before first of all spending time alone with Him. Nor would I attempt to carry on my church work without first meeting God, morning by morning. Directly after breakfast I retire to my study, close the door, and there spend the first hour alone with God.

For many years now I have observed the Morning Watch. If God has used me in any way down through the years it is because I have met Him morning by morning. I solve my problems before I come to them. Without the Morning Watch my work would be ineffective. I would be weak and helpless. It is only when I wait upon Him that I become strong spiritually.

Oswald J. Smith

June 24

SINGING SCRIPTURE: **Isaiah 52:8**

Thy watchmen shall lift up the voice; with the voice together shall they sing: for they shall see eye to eye, when the Lord shall bring again Zion.

The prince of prophets, Isaiah, paints a picture for the reader of watchmen on a wall to keep an eye out for danger or for those coming home. From the high points of walled Jerusalem, these watchmen with sharp eyes could see at a long distance anyone coming to bring good news. The idea during Isaiah's day was that when the people of God returned to the land there would be great blessing. The darkness of the hour would lift and be given over to rejoicing for there would be a time of peace and blessing.

The watchman does not merely announce the good news that God has been true to His word, but the lone voice of one rejoicing watchman is joined by the team of watchmen to praise the promises of God in a song of sweet deliverance.

The next step is that they see the Lord, Himself. This goes beyond the prophecy of Isaiah's day and reaches to the final time when everyone who loves the Lord and looks for His deliverance, will see him "eye to eye". What rejoicing and singing will take place at the entrance of the Great King, Jesus. Angelic hosts and countless powers from eternity will listen to the blessed of the Lord sing praises to their King. This is the blessed hope to the Christian, that long awaited time of final and complete rest in Jesus. Oh, what a day that will be!

Russell B. Gordon

June 25

PRAISE PSALM: **Psalm 51:15**

O Lord, open thou my lips: and my mouth shall show forth thy praise.

An Arab proverb says the thing we can never recover are: the spoken word, the sped arrow, time passed, and lost opportunity. We find definite parallels to these in the Word of God, which we should consider carefully as we raise our voices in songs of witness and worship.

The *Unbridled Tongue*: "If any man among you seem to be religious, and bridleth not his *tongue*, but deceiveth his own heart, this man's religion is vain" (James 1:26).

The *Undirected Talent*: "He that answereth a matter before he heareth it, it is folly and shame unto him" (Proverbs 18:13). "Neglect not the *gift* that is in thee" (1 Timothy 4:14).

The *Unredeemed Time*: "Sow to yourselves in righteousness, reap in mercy; break up your fallow ground: for it is *time* to seek the Lord, till he come and rain righteousness upon you. Ye have plowed wickedness, ye have reaped iniquity; ye have eaten the fruit of lies; because thou didst trust in thy way, in the multitude of thy mighty men" (Hosea 10:12, 13).

The *Uncaring Testimony*: "For what shall it profit a man, if he shall gain the whole world, and lose his own soul?" (Mark 8:36). "Be not thou therefore ashamed of the *testimony* of our Lord" (2 Timothy 1:8).

Tell or tarnish! Sing or stagnate!

"And whatsoever ye do, do it heartily, as to the Lord, and not unto men" (Colossians 3:23).

Ed Lyman

June 26

SINGING SCRIPTURE: **Amos 6:1a, 5**

Woe to them who are at ease in Zion ... That chant to the sound of the viol and invent to themselves instruments of music, like David.

In television productions, a technique known as "lip-synch" is frequently used. It is the process of mouthing the lyrics, pretending to sing, as pre-recorded music is played. The result is the impression that the performer is actually singing as the camera records the scene of sight and sound. "Woe to them ... That chant" — the Lord's people (then and NOW) who fall prey to the perfidy of spiritual "lip-service" forming the words of worship with their lips, but having hearts wandering from God. This is the music of hypocrisy and the prophet is calling God's people to task, because of their "lip-singing." They had become chanters in the corridors of complacency instead of rendering anthems of true praise as carolers in the courts of the King.

The melodic challenge to the believer from these ancient times is for a deliberate and dedicated determination to "present your bodies a living sacrifice, holy, acceptable unto God, which is your reasonable service" (Romans 12:1). "Woe to them ... That chant" finds affirmation in the apostle Paul's charge in Colossians 3:16 to "Let the word of Christ dwell in you richly, in all wisdom teaching and admonishing one another, in psalms and hymns and spiritual songs singing with grace in your hearts to the Lord."

"Now unto the King eternal, immortal, invisible, the only wise God, be honor and glory forever and ever. Amen" (1 Timothy 1:17). Since we worship the "only wise God," we find our faith to be developing and expanding as we wisely express our commitment to Him in songs and sacrifices of praise to the Creator, Comforter, and coming King!

Ed Lyman

June 27

SINGING SCRIPTURE: **Psalm 30:4**

Sing unto the Lord, O ye saints of his, and give thanks at the remembrance of his holiness.

Inspiration from this verse can be very rich and remarkably timely. Taken in context, the verse is more than a suggestion; it is an exhortation and a joyous command.

Often the Psalmist speaks of being in situations of extreme insecurity, terrifying danger, and deep anxiety. The absolute lack of any human solution to the problems originating in human sin and spiritual blindness is clearly emphasized. Threats to health, property, and life are implicit in these passages.

Upon whom can there be ultimate reliance?

It is God; alone.

Look at the context in Psalm 30. Here he states, "I will extol thee, O Lord, for thou hast drawn me up and hast not let my foes rejoice over me."

Obedient dependence upon the Lord alone is the required acknowledgment of His care. The assurance of His Lordship and salvation lies in His own Word.

His faithfulness to us produces inward peace. As we are commanded in this Psalm, we are to express this tranquillity joyfully and in songful praise.

Stephen Cushman

June 28

SINGING SCRIPTURE: **Psalm 92:3**

Upon an instrument of ten strings, and upon the psaltery; upon the harp with a solemn sound.

Here is enumerated the variety of instruments to be used in the public worship service of the congregation of Israel as they praise the Lord for His wondrous works and His marvelous dealings with His people. A gladsome response rises from the temple as the people gather on the Sabbath day to worship in song and sacrifice.

In the New Testament economy, Jesus Christ is our Sabbath, our Rest. Hebrews 4:3 states, "For we which have believed do enter into rest." He is therefore our means of entrance into the presence of

God. Jesus said, "I am the door: by me if any man enter in, he shall be saved."

Christ's incarnation was the entry of God into the human family forever. "Therefore the Lord himself shall give you a sign; Behold, a virgin shall conceive, and bear a son, and shall call his name Immanuel" (Isaiah 7:14).

His incarnation was spiritual, spontaneous, and sacrificial. "For ye know the grace of our Lord Jesus Christ, that, though he was rich, yet for your sakes he became poor, that ye through his poverty might be rich" (2 Corinthians 8:9).

Our serving, giving, and singing should also be spiritual, spontaneous, and sacrificial.

Ed Lyman

June 29

PRAISE PSALM: **Psalm 56:4**

In God I will praise his word, in God I have put my trust; I will not fear what flesh can do unto me.

The American Civil War raged on with men being killed and maimed on both sides. In May, 1864, General Sherman with 100,000 veterans broke loose from his base and started his long march through Georgia. The success of this campaign had Southern forces fleeing Atlanta by September and all of Georgia was open to Sherman and his troops. Sherman's Christmas present to President Abraham Lincoln was the city of Savannah.

During this sweeping campaign, General Sherman sent a message to his soldiers, who were defending the strategic Altoona Pass. It said, "Hold the Fort, I am coming."

After the war ended, Philip P. Bliss was told the story of this encouraging signal from the general to his men and he wrote:

Ho, my comrades, see the signal waving in the sky!
Reinforcements now appearing, victory is nigh.
See the mighty host advancing, Satan leading on;
Mighty men around us falling, courage almost gone!
See the glorious banner waving! Hear the trumpet blow!
In our Leader's name we triumph, over every foe,
Fierce and long the battle rages, but our help is near;
Onward comes our great commander — Cheer, my comrades, cheer!

Then, we hear the chorus sounding the theme of our song of praise:

"Hold the fort, I am coming, Jesus signals still;
Wave the answer back to heaven, 'By thy grace we will.' "

Ed Lyman

June 30

SINGING SCRIPTURE: **Isaiah 52:9**

Break forth into joy, sing together, ye waste places of Jerusalem: for the Lord hath comforted his people, he hath redeemed Jerusalem.

The NIV translates this verse: "Burst into songs of joy together, you ruins of Jerusalem." Can ruins sing? Can broken-down walls and decayed, rocky rubble make a joyful noise literally? Is that what this verse is saying or is it to be interpreted in a spiritual sense?

All day long in our advanced culture, we are bathed in electromagnetic radiation and sonic vibrations. The air is filled with broadcasts of noise, music, and speech, most of which is unheard and unfelt. We are not tuned to this. We use various machines and instruments to make these vibrations into visible light, sounds within the hearing range of our ears, and vibrations within the feeling capacity of other senses.

If man, by his God-given ability, can change the vibrations of rocks grinding together many thousands of feet below the surface of the earth into squiggles on a paper chart or bring sounds of a symphony orchestra from thousands of miles away to the ears of a listener by means of a box called a radio, couldn't God make rocks sing praises to the Creator at the redemption of His creation? Luke 19:38-40 tells us of the triumphal entry of Jesus into Jerusalem. The Pharisees wanted Jesus to rebuke His disciples for saying, "Blessed be the King that cometh in the Name of the LORD, peace in heaven and glory in the highest." Jesus said, "If they keep quiet, the stones will cry out." The Creator was walking the earth then — and He will walk it again!

Ev Gourlay

July

DAILY PRAISE

July 1

SINGING SCRIPTURE: **Psalm 150**

Praise ye the Lord. Praise God in his sanctuary: praise him in the firmament of his power.
Praise him for his mighty acts: praise him according to his excellent greatness.
Praise him with the sound of the trumpet: praise him with the psaltery and harp.
Praise him with the timbrel and dance: praise him with stringed instruments and organs.
Praise him upon the loud cymbals: praised him upon the high sounding cymbals.
Let everything that hath breath praise the Lord.
Praise ye the Lord.

How wonderful it is to praise the Lord, who loved us enough to send His Son. Truly it means great joy and lasting peace. Just consider for a moment our Saviour as we see Him in Luke 1:31-33. We read, "And behold ..."

Shall conceive — humility
Shall call His name Jesus — humanity

Shall be great — dignity
Shall be called Son of the Highest — deity

Shall give unto Him the throne — majesty
Shall reign — sovereignty
Shall be no end — eternity

Praise the Lord!

Fred Nader

July 2

PRAISE PSALM: **Psalm 139:14**

I will praise thee; for I am fearfully and wonderfully made. Marvelous are thy works, and that my soul knoweth right well.

Recognition of the magnificent architecture of the human body and its biological uniqueness is cause for praise; joyous songs of worship. Truly, we are "fearfully and wonderfully made." Yet, beyond the marvel of physical life, there is the spiritual creation of God, which brings us to the awareness that "if any man be in Christ, he is a new creation!" This is cause for "praise-song" from the heart and voice of every believer.

"All things are become new" (2 Corinthians 5:17), because the faithful Man (Jesus Christ) was forsaken in order that the filthy man might be changed and forgiven.

Jesus Christ, the Faithful Man, said to His Father, "I have glorified thee upon the earth; I have finished the work which thou gavest me to do" (John 17:4). As the Forsaken Man, Jesus Christ, was made "to be sin for us who knew no sin, that we might be made the righteousness of God in him" (2 Corinthians 5:21).

As a result, the filthy man "as an unclean thing, and all our righteousnesses are as filthy rags" (Isaiah 64:6), is transformed to a forgiven man. "Be it known unto you, therefore, men and brethren, that through this man (Jesus Christ) is preached unto you the forgiveness of sins; And by him all that believe are justified from all things" (Acts 13:38, 39).

Not only do we raise our voices in rapturous song for the blessing of physical life by God's creation, but we sing in grateful praise for the everlasting life we find through our spiritual new birth. "Marvelous are thy works!"

Ed Lyman

July 3

SINGING SCRIPTURE: Luke 20:42, 43

And David himself saith in the book of Psalms, The LORD said unto my Lord, Sit thou at my right hand, Till I make thine enemies thy footstool.

This song of David is found in the Psalms (110:1) and is repeated again in Acts 2:34, 35. Its repetition is very significant in light of its prophetic presentation of the scope of Christ's salvation and the centrality of God's program throughout history. In 1 Corinthians 15:20-26, Paul puts it into perspective:

But now is Christ risen from the dead, and become the firstfruits of them that slept.

For since by man came death, by man came also the resurrection of the dead.
For as in Adam all die, even so in Christ shall all be made alive.
But every man in his own order: Christ the firstfruits; afterward they that are Christ's at his coming.
Then cometh the end, when he shall have delivered up the kingdom to God, even the Father; when he shall have put down all rule and all authority and power.
For he must reign, till he hath put all enemies under his feet. The last enemy that shall be destroyed is death.

Can there be a greater song of hope.

Ed Lyman

July 4

SINGING SCRIPTURE: **Ezekiel 33:2-5**

Son of man, speak to the children of thy people, and say unto them,
When I bring the sword upon the land, if the people of the land take a man of their coasts, and set him for their watchman:
If when he seeth the sword come upon the land, he blow the trumpet, and warn the people;
Then whosoever heareth the sound of the trumpet, and taketh not warning; if the sword come, and take him away, his blood shall be upon his own head.
He heard the sound of the trumpet, and took not warning; his blood shall be upon him. But he that taketh warning shall deliver his soul.

By using the musical warning of the watchman's trumpet, the prophet is sounding the Scriptural theme that God has spoken clearly about judgment for sin. Twice in the 18th chapter of Ezekiel the statement is made "The soul that sinneth, it shall die." Throughout the Word of God the warning has been sounded. With such clear tones ringing in our ears as we turn the pages of Holy Writ, "the melody lingers on." It is a resounding warning, a call for repentance, a promise of salvation.

"For the wages of sin is death but the gift of God is eternal life through Jesus Christ our Lord" (Romans 6:23).

If you have heeded this warning sound, put your faith and trust in the Son of God, who died that you might live, and seek to do His pleasure, you, too, must become a trumpet-sounding watchman.

Ed Lyman

July 5

SINGING SCRIPTURE: **Psalm 92:1**

It is a good thing to give thanks unto the Lord, and to sing praises unto thy name, O Most High.

An army corpsman told one of the doctors visiting the ward in which the young man was assigned that on the days the band played near the sick-bay, the ill and wounded always felt better. Men who were lame the day before and needed assistance to walk got up and made their way outside to sit in the sunshine. Those who were so depressed they never thought they would return home began to pack and ask about travel schedules.

Not only does gospel music have a saving influence, it also comforts and soothes the restless spirit and troubled heart.

Many people have entered church filled with worries and anxieties and perhaps in the singing of the very first song, faith has been renewed and troubles lost their importance.

Ed Lyman

July 6

SINGING SCRIPTURE: **Isaiah 26:19**

Thy dead men shall live, together with my dead body shall they arise. Awake and sing, ye that dwell in dust; for thy dew is like the dew of herbs, and the earth shall cast out the dead.

This is a song of resurrection!

And though after my skin worms destroy this body, yet in my flesh shall I see God'' (Job 19:26).

As it is written, Eye hath not seen, nor ear heard, neither have entered into the heart of man, the things which God hath

prepared for them that love him.
But God hath revealed them unto us by his Spirit; for the
Spirit searcheth all things, yea, the deep things of God.
For what man knoweth the things of man, save the spirit of
man which is in him? even so the things of God knoweth no
man, but the Spirit of God.
Now we have received, not the spirit of the world, but the
Spirit which is of God; that we might know the things that are
freely given to us of God.
Which things also we speak, not in the words which man's
wisdom teacheth, but which the Holy Ghost teachest; com-
paring spiritual things with spiritual.
But the natural man receiveth not the things of the Spirit of
God: for they are foolishness unto him: neither can he know
them, because they are spiritually discerned (1 Corinthians
2:9-14).

Ed Lyman

July 7

PRAISE PSALM: **Psalm 56:10**

In God will I praise his word; in the Lord will I praise his
word.

This is a verse of song-sowing. By this I mean the songs of praise
and witness, which we sing are sowing seed along the highways and
byways of life. Our relationship with Christ involves our walk with
Him, our worship of Him, our witness for Him. There is a song
evangelism, which bears much fruit. It is a "sowing" as stated in
psalm 126:6, "He that goeth forth and weepeth, bearing precious
seed, shall doubtless come again with rejoicing, bringing his
sheaves with him."

The sower must have *faith* in the seed itself, which is God's word.
He must have faith in the providence of God to care for the seed and
he must have proper faith in himself as recommended in Romans
12:3, "For I say, through the grace given unto me, to every man that
is among you, not to think of himself more highly than he ought to
think, but to think soberly, according as God hath dealt to every
man the measure of faith." This kind of "self-thinking" is the
antithesis of pride. Pride is a disease, which makes everyone else
sick except the one, who has it.

The song-sower must have *hope*. In Isaiah 55:10 and 11, we are presented with the imagery of sowing seed for eventual harvest and the effectiveness of preaching the Word of God, which "shall not return unto me (God) void, but it shall accomplish that which I please."

Thirdly, the sower must have *love* for the work of the Lord. Sow with songs of love.

Ed Lyman

July 8

SINGING SCRIPTURE: **1 Chronicles 13:8**

And David and all Israel played before God with all their might, and with singing, and with harps, and with psalteries, and with timbrels, and with cymbals, and with trumpets.

I am impressed with the phrase "with all their might." The people may not have been professional musicians, yet they put everything they had into their efforts. They were performing for the glory of God.

A thought has just occurred to me. Why is it that so many Christians do not expect the same professionalism from Christian musicians as they do from secular artists? So often we tend to settle for second best. We do not make demands upon Christian musicians, which would require them to stretch their abilities. Sometimes the attitude of the musician himself is wrong: "This is a 'ministry' and God will use it even though I have not rehearsed."

My music, performed "with all my might," urges me to strive for perfection. I cannot be satisfied with a lesser attitude. I must put everything I have into my ability: rehearse, interpret, memorize, understand, feel, create, and perform. I must do this "with all my might." The reason — I want my God to have the very best of the talent He has given me, because if my attitude and performance are not the best I can accomplish, it reflects, somehow, on the One whom it glorifies.

Mark Moore

July 9

SINGING SCRIPTURE: **Exodus 19:16**

And it came to pass on the third day in the morning, that there were thunderings and lightnings, and a thick cloud upon the mount, and the voice of the trumpet exceedingly loud, so that all the people that were in the camp trembled.

"And God spoke all these words, saying, I am the Lord thy God, who have brought thee out of the land of Egypt, out of the house of bondage (Exodus 20:1, 2).

"Thou shalt have no other gods before me (3).

"Thou shalt not take the name of the Lord thy God in vain (7).

"Remember the sabbath day, to keep it holy (8).

"Honor thy father and thy mother, that thy days may be long upon the land which the Lord thy God giveth thee (12).

"Thou shalt not kill (13).

"Thou shalt not commit adultery (14).

"Thou shalt not steal (15).

"Thou shalt not bear false witness against thy neighbor (16).

"Thou shalt not covet thy neighbor's house; thou shalt not covet thy neighbor's wife, nor his manservant, nor his maidservant, nor his ox, nor his ass, nor anything that is thy neighbor's" (17).

The trumpet sound was the music of commandment (Exodus 19:13,16,19; 20:18). It announced the giving of the *law, which judges.* Man looks at himself through the mirror of this law and finds that he is wanting. However, another musical event, the angelic choir singing at the birth of the Lord Jesus Christ, announced the giving of God's *grace, which justifies.* The believer is now under the law of Christ: "For the law of the Spirit of life in Christ Jesus hath made me free from the law of sin and death" (Romans 8:2).

Ed Lyman

July 10

PRAISE PSALM: **Psalm 135:21**

Blessed be the Lord out of Zion, who dwelleth at Jerusalem. Praise ye the Lord.

This psalm-song is a chorale of contrasts between the true God and idols. We worship and adore the only God; there is none other. Yet, men refuse to accept His reign and rule in their lives. They constantly turn to their own devised idols.

Our God, the Lord Jesus Christ, surrounds us with His presence and His love.

He is *above us:* "Jesus, made an high priest after the order of Melchizedek" (Hebrews 6:20).

He is *beneath us*: "The eternal God is thy refuge, and underneath are the everlasting arms" (Deuteronomy 33:27).

He is *behind us*: "For ye shall not go out with haste, nor go by flight; for the Lord will go before you, and the God of Israel will be your rear guard" (Isaiah 52:12).

He is *before us*: "And when he putteth forth his own sheep, he goeth before them, and the sheep follow him; for they know his voice" (John 10:4).

He is *beside us*: "I have set the Lord always before me; because he is at my right hand, I shall not be moved" (Psalm 16:8).

He is *around us*: "His left hand is under my head, and his right hand doth embrace me" (Solomon 2:6).

He is *within us*: "I am crucified with Christ: nevertheless I live; yet not I, but Christ liveth in me" (Galatians 2:20).

Surrounded by the Son of God, we bless Him with songs of praise.

Ed Lyman

July 11

SINGING SCRIPTURE: **Psalm 33:3**

Sing unto him a new song; play skilfully with a loud noise.

Christianity sings of a Savior, Whose mercy is immeasurable and Whose love surpasses comprehension.

The message of salvation is timeless.

It creates new beginnings.

It develops new values.

It brings new experiences.

It produces new lives.

In this day of thrill seeking, no experience can compare with the transformation of a life by the power and presence of Jesus Christ. His love is everlasting and his mercy is enduring.

Excitement that defies any comparison awaits those who keep a faithful testimony in song, speech and deed. In the hands of the "Master Musician," the Great Conductor of the universe, the musical talent of a life dedicated to the service of Jesus Christ can become an effective and useful instrument.

This is incomparable excitement! The emphasis of Christian music is different from that of other music. The "Good News" is applicable to every culture, every age, every society. The message of Gospel songs is a challenge to life that is different from the humdrum of aimless existence.

Through music, we can share with the world around us our own awareness of God's presence, God's promises and God's power.

Ed Lyman

July 12

SINGING SCRIPTURE: **Psalm 59:16**

But I will sing of thy strength; yea, I will sing aloud of thy lovingkindness in the morning: for thou hast been my high tower, and a refuge in the day of my distress.

This note of praise occurs at the end of a prayer for deliverance — deliverance from the Psalmist's enemies. There are few occasions in our lives when we feel as if we are surrounded by "enemies" and that we must pray for deliverance. Most of us, modern-day people, pride ourselves in being so much in control of our life situations, that we would normally expect to have the option of simply walking out of the presence of our enemies.

The Psalmist, who has witnessed the cursing and lying (verse 12) of his detractors, turns his thought to the strength and lovingkindness of his God and sings aloud of His attributes. We have indication of any physical deliverance in the Psalm, but what is seen is the marvelous deliverance of the spirit. You and I enjoy the same freedom of spirit when we are surrounded by the enemies of loneliness, family problems, job pressures, financial anxieties, fears of the unknown, etc.

Many times in my memory and imagination, I have returned to a worship service over which I presided as minister of music. I was the worker, salaried to serve and bless the people of God, but my impact was as nothing compared to the effect on me by the unpaid ministry of one of the members of the congregation. A dear lady, whose witness in my life had always been profound, stood with the congregation and sang with full voice and radiant face: "Stayed upon Jehovah, hearts are fully blest; finding as He promised, perfect peace and rest." All of us knew that she had buried her husband just two days before. Was her sorrow so great that a song of praise did not lift her spirit to soar? Never! The song directed her heart to the only One, who can free the human spirit, even in life's greatest sorrow.

Ron Boud

July 13

SINGING SCRIPTURE: **Ezra 3:10**

And when the builders laid the foundation of the temple of the Lord, they set the priests in their apparel with trumpets, and the Levites, the sons of Asaph, with cymbals, to praise the Lord, after the ordinance of David, king of Israel.

The influence of David upon the worship and praise services of the people of God is once again seen as the foundation is begun for the new temple in this hostile environment by the returned remnant from Babylon. The sound of music is to be heard. It is to mark the melding of musical exaltation with the practical presentation of the workmanship of God's people. The expectation, engineering, and execution of the task of laying the foundation demanded integrity, intelligence, and initiative.

As we seek to serve the Lord Jesus Christ, we are bound to be governed by the same principles, which guided the people in this project of laying the temple foundation. The personal integrity of the workman makes him presentable for the Lord's use. His intelligent acceptance of the Lord's leading prepares him for the work ahead. His initiative is established by his trust in God's preeminent priorities.

"Let integrity and uprightness preserve me; for I wait on thee," said David in Psalm 25:21. Preservation is found in moral and spiritual soundness. This is true integrity. Intelligence comes as a result of wholly depending upon the Lord. Initiative is the outgrowth of properly placed trust. David's prayer song in Psalm 16:1 gives it to us: "Preserve me, O God, for in thee do I put my trust."

Ed Lyman

July 14

PRAISE PSALM: **Psalm 56:12**

Thy vows are upon me, O God: I will render praise unto thee.

It is good to bear in mind that in whatever circumstances we find ourselves, it cannot be necessary to disobey God. If we wish for something, the means to obtain it must be as much approved of by the Lord as the end, itself.

As if it were already upon him, David foresees His deliverance by the Lord from harassment and hostility and is prepared to present his vows of praise to God for complete safety and security within His perfect will. The song is already formed on his lips and is about to burst forth as he is consumed with a preoccupation with the presence and purpose of God. What a lesson for us today!

The mature Christian is one who has a deliberate purpose to do the will of God in all things, under all circumstances, and at all times. He never relies on just a part measure of obedience, but still running the race, his eyes are fixed on the goal. The only path of happiness and safety is prompt and unquestioning obedience to the commandments of the Lord. As in David's example, if we have a right mind, the way in which it pleases God to answer our prayers will always please us well.

Ed Lyman

July 15

SINGING SCRIPTURE: **Revelation 14:3**

And they sung as it were a new song before the throne, and before the four beasts, and the elders: and no man could learn that song but the hundred and forty and four thousand, which were redeemed from the earth.

An unknown poet has written:

Once I heard a song of sweetness as it cleft the morning air,
Sounding in its blest completeness like a tender, pleading prayer;
And I sought to find the singer whence the wondrous song was born;
Till I found a bird, sore wounded, pinioned by an ugly thorn.
I have seen a soul of sadness while its wings with pain were furled,
Giving hope and cheer and gladness that should bless the weeping world;
Soon I learned a life of sweetness was of pain and sorrow borne,
For that stricken soul was singing with its heart against a thorn!

You are told of One who loves you, of a Savior crucified,
You are told of nails that pinioned, and a spear that pierced His side;
You are told of cruel scourging, of a Savior bearing scorn,
And He died for your salvation with His brow against the thorn.
You are not above the Master! Will you breathe a sweet refrain?
Then His grace will be sufficient when your heart is pierced with pain;
Will you live to bless His loved ones though your life be bruised and torn,
Like a bird that sang so sweetly with its heart against a thorn?

Ed Lyman

July 16

SINGING SCRIPTURE:**Isaiah 30:29**

Ye shall have a song, as in the night when a holy solemnity is kept; and gladness of heart, as when one goeth with a pipe to come into the mountain of the Lord, to the Mighty One of Israel.

If the people of Judah would fully trust the Lord, they would have singing and rejoicing. The term "Mighty One" is the same used in Deuteronomy 32:4 when Moses speaks of God: "He is the Rock, his work is perfect; for all his ways are judgment; a God of truth and without iniquity, just and right is he."

A song of gladness accompanied by the music of stability is the result of placing our hope and trust on the solid Rock — "On Christ, the solid Rock, I stand; All other ground is sinking sand." The reality of the presence of the Lord Jesus Christ becomes clear as we contemplate Isaiah 28:16: "Therefore thus saith the Lord God, Behold I lay in Zion for a foundation a stone, a tried stone, a precious cornerstone, a sure foundation." Peter explains it further as he speaks of Christ as "a living stone, disallowed indeed of men but chosen of God, and precious ... the stone which the builders disallowed, the same is made the head of the corner" (1 Peter 2:4, 7).

Music can be the platform from which we center our gaze upon what God can do.

As the stone was struck by Moses in the desert and life-giving water flowed, so the Lord Jesus Christ, our Rock, was smitten in order that the Spirit of life might flow from Him to all, who would drink. Jesus said, "Whosoever drinketh of the water that I shall give him shall never thirst, but the water that I shall give him shall be in him a well of water springing up into everlasting life" (John 4:14).

Upon this Rock we can build our chorale of consecration.

Ed Lyman

SINGING SCRIPTURE: Psalm 27:6

And now shall mine head be lifted up above mine enemies round about me: therefore will I offer in his tabernacle sacrifices of joy; I will sing, yea, I will sing praises unto the Lord.

This kind of rejoicing could easily be called the music of Christian confidence; the song of optimistic certainty.

Two workmen watched in awe the performance of a huge steam shovel which took up tons of earth with each bite of its enormous scoop. One of the workers observed, "If it were not for that scoop, five hundred men might be working with shovels". "Yes", replied the other, "and if it were not for shovels, a million of us might be using spoons to move that soil".

Some say the glass is *half empty* while others say the glass is *half full.* It depends on one's point of view, doesn't it?

An artist contemplated purchasing a farm in Vermont. He asked the farmer if the view was good. "I must have a good view in order to paint". The farmer replied, "From the front porch you can see Ed Smow's barn, but beyond that is just a bunch of mountains." It depends on how we look at things as to what we see — and how we sing!

Jack Schurman

July 18

PRAISE PSALM: Psalm 63:3

Because thy loving-kindness is better than life, my lips shall praise thee.

Though we sing of the love of God throughout eternity, we'll never exhaust the scope of dimension. We cannot explain — completely — God's loving-kindness nor can we find adequate words to explain the grace that makes us kin to the Lord of the Universe. Yet it is in John 3:16 where we are given a glimpse of the magnitude of God's love, which brings salvation to mankind.

God's love is *unsought* in its *Action.* "Herein is love, not that we loved God, but that he loved us, and sent his Son to be the propitiation for our sins" (1 John 4:10).

God's love is *unmerited* by its *Object.* "Much more then, being now justified by his blood, we shall be saved from wrath through him" (Romans 5:9).

God's love is *unfathomable* in its *depth.* "Comprehend with all saints, what is the breadth, and length, and depth, and height. And to know the love of Christ" (Ephesians 3:18,19).

God's love is *universal* in its *Offer* and *unbounded* in its *Gift.* "He that spared not his own Son, but delivered him up for us all, how shall he not with him also freely give us all things?" (Romans 8:32)

God's love is *unending* in its *Character* and *broken* in its *Ministry.* "Nor height, nor depth, nor any other creature, shall be able to separate us from the love of God, which is in Christ Jesus, our Lord" (Romans 8:39).

Ed Lyman

July 19

SINGING SCRIPTURE: **Psalm 40:3**

He hath put a new song in my mouth, even praise unto our God; many shall see it and fear and trust the Lord.

Just how important is music in the life of the church and more specifically, in the life of the Christian today?

David, the Psalmist, gave a practical evaluation of this, when he said that God had put a new song on his lips, which was praise to God.

In our rehearsals do we sing as though God were listening or do we feel that we do not have to work so hard because no one is listening?

Do we do our best only before a large congregation?

Our singing should depend upon our desire to exalt the Lord and never on the size of the audience.

What will be the result of our earnest praise? We read in this passage of Scripture that many shall "see it." They will see our exuberance and joy. David also says, "they will fear." Fear? yes, for when the world sees that we have joy in this vale of tears, it will look at itself and question its lack of assurance.

What will be the final outcome?

The answer comes to us again from this same verse. They will "trust in the Lord."

Many people have been influenced to follow Christ as Lord as a result of music and a clear expression of faith and praise in song.

Don Jost

July 20

SINGING SCRIPTURE: **Leviticus 25:9**

Then shalt thou cause the trumpet of the jubilee to sound on the tenth day of the seventh month, in the day of atonement shall ye make this trumpet sound throughout all your land.

The sound of the trumpet call on the day of atonement announced the most important single day in the Hebrew year — *Yom Kippur*. The theological term "atonement" encompasses the complete sacrificial and redemptive work of the Lord Jesus Christ in His death and resurrection. However, the meaning of the Old Testament term as it relates to the children of Israel means "covering" or "to cover." At this particular time of year, the sins of the people were covered by the required sacrifices until Christ came to nail them to His cross, where, as God's sacrificial Lamb, He made full redemption.

The music of this trumpet call can be likened to tuning up an orchestra. It was the sounding of the "A" — a "shadow of good things to come and not the very image of the things" (Hebrews 10:1). The sacrifice on that day was the tune-up, but the work of the Lord Jesus Christ was the playing of the full symphony of salvation.

When the trumpet sound on the day of atonement also announced the year of jubilee, it proclaimed "liberty throughout all the land unto all the inhabitants thereof: it shall be a jubilee unto you; and ye shall return every man unto his possession, and ye shall return every man unto his family" (Leviticus 25:10). It was as if all things had become new.

This is our trumpet sound of witness today. As Christians we tell of "the liberty with which Christ hath made us free" (Galatians 5:1). It is the sound of a new possession — eternal life. It is the call of a new relationship — children of the Heavenly Father.

Ed Lyman

July 21

SINGING SCRIPTURE: **Isaiah 38:9-17 (This is called "Hezekiah's Song")**

The writing of Hezekiah king of Judah, when he had been sick, and was recovering from his sickness:

I said in the cutting off of my days, I shall go to the gates of the grave: I am deprived of the residue of my years.

I said, I shall not see the Lord, even the Lord, in the land of the living: I shall behold man no more with the inhabitants of the world.

Mine age is departed, and is removed from me as a shepherd's tent: I have cut off like a weaver my life: he will cut me off with pining sickness: from day even to night wilt thou make an end of me.

Like a crane or a swallow, so did I chatter: I did mourn as a dove: mine eyes fail with looking upward: O Lord, I am oppressed; undertake for me.

What shall I say? he hath both spoken unto me, and himself hath done it: I shall go softly all my years in the bitterness of my soul.

O Lord, by these things men live, and in all these things is the life of my spirit: so wilt thou recover me, and make me to live.

Behold, for peace I had great bitterness: but thou hast in love to my soul delivered it from the pit of corruption: for thou hast cast all my sins behind thy back.

Hezekiah

July 22

PRAISE PSALM: **Psalm 135:1**

Praise ye the Lord. Praise ye the name of the Lord; praise him, O ye servants of the Lord.

"For unto us a child is born, unto us a son is given, and the government shall be upon his shoulder; and his name shall be called Wonderful, Counselor, The Mighty God, The Everlasting Father, The Prince of Peace" (Isaiah 9:6).

"Now all this was done, that it might be fulfilled which was spoken by the Lord through the prophet, saying, Behold, the virgin shall be with child, and shall bring forth a son, and they shall call his name Immanuel, which, being interpreted, is God with us" (Matthew 1:22, 23). This was a direct quotation of the passage in Isaiah 7:14 and although the Lord Jesus Christ was not actually called "Immanuel," the Hebrew usage of the name does not imply a title, but rather, a characterization. The name "Immanuel" shows that Jesus really was "God with us." His Deity was stated at the very beginning of the New Testament in no uncertain terms.

To Joseph, the angel said, "And she (Mary) shall bring forth a son, and thou shalt call his name JESUS; for he shall save his people from their sins" (Matthew 1:21). Jesus is the Greek form of the Hebrew, *Jehoshua*, which means Jehovah is Salvation.

The Lord Jesus Christ is, by His birth, His life, His death, His resurrection, truly "God our Salvation." The music of praise belongs to Him "for there is none other name under heaven given among men, whereby we must be saved" (Acts 4:12). He is our "Salvation Song."

Ed Lyman

July 23

SINGING SCRIPTURE: **Psalm 87:7**

> *As well the singers as the players on instruments shall be there: all my springs are in thee.*

Music and song were important features in worship services during the time of David's reign as King of Israel. The Jewish people were known by the nations of the world for their musicianship.

As we read this Psalm, we find the people rejoicing in a special festive occasion and marching in a triumphant procession playing musical instruments and raising their voices in song.

In the presence of God there is joy unspeakable and full of glory.

When a church sees spiritual growth and conversions resulting from its ministry, praise to God is exuberant and seeks ways of expression.

The musicians we read about here are united in song and make a happy procession to the temple of God.

They are not inspired as the worshippers of heathen gods are inspired by wine and strong drink, but by drinking from the springs of living water from the fount of God.

Happy is the man, who can say, "all my springs are in thee." These "springs" are a man's posterity: his friends, family, children, and associates, who are entitled to the glorious privileges of God's elect and enjoy His favor and protection.

Ed Lyman

July 24

SINGING SCRIPTURE: Zephaniah 2:14

And flocks shall lie down in the midst of her, all beasts of the nations: both the cormorant and the bittern shall lodge in the upper lintels of it; their voice shall sing in the windows: desolation shall be in the thresholds: for he shall uncover the cedar work.

Ninevah had been a magnificent city. It escaped the destruction God had predicted when it repented after Jonah had preached the Lord's message. Now, it had become idolatrous, rejecting the Lord and despising His people. Zephaniah prophesied its coming downfall.

Just as a condemned building is ravaged and razed, so Ninevah will see its splendor tarnished and its position among nations brought low. Its demise will be thorough and the thresholds or gates, which once opened to wealth and beauty from the nations of the world, will be broken down and cattle will graze in the city streets and once lush gardens. The windows of this mighty city, which once allowed the entrance of light and were the eyes through which scenes of life were beheld and through which the melodies of life were wafted, and will be marred by decay and disfigured. They shall only act as tunnels through which the sounds of the cormorant and bittern echo.

The cormorant, a kind of pelican, and the bittern, a member of the heron family, are not known for their singing. They are noisemakers! The prophet is graphically illustrating the mockery of the pursuit of pleasure and self-indulgence. It is not music to the ears, but a continual, raucous reminder of "whatsoever a man soweth, that shall he also reap." Ninevah's true character is to be completely uncovered.

Such is also the picture of that person, who permits the entanglements of the world to take priority over the enlightenment of the word. David said: "The entrance of thy words giveth light." Too often we are willing to exchange the harmonic patterns of beautiful music for the discord of mundane pursuits.

Ed Lyman

July 25

SINGING SCRIPTURE: Isaiah 42:11

Let the wilderness and the cities thereof lift up their voice, the villages that Kedar doth inhabit; let the inhabitants of the rock sing, let them shout from the top of the mountains.

This brilliant exclamation of praise comes before some important reminders to the nation of Israel found in Isaiah 44:21, 22: (1) "I have formed thee," (2) "Thou art my servant," (3) "Thou shalt not be forgotten," (4) "I have blotted out thy transgressions," and (5) "I have redeemed thee."

This embodies creation, relationship, forgiveness, and redemption. What remains? God has done it all. From creation to consummation, God has designed and will implement a perfect plan. He is still in control.

In our lifetime we have the assurance of a loving Master-servant relationship, and — we will not be forsaken. The impact of the reality alone makes living an extraordinarily beautiful symphony.

We have the potential for dealing a fatal blow to the drug industry if we dare to comprehend and experience the truth of having our transgressions blotted out. No longer does guilt need to be that which debilitates us.

Is it any wonder that the heavens are admonished to sing? That the lower parts of the earth are told to shout? That every mountain and forest should break forth into song? Shouldn't you and I celebrate in song?

Ron Boud

July 26

PRAISE PSALM: Psalm 48:1

Great is the Lord, and greatly to be praised in the city of our God, in the mountain of his holiness.

"And I will dwell in the House of the Lord for ever" (Psalm 23:6b). Be ever mindful of this fact. The bride of the Lord Jesus Christ is composed of those whose robes have been washed and made white in the blood of the Lamb; those, who have inherited eternal life by being born again "not of blood, not of the will of the flesh, nor of the will of man, but of God" (John 1:13). This trust was explained so clearly to inquiring Nicodemus: where the Bridegroom dwells, there will the bride be also.

As His bride, we shall reign with Him in a land where there shall be no more tears, where death and sorrow and crying and pain are unknown. Eternity will be all too short for the unfolding of the things, which the Lord, the Bridegroom, has laid up for the enjoyment of His bride. Being the bride of the Lord Jesus Christ is indicative of nearness, of close relationship, of kinship; thus, the bride will inherit all things in Him and with Him. The innumerable angelic hosts — who move in marshalled precision more swiftly than light to do His bidding — will be in constant attendance upon Him and upon His bride, His blood-bought betrothed ones. He will adorn with heavenly impartial splendor. How privileged will we be at seeing the world bowed down before the Lamb seated upon the throne. Is that not a prospect to elicit your song of praise?

George S. Schuler

July 27

SINGING SCRIPTURE: **Luke 19:37**

And when he was come nigh, even now at the descent of the mount of Olives, the whole multitude of the disciples began to rejoice and praise God with a loud voice for all the mighty works that they had seen;

What a scene! The Lord of Glory enters Jerusalem and the disciples express their joy and praise.

Blessed be the King that cometh in the name of the Lord: peace in heaven, and glory in the highest.

In Psalm 118 this event is prophesied and later in Isaiah 40, the prophet says, "Prepare ye the way of the Lord, make straight in the desert a highway for our God."

In Ephesians we read that "he (Jesus) is our peace" and if we have allowed Him to reign as Sovereign of our lives, we too can sing with the disciples:

Hosanna; Blessed is he that cometh in the name of the Lord:
Blessed by the kingdom of our father David, that cometh in
the name of the Lord: Hosanna in the highest.

Ed Lyman

July 28

SINGING SCRIPTURE: **Isaiah 26:1**

In that day shall this song be sung in the land of Judah;

We have a strong city; salvation will God appoint for walls and bulwarks.

Open ye the gates, that the righteous nation which keepeth the truth may enter in.

Thou wilt keep him in perfect peace, whose mind is stayed on thee: because he trusteth in thee.

Trust ye in the Lord forever: for in the Lord JEHOVAH is everlasting strength.

Because of the unique relationship the Christian has with the Lord, he has the complete confidence that "all things work together for good to them that love God." This is not presumption; it is expectation resulting from faith.

Ed Lyman

July 29

SINGING SCRIPTURE: **Exodus 15:20, 21**

And Miriam the prophetess, the sister of Aaron, took a timbrel in her hand; and all the women went out after her with timbrels and with dances. And Miriam answered them, Sing ye to the Lord, for he hath triumphed gloriously; the horse and his rider hath he thrown into the sea.

After 400 years of enslavement, Israel escaped from Egypt, but Pharaoh followed in hot pursuit. The people of God faced a three-cornered dilemma. On the sides were cliffs. Behind was the

Pharaoh. Ahead, the sea. Panic broke out until Moses shouted, "Fear not, stand still, see the salvation of the Lord." The waters were parted and they passed over in "walking faith" on dry ground. When Pharaoh pursued, the waters closed over his army.

Then, Miriam took a timbrel and played as she danced and sang! All the women came after her with music. A national anthem came into being. It is sung over and over in every generation: "Sing ye to the Lord, for he hath triumphed gloriously; the horse and his rider hath he thrown into the sea." That was Miriam's shining hour. She helped a nation to be born.

Though Miriam later died, her song of exultation never did for we still say, "Let us sing unto the Lord." Miriam tried to teach us that our faith should have a lifting quality, a lilt.

After hearing a particularly moving sermon, a woman commented to her friend, "Ah, yes, but he ought to have sung the last part." Christian service and worship ought always to be on the verge of breaking into song.

Paul said it often, "Again, I say rejoice."

Ed Lyman

July 30

SINGING SCRIPTURE: **Psalm 81:3**

> *Blow up the trumpet in the new moon, in the time appointed, on our solemn feast day.*

This psalm opens with a hymn of praise. It is a summons to the opening ritual of a great feast. The people have been called to join their voices in a joyful praise song to the Lord. The priests are commanded to sound the horns. Before the whole congregation, God's relationship to Israel is to be recited.

Israel had been prepared by God and given principles and precepts by which to live in close harmony with His purposes. Through this special people, the whole world was to be blessed. The festival was a time of witness.

"Blow the trumpet" is a call to us today to be faithful ambassadors for the Lord Jesus Christ. Matthew 28:18 speaks of the *Power He Possesses*, which will enable us to witness: "All power is given unto me in heaven and in earth." Matthew 28:19 puts forth the *Program He Prefers* in our witness: "Go ye therefore, and teach all nations." Matthew 28:20 assures us of the *Presence He Promises* as we witness: "And, lo, I am with you alway even unto the end of the world."

The trumpet call is clear. It is the call of loyalty to the Lord Jesus Christ.

Ed Lyman

July 31

PRAISE PSALM: **Psalm 63:5**

My soul shall be satisfied as with marrow and fatness, and my mouth shall praise thee with joyful lips.

This is a song picture of the saint, who is satisfied by the sufficiency of the Savior and it corresponds to the theme of Christian experience, which we find in the Philippian Epistle.

It is a song of our *position in Christ.* "To all the saints in Christ Jesus" (Philippians 1:1).

It is a song of our *privilege* in *preaching Christ.* "Notwithstanding, every way, whether in pretense or in truth, Christ is preached; and in that I do rejoice, yea, and will rejoice" (Philippians 1:15).

It is a song of our *purpose* to *live Christ.* "For to me to live is Christ, and to die is gain" (Philippians 1:21).

It is a song of our *prospect with Christ.* "For I am in a strait between two, having a desire to depart and to be with Christ, which is far better" (Philippians 1:23).

It is a song of our *prize in winning Christ.* "Yea doubtless, and I count all things but loss for the excellency of the knowledge of Christ Jesus, my Lord; for whom I have suffered the loss of all things, and do count them but refuse, that I may win Christ" (Philippians 3:8).

It is a song of our *perfection* when we are *like Christ.* "Who shall change our lowly body, that it may be fashioned like his glorious body, according to the working by which he is able even to subdue all things unto himself" (Philippians 3:21).

Ed Lyman

August

DAILY PRAISE

August 1

SINGING SCRIPTURE: **Psalm 42:8**

Yet the Lord will command his lovingkindness in the daytime, and in the night his song shall be with me, and my prayer unto the God of my life.

Do you know the difference between kindness and loving-kindness?

When I was a boy, I would come home from school very hungry. I could smell the hot, fresh, golden brown bread my mother had baked. I would ask her for the crusty heel served with real, farm-churned butter. If mother granted my request, she was exercising kindness to me. However, if she gave me the crust of bread with butter but also loaded it with peanut butter and jelly, then she would be exercising lovingkindness.

The psalmist knew this kind of treatment from God and because of his appreciation for this lovingkindness, he could sing in the darkest night and had confidence that his prayers would be answered.

Is it possible that because of our thanklessness we have lost the joy of singing? Is prayerlessness an indication of our lack of trust?

Many of God's people are so busy complaining that they forget how to praise. The world today is asking the same question the people asked David in the third verse of this Psalm: "Where is God?" They will not be attracted to our God unless we find him a God worthy of our praise.

Don Jost

August 2

SINGING SCRIPTURE: **Nehemiah 12:46**

For in the days of David and Asaph of old there was a chief of the singers, and there were songs of praise and thanksgiving unto God.

God's people had returned to the land of Israel from their captivity in Babylon and had rebuilt the walls of Jerusalem. As the worship procedures were restored, music once again became prominent in their praise and thanksgiving. As captives in a strange land, their sorrow and humiliation had so controlled their outlook, they could not sing. Had their faith in Jehovah overcome their circumstances, they could have sung as an expression of their continued reliance upon the Lord even though their homeland was in desolation. By thinking of their plight and their situation, they neglected their responsibility as bearers of the truth of God.

In Babylon, they could have been witnesses to their captors about the true God, but they made themselves impotent by brooding over their misfortunes. They were so depressed that they just hung their "harps upon the willows." They missed a great opportunity.

Had they lifted up their eyes to heaven and turned their hearts to God, they would have found strength, confidence, and the joy of service by "singing the Lord's song in a strange land."

Now, finally having returned and completed the wall around Jerusalem, which had been destroyed so many years before, they recognized the hand of God in leading them back from captivity. Music now is focused upon the kindness and mercy of the Lord. It is a wonderful witness to the true God, Jehovah, Who lives and loves His people.

A Christian's harp should never be hanging "upon the willows", out of use.

Ed Lyman

August 3

SINGING SCRIPTURE: Isaiah 24:14

They shall lift up their voice, they shall sing for the majesty of the Lord, they shall cry aloud from the sea.

A little girl was sitting at the kitchen table enthusiastically rubbing her crayons over a large sheet of construction paper as her mother prepared the evening meal. Seeing the flurry of activity taking place, the mother asked, "What are you doing over there?"

"I'm drawing a picture of God," came the reply.

"But, Honey, nobody knows what God looks like."

Quickly the little girl looked up from her work and with red crayon poised to begin the next strokes, she replied, "They don't know now, but they will when I finish."

It has been truly stated that sometimes the only picture a lost person, friend or neighbor may have of God is what he sees in us. Can they "lift up their voice" or "sing for the majesty of the Lord" because we have been faithful in our own place of service?

Ed Lyman

August 4
PRAISE PSALM: **Psalm 52:9**

I will praise thee forever, because thou hast done it; and I will wait on thy name, for it is good before thy saints.

Without going into the details of a commentary on the full passage of Scripture, which allows us to see that desolation follows the refusal to follow the precepts of the Lord, we are however confronted with the practical truth that trusting God brings a song of satisfaction for time and eternity.

If we train a child in the way he should go, then when he is old he cannot escape the truth. With this in mind, we must recognize the tremendous importance of using music properly in the evangelism and Christian education of children. Young minds are receptive to music and singing. What we teach musically is remembered on wings of song for a lifetime. They will never escape it!

How often have I been reminded of the love and watchcare of my Heavenly Father by a song, which crept into my thoughts when I've been concerned about problems and decisions.

No methods of instruction have such lasting qualities as when truths of God are put to music — training a child in the way he should go. The content must be accurate, Biblical, and properly convey the message of God's Word. It may be child-like, but it should not be childish.

Winfield F. Ruelke

August 5
SINGING SCRIPTURE: **Psalm 43:4**

Then will I go unto the altar of God, unto God my exceeding joy, yea, upon the harp will I praise thee, O God my God.

We can approach God, claiming Him as our exceeding joy, with a song of thanksgiving upon our lips only when we are secure in our relationship to Him. To be able to say, "O God my God", emphasizes a personal relationship representing present and eternal security. This is the meaning of 1 John 5:10-12.

Eternal life is a Present Possession. Verse 10 says, "He that believeth on the Son of God *hath* the witness in himself." We can be as sure of heaven as though we were already there.

Eternal life is a Gift. The 11th verse tells us, "God *hath given* to us eternal life." Romans 6:23 reminds us, "The gift of God is eternal life," when we accept Jesus Christ as Savior.

Eternal life involves a Person. The last part of the 11th verse states that eternal life is "in His Son." This involvement with the Son of God is in a *relationship* and a *fellowship*. The relationship is established when we are saved and the fellowship continues as we follow Him.

Eternal life has a Consequence. Verse 12 says, "He that hath the Son hath life; and he that *hath not* the Son of God *hath not* life."

Decision determines destiny!

John DeBrine

August 6

SINGING SCRIPTURE: 2 Chronicles 7:6

And the priests waited on the offices: the Levites also with instruments of music of the Lord, which David the king had made to praise the Lord, because his mercy endureth forever, when David praised by their ministry; and the priests sounded trumpets before them, and all Israel stood.

Solomon had postponed the dedication of the temple for months in order that it might coincide with the harvest feast of Tabernacles, the Day of Atonement, and the regular Feast of Tabernacles. The people gathered from the far corners of Israel and Solomon made an offering of twenty two thousand oxen and one hundred and twenty thousand sheep, a staggering number, as "peace offerings."

With the music sounding forth and the people rejoicing, this was a magnificent celebration of praise to the Lord and "the glory of the Lord filled the house."

When the people saw this, they bowed and worshipped and praised the Lord, their God, saying, "For he is good; for his mercy endureth forever."

When we bow, we acknowledge the Lord Jesus Christ as Savior and Sovereign. Then, our worship is the natural expression of our faith and our praise is the result of our position in the family of God.

Ed Lyman

August 7

PRAISE PSALM: **Psalm 65:1**

Praise waiteth for thee, O God, in Zion; and unto thee shall the vow be performed.

The vows, which are spoken of in this harvest song of praise, were made by the people of God not as a means of putting some kind of intimidating pressure on the Lord or even of driving a bargain with God. Instead, these vows were recognitions that active consecration had to accompany their petitions for the blessings of Jehovah. They vowed that they would give themselves and their possessions as their offerings of thanksgiving. They were not merely paying some flippant lip service to thank God for His bounty and blessing. Therefore, it is evident that songs of praise and these vows of dedication are due to the beneficent Lord and they result from the experience of the presence of God, Himself.

Within the compass of this verse and those to follow, there is also the careful and considered consciousness that before praise songs can be lifted to God on high, forgiveness is needed for the transgressions of the flesh and spirit.

The goodness of God in providing a bountiful harvest is only a molecule of the full-measured joy of experiencing the presence of the Provider, Creator, and Savior in the total life-style of the believer. To know His blessing at any one point in life is to want Him at every other point in all of His fulness. Praise then waits on every hand.

Ed Lyman

August 8

SINGING SCRIPTURE: **Revelation 15:2**

And I saw, as it were, a sea of glass mingled with fire, and them that had gotten the victory over the beast, and over his image, and over his mark, and over the number of his name, standing on the sea of glass, having the harps of God.

It can be said the "expression of joy in song is rejoicing" and rejoicing with gladness is a privilege the Christian has because of his unique position of security in the Lord Jesus Christ. "And it shall be said in that day, Lo, this is our God; we have waited for him, and he will save us: this is the Lord; we have waited for him, we will be glad and rejoice in his salvation" (Isaiah 25:9). This relationship with Christ produces joy and "believing, ye rejoice with joy unspeakable and full of glory."

We are not talking about happiness. Happiness comes from the word "happen," which has a "chance" character to it. The joy in rejoicing is more stable; it is joy in the NOW.

Enjoying the NOW is part and parcel of the Christian life, because the FUTURE is secure, the PAST is forgiven, and what we have NOW is the challenge of putting JOY to work — in our singing, in our witnessing, and in our daily living —" kept by the power of God through faith unto salvation ready to be revealed in the last time. Wherein ye GREATLY rejoice."

Ed Lyman

August 9

SINGING SCRIPTURE: **Ecclesiastes 7:5**

It is better to hear the rebuke of the wise, than for a man to hear the song of fools.

An apt illustration of this is found in Matthew 27:24 through 27. Jesus tells the story of the wise man, who builds his house upon a rock. When the storms came, the house stood upon a firm foundation and was secure. However, the foolish man put his house on sand and the storms washed the house away.

As I drove in a rented car through a darkness of the wee hours of the morning after a concert to catch a plane at the airport in another part of the state, I was listening to a radio broadcast. It was a program of sacred music with comments by the announcer. At one point, he presented a brand new song and he challenged his audience to listen to the message. Had he not said this, I'd not have listened as carefully. For the next few minutes I heard a lovely orchestral background, a fine voice singing, and a nice ballad — a love song — but I did not hear the gospel! In fact, I didn't hear the words "God", "Jesus", "Lord", or one single word to identify Deity. The only pronoun used was "you." It could have been a lover, wife, or husband. I was not pointed to God nor did the theme of the song provide a Biblical approach to the "relationship" presented.

The song of vague concepts and clouded innuendo cannot put the mind of the seeker in tune with the orchestrator of the heavens. To build a song on the sand of sentimentality brings about an unresolved discord, but good hymnology built on solid theology results in a great doxology of praise.

Ed Lyman

August 10

SINGING SCRIPTURE: 1 Chronicles 15:19

So the singers, Heman, Asaph, and Ethan, were appointed to sound with cymbals of brass.

Those, who minister to the Lord in song travel in great company! Before the Temple was built in Jerusalem by Solomon, David appointed three men to direct choirs. They took regular turns of duty singing in the Tent of the Lord. Heman, Asaph, and Ethan were chosen by King David to direct the music in this early Tent-Home of the Lord prior to the building of the magnificent Temple.

Any home is very important to God, whether it be a church home or our own dwelling, and He should be honored there through worship, faith, and prayer. The joy we know from this relationship should be expressed in meaningful song. Even though the home be only temporary, as was the Tent in which the Israelites worshipped, King David recognized the importance of praising the Lord through song. Let your home and your church home be full of the joy which comes from faith in God. Isaiah once observed, "This is refreshing."

We can draw strength from the refreshing of song through faith and it will light up our lives and give us peace that only is known in Christ. Let this be our refreshing.

Jack Schurman

August 11

SINGING SCRIPTURE: **Psalm 81:2**

Take a psalm, and bring hither the timbrel, the pleasant harp with the psaltery.

Music is a marvelous means by which man may magnify the Lord. That's the significance of this charge to serve the Lord. Take some music — a song, some singers, and instruments — and praise the Lord. The uniting of vocal and instrumental music into a presentation of musical praise to the God of glory is echoed in Romans 12:1. "I beseech you therefore, brethren, by the mercies of God, that ye present your bodies a living sacrifice, holy, acceptable unto God, which is your reasonable service."

The believer serves as a priest before the Lord. True Christian service ought to be the presentation of every activity as an act of worship. In this light, the distinction between secular and sacred disappears as our service is channeled through the direction of the Holy Spirit. This is the key. In order for service to be affective and not tiring or boring, it must be rendered to God as an act of worship and the one serving must perform under the controlling presence of the Holy Spirit.

The worship of God through our service, whether in the area of music or other activities, becomes meaningful as we carefully and prayerfully consider the Person we are called to worship and the people we are called to be.

Ed Lyman

August 12

PRAISE PSALM: **Psalm 119:171**

My lips shall utter praise, when thou hast taught me thy statutes.

We are told of a reply given by a young woman when she was asked to explain what her devotional reading of the Bible meant. "Yesterday morning," she said, "I received a letter from one to whom I have given my heart and devoted my life. I freely confess to you that I read that letter five times; not because I expected to commend myself to the author by frequent reading of his epistle. It was not with me a question of duty, but simply one of pleasure. I read it because I am devoted to the one who wrote it."

Reading God's Word and meditating upon it in such a way as this is truly making it a love letter from the Lord and by doing so, we come to the place, where God's Word becomes an integral part of our being. Our praise song forms upon our lips as a joyous response to the overwhelming revelation and recognition of God's mindfulness of our needy condition. God's Word actually speaks to us as individuals and it is with awe and reverence that we should open our ears to what He has to say. In the statutes of the Lord, we find the secrets of safety, of certainty, and of enjoyment.

Ed Lyman

August 13

SINGING SCRIPTURE: **Job 30:9**

And now I am their song, yea, I am their byword.

No one, who has ever read the story of Job, will ever say that this ancient man did not have a difficult time of testing, trouble, and tribulation. Everything went wrong for him and his whole world came tumbling down around his feet. As in the nursery tale about Humpty Dumpty, it seemed that nothing could put Job "back together again." So, he was complaining that he was in such a miserable condition that people were even singing songs about his predicament.

Yet, God tells us that though sickness, sorrow, and distress may beset us "all things work together for good to them that love God."

Have you ever listened to a brass band? If you take the instruments separately, you will find that some of the sounds just are not the most pleasant you have ever heard. The tenor horn sometimes gives a lonely, shrill sound when it is played alone. It takes the combined sounds of the instruments playing together to make sweet music.

Life is often like the tones of the tuba; not too much pleasantness. However, if we allow God to bring together the other instruments, there is a wonderful harmony.

If we constantly sound the horn of distress and listen for the tuba tones of disappointment, we will fail to recognize the sound of "tuning up" for the glorious harmony of God's orchestra.

Ed Lyman

August 14

SINGING SCRIPTURE: **Psalm 47:7**

For God is the King of all the earth: sing ye praises with understanding.

Understanding implies knowledge of God and a personal relationship with Him. You can only sing praises to Him with understanding if you can answer these two questions correctly.

Are you a Christian? What did you do to become one?

Those two questions I asked hundreds of servicemen just before they headed overseas to battle. I had only a few minutes with each one. I needed specific questions and a "penicillin" verse to make their spiritual condition clear to them. Penicillin, at the time, was considered as an all-purpose drug. The verse would have to cover all possibilities. John 1:13 was it! "Who were born, not of blood, nor of the will of the flesh, nor of the will of man, but of God."

Most of the men claimed to be Christians, but most failed to answer the next question in the way God would accept. The three answers most of them gave are found in this verse.

"I'm a Christian, because I was born in a Christian family." (Blood)

"I'm a Christian, because I'm trying to do good." (Will of the Flesh)

"I'm a Christian, because I joined the church." (Will of Man)

John 1:13 clearly states that these reasons are wrong. To be a Christian, a man must be born of God. The right answer is found in John 1:12: "But as many as received him, to them gave he power to become the children of God, even to them that believe on his name."

If Jesus Christ has become King of your life, then it follows that you will be able to sing praises with true understanding.

John DeBrine

August 15

PRAISE PSALM: **Psalm 66:8**

Oh, bless our God, ye people and make the voice of his praise to be heard.

Two things face us in this passage of Scripture: a song of blessing and a signal for broadcasting God's message. To accomplish them, we envision certain goals, which follow the pattern of Ephesians 5:15: "See, then, that ye walk circumspectly, not as fools but as wise."

Redeeming the time (Ephesians 5:16) is to take advantage of every opportunity to minister and worship. It is a continual walk in the fullness of God's power as we live His life. Why? "Because the days are evil!"

Be ye not unwise (Ephesians 5:17). Don't be unmindful or without your mind when it comes to the world and the Word of God. We should not allow spiritual fatigue to develop. Instead, we should be vulnerable to the Lord in order to understand His will and to do it.

Speaking to yourselves (Ephesians 5:19) is manifest in the Christian experience, "In psalms and hymns and spiritual songs, singing and making melody in your heart to the Lord." This is sincere sensitivity to others through the Lord.

Giving thanks always (Ephesians 5:20) becomes specifically significant when we read that this thanksgiving ... always ... is "for all things". "Lord, thank you for this situation and I am looking forward to what you will do through it for your glory."

Submitting yourselves one to another (Ephesians 5:21) is the vital link in the "oneness" of all believers. It is to be done in the "fear of God". This is not dread, but holy respect.

Ed Lyman

August 16

SINGING SCRIPTURE: **Genesis 31:27**

Wherefore didst thou flee away secretly, and steal away from me: and didst not tell me, that I might have sent thee away with mirth, and with songs, with tabret, and with harp.

Once again we are reminded that special occasions are times for gladness and singing even though in this case, the intentions were cunningly obscured by false intentions. Jacob had worked for his uncle, Laban, fourteen years for Rachel and Leah, and six more years for his cattle. Now, having been commanded by the Lord to return to his own country, for fear that Laban would send him away alone and penniless, Jacob slips away with his wives, children, servants, and herds. Discovering the stealthy exodus, Laban overtook them and were it not for his deceitful personality, it would appear that his rebuke was meant to show a sincere desire for a "fond farewell." Instead of an expression of love, care, and appreciation, it was an empty chastisement.

What a difference if Laban had been kind and considerate instead of calculating and greedy! The departure of his loved ones would then have been a time of joy and the music of the occasion could have dispelled the tedium of the journey and would have lightened heavy hearts: music with a purpose.

> If I can right a human wrong,
> If I can help to make one strong,
> If I can cheer with smile or song,
> Lord, show me how.

Ed Lyman

August 17

SINGING SCRIPTURE: **Isaiah 24:9**

> *They shall not drink wine with a song; strong drink shall be bitter to those who drink it.*

The prophet looks at the future and sees the way before God's people crumbling as spiritual corruption and disinterest in the things of the Lord infest their lives. Soon they would be marched off into captivity by the Babylonian conquerors and the land would become desolate. Since their lives had become barriers to the flow of God's program, their singing would soon cease and the music of merriment would stop. The bridge of blessing from God to man was about to collapse.

In a book I've enjoyed since I was a teenager, *The Rubaiyat of Omar Khayyam*, one particular refrain especially characterizes this situation. It is poignant music for our contemplation as the poetry of the ancient Persian challenges us as we live Christ before our neighbors.

> *The Moving Finger writes: and having writ,*
> *Moves on: nor all your Piety or Wit*
> *Shall lure it back to cancel half a line*
> *Nor all your tears wash out a Word of it.*

Thought provoking! The Persian poet reflects a Biblical truth. We must realize that we can either be a bridge over which God's blessings can travel or a barrier to the proclamation of God's Good News.

Ed Lyman

August 18

SINGING SCRIPTURE: **Psalm 57:9**

I will praise thee, O Lord, among the peoples; I will sing unto thee among the nations.

As the Apostle Paul traveled about proclaiming Christ as redeemer and Lord, he suffered as much or more than any of us. He was beaten, stoned and imprisoned. He suffered hunger and privation of every kind, and yet, he could write with confidence, "We are troubled on every side, yet not distressed; we are perplexed, but not in despair; persecuted, but not forsaken; cast down, but not destroyed; always bearing about in the body the dying of the Lord Jesus, that the life also of Jesus might be made manifest in our body" (2 Corinthians 4:8-10). How do we account for this wonderful peace?

The answer is very simple. Paul knew the Lord and trusted Him for everything. That's why he could praise Him among all the peoples with whom he came in contact and he could sing of Him in the many nations where he went even though the hostility of non-believers attempted to drag him down.

On the Damascus highway, the proud, resistant unbeliever, Saul, was suddenly broken before God, Christ became his Savior, and from that moment on, he was a different man. As a result, he knew the joy of living and the peace that God alone gives. Such peace and security makes for a song of praise in the midst of crises all around us. Jesus said, "peace I leave with you, My peace I give unto you: not as the world giveth, give I unto you. Let not your heart be troubled, neither let it be afraid."

J. Allen Blair

August 19

PRAISE PSALM: **Psalm 116:18, 19**

I will pay my vows unto the Lord now in the presence of all his peoples, In the courts of the Lord's house, in the midst of thee, O Jerusalem. Praise ye the Lord.

Dr. John Cumming said, "The empire of Caesar is gone, the legions of Rome are mouldering in the dust; the avalanches that Napoleon hurled upon Europe have melted away; the pride of the Pharaohs is fallen; Tyre is a rock for bleaching fishermen's nets; Sidon has scarcely left a wreck behind; but the Word of God still survives. All things that threatened to extinguish it, have only aided it; and it proves every day how transient is the noblest monument that man can build, how enduring is the least word God has spoken."

Although the believer is not *of* the world, he is *in* the world; and, as a result, the constant and continual influences, which surround them, tend to make them lose touch with and sight of the spiritual life. The life of the Christian is then robbed of its fragrance and clarity. To defend against this tendency, the believer renews his vows before the Lord daily. This is a sacred exercise.

George Muller wrote, "It has pleased the Lord to teach me a truth, the benefit of which I have not lost for more than fourteen years. The point is this: I saw more clearly than ever that the first great and primary business to which I ought to give my attention every day was to have my soul happy in the Lord. The first thing to be concerned about was not how much I might serve the Lord, but how I might get my soul into a happy state, and how my inner man might be nourished."

Ed Lyman

August 20

SINGING SCRIPTURE: **1 Corinthians 13:1-13 (This is the "Believer's Love Song")**

Though I speak with the tongues of men and of angels, and have not *love*, I am become as sounding brass, or a tinkling cymbal.

And though I have the gift of prophecy, and understand all mysteries, and all knowledge; and though I have all faith, so that I could remove mountains, and have not *love*, I am nothing.

And though I bestow all my goods to feed the poor, and though I give my body to be burned, and have not *love*, it profiteth me nothing.

Love suffereth long, and is kind; *love* envieth not; *love* vaunteth not itself, is not puffed up,

Doth not behave itself unseemly, seeketh not its own, is not easily provoked, thinketh no evil,

Rejoiceth not in iniquity, but rejoiceth in the truth;

Beareth all things, believeth all things, hopeth all things, endureth all things.

Love never faileth; but whether there be prophecies, they shall be done away; whether there be tongues, they shall cease; whether there be knowledge, it shall vanish away.

For we know in part, and we prophesy in part.

But when that which is perfect is come, then that which is in part shall be done away.

When I was a child, I spoke as a child, I understood as a child; but when I became a man, I put away childish things.

For now we see in a mirror, darkly; but then, face to face; now I know in part, but then shall I know even as also I am known.

And now abideth faith, hope, *love*, these three; but the greatest of these is *love*.

Paul, the Apostle

August 21

SINGING SCRIPTURE: **Psalm 9:2**

I will be glad and rejoice in thee: I will sing praise to thy name, O thou Most High.

According to Rev. William Bates, an old lady was reminiscing about a trip she had made one night on a train from Chicago to St. Louis. There were no Pullman cars then and the seats were small and cramped. With her shawl over her head, she was able to fall asleep only to be awakened some hours later by the entrance of some ladies and a very tall, homely man to her car. The man took a seat opposite hers and with the first light of morning, he "threw up the sash, leaned his head out, and held his hat in place with his right hand, while his body filled the seat and his legs extended to the middle of the aisle."

She noted that he seemed almost overcome by the beauty of the sunrise and "unconscious of the presence of anyone, he began to croon, in a tender, reflective voice." Soon she caught the words:

"When all thy mercies, O my God,
My rising soul surveys,
Transported with the view, I'm lost
In wonder, love, and praise."

She said he repeated this verse over and over again. The next time the conductor passed, she asked, "Who is this man?"

He quietly replied, "Abraham Lincoln."

Ed Lyman

August 22

SINGING SCRIPTURE: **Zephaniah 3:17**

The Lord thy God in the midst of thee is mighty; he will save, he will rejoice over thee with joy; he will rest in his love, he will joy over thee with singing.

Certainly, the Christian finds rest in the love of God and joy in His presence. Christians should be singing people. Whatever the source of problems and difficulties, if a person is in God and completely surrounded by him, all perplexities must pass through Him before they pass on to the Christian.

Spurgeon, the preacher, once told this story: "We once saw a man draw some black dots. We looked and could make nothing of them but an irregular assemblage of black dots. Then he drew a few lines, put a few rests and a clef at the beginning and we saw the black dots were musical notes. On sounding them, we were singing, 'Praise God from Whom All Blessings Flow.' There may be many black dots and black spots in our lives and we cannot understand why they are permitted to be there or why God allowed them to come, but if we let God come into our lives and adjust the dots in the proper way and draw the lines he wants and separate this from that and put the rests in the proper places; out of the black dots and spots in our lives, He makes glorious harmony. Let us not hinder this work."

Ed Lyman

August 23

PRAISE PSALM: **Psalm 54:6**

*I will freely sacrifice unto thee; I will praise thy name, O Lord;
for it is good.*

One of the great dividends of knowing Christ is the wide range of
opportunities He gives. We are not shut-ins or victims to the enemy.
Our feet are set in a large room. David says this in his song of praise
in Psalm 31:8. John Wesley reiterates it in his statement that the
world was his parish. Our prayers and interests as Christians can
span the globe. Similarly, the town we live in and our immediate
neighbors comprise an urgent mission field.

The idea of "working oneself out of a job" is a misnomer. The
Christian always has a job. He never retires from witness to the
One, Who saved him. But unless he walks close to God, he will not
see the opportunities, which lie in people right around him. The
French boy across our street used to come over and shoot the breeze
about nothing in particular. We all became his friends. He was
reaching out for the understanding he didn't receive at home.
Naturally, in communicating, we shared Christ. Soon he was a
believer. God has set our feet in a room teeming with opportunities.
Are we taking them? What is your praise song saying?

The Lord can give us strength at every weak point, reinforce our
weaknesses, and shore up our resolve. The strength is there,
because the Lord Jesus lives in us. He never tires. He's never
perplexed. He gives energy, because He is the Source of life itself.

Robert P. Evans

August 24

SINGING SCRIPTURE: **Isaiah 5:12**

*And the harp, and the viol, the tabret, and pipe, and wine are
in their feasts; but they regard not the work of the Lord,
neither consider the operation of his hands.*

It seems that everywhere we go in these days of rush and run, we
hear "Pop" music whispering or screaming at us in malls, banks,
department stores, buses, and planes. We can't help but hear it, but
do we really listen? Though pop musicians appear to lead glamorous

lives of fame, success, and popularity, there comes through an underlying desperation, a searching for truth and life and answers. Listening to their lyrics instead of just hearing the musical presentation gives us a picture of frustration, hopelessness, and craving for love and affection. These songs express the idea, the feeling, the philosophy that nothing lasts, nothing makes any difference. All of this is expressed in the popular music of our generation — music in their feasts, "but they regard not the work of the Lord".

Having grown up in a home where music was a daily part of our lives, I often heard my father comment on some song he was learning for a concert or program. He was concerned with the grammar and the rhyme, but he would frequently express his conviction that the song should say something positive and specific to those, who would be listening. If the church leaders of the past put their theology into songs as a way of helping the people to learn about their faith, we must also give a positive answer to the musical questions of the world around us.

Talin Lyman

August 25

SINGING SCRIPTURE: **Psalm 9:11**

Sing praises to the Lord, who dwelleth in Zion; declare among the people his doings.

God does not ask us to do what we cannot do in serving Him. The story found in Mark 14 is an apt illustration of this. When the woman broke the alabaster box and poured the ointment on Him, Jesus rebuked those, who criticized her for wasting this precious perfume, and said, "She hath wrought a good work on me."

Witnessing may be classified as "good works." Though we are saved by grace through faith and not of works "lest any man should boast," good works are part and parcel of the Christian life. In 1 Thessalonians 1:3 we read, "Remembering without ceasing your work of faith, and labor (drudgery) of love, and patience of hope in our Lord Jesus Christ, in the sight of God and our Father."

Good works are:
Commanded in God's Word
A result of faith
Stimulated by the Holy Spirit
Must be for the glory of God

The woman's act of good works measured up in each of these areas and Jesus said, "She hath done what she could.... Wherever this gospel shall be preached throughout the whole world, this also that she hath done shall be spoken of, for a memorial of her."

Nothing is ever wasted if it is lavished on Christ. When God's people do what they can, they will raise a memorial — and that means declaring among the people His doing as we "sing praises to the Lord."

Ed Lyman

August 26

SINGING SCRIPTURE: **Exodus 15:2**

The Lord is my strength and song, and he is become my salvation: he is my God, and I will prepare him an habitation; my father's God, and I will exalt him.

The statement occurs three times in the Bible: "The Lord is my strength and song, and he is become my salvation." This is the first time we see it. Then, it appears in Isaiah 12:2 and in Psalm 118:14.

There are lessons to be learned from the appearances of this statement. The first and second times we read these words, they teach that Israel's deliverance is a prophetic picture of the redemption in Christ. The third time, long after the first two times, they are uttered privately; teaching that every person in every age has the power of God working for him.

The words themselves make plain that true faith appropriates the Father's universal mercy as a personal possession. We read "my" strength, "my" salvation, and "my" God.

Every single act of mercy should show God more clearly as "my" strength. The word "and" in the second clause is not used as a conjunction, but it rather means "for". It designates the reason for the assurance that the Lord is my "strength and song."

Because of the experiences of deliverance and added blessings, an increase of faith becomes a most happy strengthening of the heart.

The result of God's deliverance is praise! "He is my song."

Ed Lyman

August 27

PRAISE PSALM: **Psalm 118:19**

Open to me the gates of righteousness; I will go into them, and I will praise the Lord.

It has been said that when it gets darker and darker in the valleys of life, the pupil of the soul of the believer enlarges and he sees more plainly the presence of the Lord. It is the Will of God that His people obey Him and by their obedience they will then enjoy His provision and protection.

Happiness is the outward expression or the outworking of the inward experience. To be able to say to God, "Open to me the gates of righteousness", is to have a heart already prepared for His use. Fullness of self is spiritual emptiness. If you want to be Holy tomorrow, be Holy now! Psalm 86:2 states, "Preserve my soul; for I am holy, O thou my God, save thy servant who trusteth in thee." The present condition of the believer allows him to expect the Lord's provision. When you give anything to God, it is never normal again. When you give yourself to God, you are not normal, you are Holy! — for God's use!

Psalm 86:4 says, "Rejoice the soul of thy servant; for unto thee, O Lord, do I lift up my soul." Why is such an expectation possible? The answer is found in the very fact that we can trust God. By faith, not seeing, we believe.

The servant of the Lord rejoices in unbounded song as he praises God for those things which preserve and prepare him for the work of the ministry of witnessing.

Ed Lyman

August 28

SINGING SCRIPTURE:**Psalm 65:13**

The pastures are clothed with flocks; the valleys also are covered with corn; they shout for joy, they also sing.

I stood in the heart of Ethiopia with the missionary and the fields around us stretched for miles. I felt alone. Soon, a sound fell upon our ears. At first, it was there and then it was gone — but soon it became steady and gradually increased in volume. It was a familiar hymn and I found myself humming. Off to my left, little dots appeared on the horizon. They came closer and the music became louder. Soon more dots were coming from every direction. People arrived from far and near. The music of these Ethiopian Christians preceded them — faith music!

Here was the fruit of the missionary effort. The flocks, who had found their place with the Good Shepherd, seemed to cover the fields. One after another of the national evangelists challenged them and then they took their missionary offering to support evangelists, who would go to other tribes, where the Gospel had not been heard. It was an amazing and moving experience. First, they gave all their money, which was little. Next, they brought their shoes, hats, and clothing, and placed them on a pile, which mounted higher than my head. Finally, they made faith-promises of cows, corn, and material possessions at home. Then, I saw something I could not believe. One after another began to shed tears. They were weeping, because they had nothing more to give. They knew what it meant to give sacrificially. When they left the conference, some, who had shoes when they came, walked on bare feet; some, who had hats to protect them from the sun, walked under a broad leaf and they were singing! They were singing, because Christ was their life.

Kenneth E. Moon

August 29

SINGING SCRIPTURE: Psalm 18:49

Therefore will I give thanks unto thee, O Lord, among the heathen (nations), and sing praises unto thy name.

Often as I travel the length and breadth of North America, I feel a kinship with a person or a family, never having ever met them before, when I glance across a restaurant table and see heads bowed over lunch in thanksgiving. This is a testimony, which encourages other Christians and reminds those, who are lost, of a God, who loves them.

Billy Sunday, the baseball player turned evangelist, said, "Good men leave footprints; bad men leave finger prints." The kind of prints we leave in this world of "get everything you can" may be the only testimony some people will ever have.

As we meditate on God's Word in a daily encounter with the Creator of the universe and the Savior of mankind, we should seek to apply the truths we find to our own lives. In this way, we begin to witness naturally and not because of a self-inflicted conviction of necessity. Our meditation should be attention with intention.

The living of the natural, normal Christian life has an aura, which permeates our environment and strikes the keynote of the song of praise.

Ed Lyman

August 30

PRAISE PSALM: **Psalm 67:3 and 5**

Let the people praise thee, O God; let all the people praise thee.

This psalm could very well be a kind of national anthem for the believer. The setting for the psalm is the Feast of Tabernacles. Thanksgiving is offered to the Lord for His provision and for His salvation. There is also the expectation for God's reign and rule over the whole world. The blessings God has showered upon His people, Israel, are a foreshadowing of what He will provide for all people.

This psalm is an example of "responsive singing". The priest sang of God's blessing and then the assembled people sang in response, "Let the people praise thee, O God; let all the people praise thee."

As the Israel of God, believers recognize that their security is in the governing grace of God and the guidance of His Spirit, even as He ruled over the tribes of Israel and led them through their wilderness experiences.

The continual care and kindness of God in His dealings with His chosen people provide the firm basis of confidence the believer is entitled to as a member of God's family today.

Thus, the Christian can join with the assembly of ancient Israel and sing, "Let the people praise thee, O God; let all the people praise thee."

Ed Lyman

August 31

SINGING SCRIPTURE: **Job 35:10**

> *But none saith, Where is God my maker, who giveth songs in the night;"*

Elihu, one of Job's friends, states that men can neither take away from nor add to the glory of Him, who is exalted above the heavens. God's justice is not conditioned by man's fear of Him nor by man's "goodness" toward Him. However, this does not mean that God is indifferent to our virtue or vice. In our relationships with other people, our sins may affect their lives and hurt them or our good deeds may be helpful to them, but God's righteousness and justice is not affected by man's whims.

It is not that God sits afar off and is indifferent to men, but rather that men are indifferent to Him. They do not seek Him for His own sake; they are content to sing praises in the midst of trials and troubles if only He will be their portion.

Thus we come to this verse, which concludes that oppressed and burdened people may shriek and cry and plead beneath their ills and wrongs, but they fail to seek after God alone "who gives songs in the night" and comforts the troubled soul. Job is reminded of his attitude in the first chapter when he recognized that he could not resist the sovereign Lord and in the midst of adversity maintained his spiritual composure and even found in his adversities occasion for praise. Stripped of all his worldly possessions, Job was unusually sensitive to God's presence.

The redeemed heart in the presence of God responds with the doxology: "Whom have I in heaven but thee? and there is none upon earth that I desire beside thee" (Psalm 73:25).

Ed Lyman

September

DAILY PRAISE

September 1

SINGING SCRIPTURE: **Luke 15:25-27**

Now his elder son was in the field; and as he drew nigh to the house, he heard music and dancing. And he called one of the servants, and asked what these things meant. And he said unto him, Thy brother is come; and thy father hath killed the fatted calf, because he hath received him safe and sound.

In this story of the prodigal son, music meant merriment. It was a sign of joy and delight in the household; something the elder brother hadn't heard in a long, long time. However, when he was told why there was this singing and happiness, the brother became angry.

When his jubilant father begged him to join the celebration, he answered, "Lo, these many years do I serve thee, neither transgressed I at any time thy commandments; and yet thou never gavest me a kid, that I might make merry with my friends. But as soon as this, thy son, was come, who hath devoured thy living with harlots, thou hast killed for him the fatted calf" (Luke 15:29, 30).

The actions of this brother and of all of us have specific roots. Some people are always complaining that they didn't get the "breaks" needed to put them in good social positions. Others blame the environment in which they had to grow up. The Word of God states that our actions have roots in our thinking processes. We can almost program our life-styles according to the way we think. Morality, business deals, and interpersonal relationships have their roots in the thought processes of the people involved. In essence the elder brother was saying, "The music isn't for me, so you don't love me." If he had thought positively and spiritually about the return of his brother, he would have joined the happy celebration and participated in the meaningful music of redemption. With Christ dwelling in our hearts by faith, we should be "rooted and grounded in love" (Ephesians 3:17) and not tossed to and fro by the winds of warped and worldly thinking.

Ed Lyman

September 2

SINGING SCRIPTURE: **Isaiah 12:2**

Behold, God is my salvation; I will trust and not be afraid: for the Lord JEHOVAH is my strength and my song; and he also is become my salvation.

When you know God intimately you realize that you can never be alone again, and if you are separated from other human beings you are not unhappy or afraid because your best Friend is always with you.

I do not say that you should choose to be alone, or want to be alone, but when you are forced to be alone you can do so without fear.

If Christianity does not give us a relationship with God that governs this area of our lives, then it is not much at all. I am grateful to God that the Bible portrays Him as one who is with us at all times and because He is our "Helper" we need not "be afraid".

Paul B. Smith

September 3

PRAISE PSALM: **Psalm 118:21**

I will praise thee; for thou hast heard me, and art become my salvation.

What a thought to ponder! The Creator of the heavens, the galaxies innumerable, hears the prayers of mortal man. Contemplation of such is the preliminary "tune-up" for the concert of praise offered by the believer.

"Beloved, if our heart condemn us not, then have we confidence toward God. And whatever we ask, we receive of him, because we keep his commandments, and do those things that are pleasing in his sight" (1 John 3:21, 22).

The very first prayer of the man who sees his condition before the Lord must be *"Save me!"* Until this petition for salvation is presented to God, man is lost and undone; still in his sin. Peter had started to walk toward the Lord Jesus Christ on the water, "But when he saw the wind boisterous, he was afraid; and beginning to sink, he cried, saying, Lord, save me" (Matthew 14:30). The very words of Peter's cry were proof of his belief in the Lord's ability to save him. This is the essence also of Acts 16:31: "Believe on the Lord Jesus Christ, and thou shalt be saved."

David cried unto the Lord, "*Search me*, O God, and know my heart; try me, and know my thoughts" (Psalm 139:23). After our experience of salvation, we are confronted with the constant corruption of the world around us and we need the guidance and cleansing of the Lord in order to walk in His Way. Once we've been saved by God's Grace and searched by God's Holiness, we can call upon Him, as Moses did, to show us His Will: "Now therefore, I pray thee, if I have found grace in thy sight, *show me* now thy way, that I may know thee" (Exodus 33:13).

Ed Lyman

September 4

SINGING SCRIPTURE: **Isaiah 65:14**

Behold, my servants shall sing for joy of heart, but ye shall cry for sorrow of heart, and shall howl for vexation of spirit.

Many of us sing but not all of us because we have a recognized singing ability or expect to bring delight to others. However, we are impelled to sing as a natural expression of the Lord's redeeming presence within us. That we are privileged to be His servants is indeed stimulating.

The believer's ultimate triumph over sin and death not only excites glorious contemplation, but causes one's spirit to break forth in melodies "almost divine," sometimes silently to one's self or articulately before others. While the opposite is true of those, who reject Him, to the child of God, there is blessed "rightness" about his relationship with Christ. In body, soul, and spirit, we sense that it is well to belong to His family.

Moses and the children of Israel sang unto the Lord. Even the "morning stars sang together." Should we not then, as the sweet singer of Israel exhorts, "Come before his presence with singing?"

Merrill Dunlop

September 5

SINGING SCRIPTURE: **1 Chronicles 25:1a, 7**

Moreover David and the captains of the host separated to the service of the sons of Asaph, and of Heman, and of Jeduthun, who should prophesy with harps, with psalteries, and with cymbals:
So the number of them, with their brethren that were instructed in the songs of the Lord, even all that were cunning, was two hundred fourscore and eight.

This appointment to the musical ministry clearly confronts us with the marvelous opportunity for worship and witness we have in music with a purpose. Not only is this apparent from the passage we have read, but there is also the truth set forth, which brings us to the conclusion that ministers of music are members of a team. "For as the body is one, and hath many members, and all the members of that one body, being many, are one body, so also is Christ" (1 Corinthians 12:12). Paul then states that "the body is not one member, but many" and that "God hath set the members, every one of them, in the body, as it hath pleased him" (1 Corinthians 12:14, 18). To understand this, we begin to appreciate each other and endeavor to increase the effectiveness of each other's gifts.

In 1 Thessalonians 1:4, we have a pattern for teamwork: "Knowing, brethren beloved, your election of God." These first three words give us the points of the pattern. Let's start with the word "brethren". To be a member of the team, we must be CONVERTED; knowing the Lord Jesus Christ personally. Next, "beloved" indicates COMPATIBILITY; accepting one another in the family and fellowship of believers. Thirdly, "knowing" emphasizes the fact that we are CONVINCED that our message of salvation through the Lord Jesus Christ can change lives.

David's conviction that the songs of the Lord could make a difference, enabled him to develop a team, which would honor the Lord and present His glory to the nations. This is music with a message!

Ed Lyman

September 6

SINGING SCRIPTURE: **Leviticus 23:24**

Speak unto the children of Israel, saying, In the seventh month, in the first day of the month, shall ye have a sabbath, a memorial of blowing of trumpets, as an holy convocation.

The trumpets are symbols of testimony. The Feast of Trumpets was a special time. It was a remembrance of God's unique covenant with His children. The music was a call to prepare for service and worship before the Lord.

In light of the believer's New Testament position in Christ, the "blowing of trumpets" signifies an energizing of the Christian's commitment.

Our trumpet call is testimony to the believer's FOCUS on Christ, Who removes the darkness of sin — "In whom are hidden all the treasures of wisdom and knowledge" (Colossians 2:3).

Our trumpet call is testimony to the believer's FORGIVENESS through Christ, Who removes the depression of sin — "And you, being dead in your sins ... hath he made alive together with him, having forgiven you all trespasses" (Colossians 2:13).

Our trumpet call is testimony to the believer's FREEDOM in Christ, Who removes the domination of sin — "Blotting out the handwriting of ordinances that was against us ... and took it out of the way, nailing it to his cross" (Colossians 2:14).

Our trumpet call is testimony to the believer's FELLOWSHIP with Christ, Who removes the detachment of sin — "... from whom all the body by joints and bands having nourishment ministered, and knit together, increaseth with the increase of God" (Colossians 2:19).

Paul sounds a similar trumpet call when he says, "And he gave some, apostles; and some prophets; and some, evangelists; and some pastors and teachers; For the perfecting of the saints for the work of the ministry for the edifying of the body of Christ" (Ephesians 4:11, 12).

Ed Lyman

September 7

PRAISE PSALM: **Psalm 69:34**

Let the heaven and earth praise him, the seas, and every thing that moveth therein.

We only read this exhortation to praise after David has reviewed the calamity of his predicament. This Psalm is a song of wrath penned by Israel's king in the time of his life when all that was and could be safe had turned to disaster. His beloved son had turned against him. Those he trusted most had left his side. He was caught in the river of despair and disappointment.

To remind God's people of what their lives and hearts should be, he writes this heart-rending Psalm. He speaks of the ultimate end of those, who go against the purposes, plan, and man of God and he asks the Lord to deal with them in judgment. When the apple of God's eye is touched by the ungodly, God pronounces his wrath and judgment upon them.

Using an instrument called *Shoshannim*, instrument of lilies, this Psalm was sung during the time of Passover to instruct concerning the Lord's dealings with those, who hurt, hinder, or destroy the work of God and the servant appointed by the Lord. Music becomes an instructor, corrector, and informer of God's relations with man.

A song of praise then rises as an AMEN to the truth of God's righteousness.

Russell B. Gordon

September 8

SINGING SCRIPTURE: **Psalm 21:13**

Be thou exalted, Lord, in thine own strength; so will we sing and praise thy power.

David expressed the everlasting truth concerning the sovereignty of God, which brings everything about the glory, majesty, and love of God into proper focus. Our God is exalted because of His own strength and power. In Psalm 62:11, he again puts this power into positive perspective: "God hath spoken once, twice I have heard this, that power belongeth unto God."

We sing and praise the Searching Power of God's Word: "For the word of God is quick, and powerful, and sharper than any two-edged sword, piercing even to the dividing asunder of soul and spirit, and of the joints and marrow, and is a discerner of the thoughts and intents of the heart" (Hebrews 4:12).

We sing and praise the Saving Power of the Gospel: "For I am not ashamed of the gospel of Christ; for it is the power of God unto salvation to everyone that believeth" (Romans 1:16).

We sing and praise the Sustaining Power of God: "Who are kept by the power of God through faith unto salvation" (1 Peter 1:5)

We sing and praise the Strengthening Power of the Holy Spirit: "But ye shall receive power, after the Holy Ghost is come upon you; and ye shall be witnesses unto me" (Acts 1:8).

We sing and praise the Stimulating Power of the Resurrected Lord: "It is sown in dishonor; it is raised in glory. It is sown in weakness; it is raised in power. It is sown a natural body; it is raised a spiritual body" (1 Corinthians 15:43, 44).

Ed Lyman

September 9

SINGING SCRIPTURE: **Proverbs 29:6**

In the transgression of an evil man there is a snare, but the righteous doth sing and rejoice.

Imagine two men: one evil and the other righteous. The righteous man's life is marked by his rejoicing and the song he sings. The evil man's life is one of transgressing God's Word, resulting in his entrapment in a snare. The righteous man is free; the evil man is trapped. The difference is that the righteous man has invited Jesus Christ to walk with him. The New Testament states that if we know the Truth, Jesus Christ, then we are truly free.

It might be said, "When one walks with God, life is a song." I realize that the Christian's life is not always a bed of roses, but when Jesus walks with us, we can sing and rejoice — no matter what the circumstances.

Sin, when it is finished with us results in death, separation from God. This is just one of the snares or traps experienced by the evil man. Guilt, dissatisfaction, insecurity, helplessness, eternal purposelessness, and hopelessness are just a few more of the snares. Sin is forgiven, guilt is absolved, the future secured, and help for the helpless is provided through Jesus Christ. The man, who commits his life to Jesus Christ receives the righteousness of God. Then, with the snares removed, he can rejoice and say the Lord has put a new song in his heart — for "He walks with me and He talks with me...."

Keith Whiticar

September 10

SINGING SCRIPTURE: **Amos 5:23**

Take away from me the noise of thy songs: for I will not hear the melody of thine harps.

God is admonishing His people. He declares that their worship without righteousness is an abomination to Him: "I hate, I despise your feast days, and I will not smell in your solemn assemblies. Though ye offer me burnt offerings and your meal offerings, I will not accept them: neither will I regard the peace offerings of your fat beasts (Amos 5:21, 22)."

Information without application produces lethargy — and empty religion.

No longer does the music of the soul make sense when we have fallen victim to the hit and miss philosophies of humanism. God calls this "noise", but when we walk with the King in harmony with our God, we sing with a soul set free. How, therefore, can we make music from dismay?

1. Live one day at a time. It's all you have.
   It's all you can handle.
   It's all God promised to make possible.
2. Keep gratitude to a MAXIMUM.
3. Keep self pity to a MINIMUM.
4. Don't give in to a defeated spirit.
5. Learn to shift your worries on the Lord: "Casting all your care upon him; for he careth for you."

Ed Lyman

September 11

PRAISE PSALM: **Psalm 71:6**

By thee have I been held up from the womb; thou art he who took me out of my mother; my praise shall be continually of thee.

Some time ago, a man who would perform daring climbing feats, called the "human fly", slowly and prudently ascended the face of a building gripping window ledges, jutting bricks, moldings, and cornices. Up he went as the crowd watched from the ground. It was amazing. Using only his hands and feet, he was able to overcome the difficulties of mounting the sheer face of that edifice. He neared the top and felt for a hand-hold to the left and then to the right. Looking over his head, he spied something, which he thought would be firm enough to hold his weight. He carefully stretched out his arm extending his fingers, but it was beyond his reach. As the people below urged him on, shouting encouragement, he made a spring-like jump to grasp the protuberance. For a brief instant, he was seen as a kind of focal point for a stop-action camera shot before he plummeted to earth before the many shocked spectators. In his clenched fist, they found the wispy strands of a spider's web, which he mistakenly thought would be solid structural material for bearing his weight.

Many feel they can climb their way to heaven by their own effort. They venture to base their hope on just such a wisp of spider's web, called "works". They fall short. Eternal life is not in works, but in the Son of God. However, the work of the Lord, such as the ministry of music, and the testimony of the believer, only "holds up" if it too is firmly placed in the Word of God and the power of "His might" — not presented in the spider web of self-fullness. Salvation and service are sound only when they are resting in Christ.

Ed Lyman

September 12

SINGING SCRIPTURE: **Psalm 28:7**

The Lord is my strength and my shield; my heart trusted in him, and I am helped: therefore my heart greatly rejoiceth; and with my song will I praise him.

Satan, himself, preaches one of the most important truths in God's Word when he admits his impotence in dealing with Job by asking God, "Hast not thou made an hedge about him?" It is an eternal truth that nothing can happen to the Christian without first passing through the WILL OF GOD. There are NO accidents in the life of the believer.

Job knew the Source of his power and protection — his strength and shield — was the Lord. Therefore, He NEVER "charged God foolishly (with folly)." He remained faithful to God throughout his ordeal and he did not fall into a frenzied emotional pattern. He asked many questions and his friends probed for some secret sin by which to blame Job for his punishment. Job put on no airs and he was honest before the Lord and his companions.

Bowing his head, he opened his heart and learned of God. When he did this, he found something we all can understand. Suffering may come our way in order that we may help others, who are afflicted; to illustrate the doctrine of God's grace; to learn obedience;

as a means of Divine discipline, or to make us more aware of our Savior.

Job's triumphant song of praise is one of a heart helped through trusting God. "Trust in the Lord with all thine heart, and lean not unto thine own understanding. In all thy ways acknowledge him, and he shall direct thy paths" (Proverbs 3:5, 6).

Ed Lyman

September 13

SINGING SCRIPTURE: **Revelation 18:22**

And the voice of harpers, and musicians, and of pipers, and the trumpeters shall be heard no more at all in thee; and no craftsman, of whatever craft he be, shall be found any more in thee; and the sound of a millstone shall be heard no more at all in thee.

Some time ago, while I was on one of the San Blas Islands just off the Atlantic Coast of Panama, a witch doctor reportedly told some people on one of the islands that the gods were angry and would make the waters very rough so the fishing fleets could not go out unless a sacrifice was offered. I was shocked and surprised to learn that a human sacrifice was demanded. In this day and age? These Indians have seen jet planes flying over their villages, they've had contact with modern society, and missionaries have brought the Gospel of Christ to them. Yet, many still cling to superstition, pagan ceremonies, and the witch doctors' incantations. By the consent of parents and relatives, a little crippled boy was thrown into the sea to pacify the angry water gods. Here was a pagan performance to pacify impotent gods. There was no song of joy. Wailing was the witness to this worthless waste of human life. Refusing the glory of the Gospel, they clung to witchcraft.

The theme of Revelation 18 is that God's judgment is inevitable upon willful and wanton disregard of His rightful place. "For true and righteous are his judgments" (Revelation 19:2).

Many people in our society emulate the paganism of the primitive peoples of the world by sacrificing their lives on the altar of worldly affections and selfish investments and involvements when they could be a part of a magnificent destiny and a great adventure in faith and witness. The harps and pipes of worldly pursuits become silent symbols of man's attempt to "be somebody" without God's presence and mourning follows. However, a glad song of service is sweet music for the saints, who seek His will.

Ed Lyman

September 14

SINGING SCRIPTURE: **Isaiah 24:16a**

From the uttermost part of the earth have we heard songs, even glory to the righteous.

It was December. I had promised my family early in the year that I would go with them on vacation to Costa Rica. Until then, my custom was to organize a crusade during my vacation time.

That year, a few weeks before vacation time, my mother became ill and was hospitalized and I had to go to my hometown, Zacatecas, to care for her. Vacation plans were laid aside. Finally, the doctor told us that she had just a very short time to live. Just a few days before our scheduled departure for Costa Rica, the cancer completed its job and my mother went home to be with the Lord. My family was very supportive of me and willingly recommended that we cancel our trip. It was a blessing to know their loving care at that time and I remember saying, "Let's go anyway, just let me ride along. You enjoy yourselves." After we started driving, we discovered our passports were missing and that delayed us more. I had accepted a preaching invitation for the 24th of December and we had planned to stay overnight in Managua on the 23rd. Now, behind schedule, we were driving through Guatemala when we heard the news on the radio as a reporter almost crying told what was happening in Managua; it was the great earthquake. I'd not be writing these lines had the Lord not delayed our departure, because we were to be sleeping in one of the places which was completely destroyed. Through that experience, I learned that His ways are always the best and it was as if I were hearing a song. At that time I wrote music for Proverbs 10:22: "The blessing of the Lord, it maketh rich, and he addeth no sorrow with it." It is glory to the righteous.

Juan Isais

September 15

SINGING SCRIPTURE: **2 Chronicles 35:15**

And the singers the sons of Asaph were in their place, according to the commandment of David, and Asaph, and Heman, and Jeduthun the king's seer; and the porters waited at every gate; they might not depart from their service; for their brethren the Levites prepared for them.

At first reading, this verse seems to carry no particular challenge to the Christian of today. However, a closer examination comes up with some very interesting observations. Notice, the singers "were in their place" ready to do the job assigned to them. The porters "waited at every gate" in order that they "might not depart from their service." Finally, the "Levites prepared for them," suggesting that those, who were teachers of the Word of God not only prepared specific service responsibilities, they also prepared hearts for the work of the Lord. The musicians, the ushers, and the preachers were all ready, willing, and able to involve themselves when they were needed in the worship and service of the God, who loved them.

This passage is an Old Testament illustration of Ephesians 4:11, 12: "And he gave some, apostles; and some, prophets; and some, evangelists; and some, pastors and teachers: For the perfecting of the saints for the work of the ministry, for the edifying of the body of Christ."

Are you in your "place" today?

Ed Lyman

September 16

PRAISE PSALM: **Psalm 119:7**

I will praise thee with uprightness of heart, when I shall have learned thy righteous judgments.

The same Hebrew word, which has been translated "judgments", is also the word for "ordinances" and the meaning, therefore, is that which has to do with the decisions God has made concerning His people. This word is one of eight synonyms, which are found throughout Psalm 119 for the Will of God. One of these words is found in every verse except verse 122. The other seven are:

Commandments; rules, which demand obedience

Statutes; rules, which are unchangeable requirements (carved in granite)

Law; teachings given by verbal communication

Word; teaching such as are given by parents in guiding their children

Ways; rules, which have to do with habitual living and thinking

Testimonies; having to do with the content of God's rules

Precepts; rules, which have been imposed by authority

As we become attuned to the Will of God, begin to understand His great love and provision, establish a proper relationship to Him, we find the loving-kindness and comfort we seek from a Father, Who is always present. The prayer to the Lord in this psalm is to be "quickened" by God's Will as it is found in these eight word symbols. This is true revival. It is revitalizing the outlook. It is ZIP — Zeal In Perspective! As we perceive God's purpose and plan, we zealously proclaim His Word and praise His Wisdom "with uprightness of heart".

Ed Lyman

September 17

SINGING SCRIPTURE: **Exodus 28:33-35**

And beneath upon the hem of it thou shalt make pomegranates of blue, and of purple, and of scarlet, round about the hem thereof; and bells of gold between them round about: a golden bell and a pomegranate, a golden bell and a pomegranate, upon the hem of the robe and round about. And it shall be upon Aaron to minister: and his sound shall be heard when he goeth in unto the holy place before the Lord, and when he cometh out, that he die not.

This portion of God's Word means much as we see the Lord Jesus Christ in it. Aaron's garments are a prefigure of Christ. The ornamentation of the robe, as described in our passage, presents a significant type of the Lord's ministry.

The golden bell and its tongue symbolized speech, the pomegranate symbolized conduct, and the blue of the robe symbolized the heavenly color. Applying these to Christ, we are reminded of His testimony, His conduct, and His heavenly character.

The golden bells speak of His Godly profession, His perfection of words, and His heavenly conversation. As Jesus preached along those dusty roads, spoke at the seashore, or taught on the hillsides, those golden bells rang true; never a false note. The bells were sewn on the garment in such a way that they might give the sound, which God intended, as Aaron performed his ministry. A bell is of very little use unless it rings. In like manner, Christians are not called to be silent shells, but to be ringing bells giving forth the sound of witness.

The pomegranates symbolized Godly practice, His perfection in works, and His heavenly conduct.

The number of bells and pomegranates was equal typifying the perfect harmony in the life of the Lord. The heavenly calling for the Christian is for harmony in works and witness.

Ed Lyman

September 18

SINGING SCRIPTURE: **Psalm 71:22**

I will also praise thee with the psaltery, even thy truth, O my God: unto thee will I sing with the harp, O thou Holy One of Israel.

It was dark when my bedside phone rang at eighteen minutes to four in the morning on December 7, 1980. I heard the voice of my daughter-in-law asking me to come next door and stay with the children while she took my son to the emergency room. "I'll be right there," I replied.

At 4:12 a.m. my son died of a massive heart attack though he had no history of heart trouble. He was 38 years old. He is greatly missed, but we have faith and know we will see him again. Though we cannot always understand, we can thank God for all things, because we know His timing is perfect and He makes no mistakes.

Psalm 70:4 in the Living Bible says, "But fill the followers of God with joy. Let those who love your salvation exclaim, 'What a wonderful God he is'." Yes, we can sing and praise His truth. It endures forever! What do people do, who don't know our precious Heavenly Father? I'm so thankful that I know "What a wonderful God he is" and that He loves me!

Dorothy Lyke

September 19

PRAISE PSALM: **Psalm 115:18**

But we will bless the Lord from this time forth and for evermore. Praise the Lord.

"The slothful man roasteth not that which he took in hunting (Proverbs 12:27)." This illustrates the fact that searching for truth, finding it, and then doing nothing about it does the seeker no real good. Studying God's Word and God's Ways fills the head with knowledge, but meditation upon the things of the Lord involves the heart also. We do not want to become spiritual tadpoles; all head and no body. We should strive for balance and this is found in the study of the Word and meditation upon it. The man in Proverbs 12:27 took real pleasure in the hunt, but he did nothing with his catch and therefore missed the nourishment it could provide.

To appropriate the promise and the praise of our text today and "bless the Lord from this time forth", it takes an honest application of Romans 12:1 and 2: "I beseech you therefore, brethren, by the mercies of God, that ye present your bodies a living sacrifice, holy, acceptable unto God, which is your reasonable service. And be not conformed to this world, but be ye transformed by the renewing of your mind, that ye prove what is that good, and acceptable, and perfect, will of God."

A filled notebook of "How to" but an empty heart shows only the acquisition of information without application. Paul told Timothy (1 Timothy 4:13 and 15), "Till I come, give attendance to reading, to exhortation, to doctrine. Meditate upon these things; give thyself wholly to them, that thy profiting may appear to all."

Ed Lyman

September 20

SINGING SCRIPTURE: **Numbers 10:10**

Also in the day of your gladness, and in your solemn days, and in the beginnings of your months, ye shall blow with the trumpets over your burnt offerings, and over the sacrifices of your peace offerings; that they may be to you for a memorial before your God: I am the Lord your God.

The sound of the trumpet has been a signal for respect of royalty, recognition of rulership, and the presence of sovereignty throughout the ages. At those times when Israel presented sacrifices in thanksgiving and praise, the music of the trumpet was a call to the children of Israel to remember the majesty and glory of the Lord their God. During feast days and special occasions, it was a clear challenge for involvement in the worship and work of the Lord.

When one day I face the Lord, He will not ask me, "Why were you not a Moses, a Paul, a Stephen?" No, He'll not question me that way, but neither do I want Him to ask, "Why were you not Ed Lyman?"

"Stand up, stand up for Jesus, the trumpet call obey."

Ed Lyman

❀

September 21

SINGING SCRIPTURE: **Psalm 30:12**

To the end that my glory may sing praise to thee, and not be silent. O Lord my God, I will give thanks unto thee for ever.

David is expressing the combination of things which make up the pillars of productivity in the life of a believer. The song of praise broadens into an anthem of witness in direct proportion to the conformity of the Christian to God's will.

This conformity has two dimensions. These are proposed by David and also clearly stated in Ezekiel 1:8 as the prophet describes the four living creatures. "And they had the hands of a man under their wings on their four sides." The "wings" speak of worship; the heavenly dimension, and "hands" show service; the human dimension. Our praise is manifest in a combination of worship and work. However, as we have seen in the Ezekiel passage, the hands are under the wings signifying the proper order. First we worship, then we work.

Next, there is the direction for our worship and service which brings a productivity to the song of the saints. This direction is straight ahead. In Joshua 6:20, the conquest of Jericho is described and after the priests blew the trumpets, "the people went up into the city, every man straight before him." Our aim must be straight before us, not sideways out of God's will.

David determined not to let circumstances deter him from proper praise and service. The believer's song of praise has dimension, direction, determination and finally, it has a Director, the Holy Spirit.

Ed Lyman

September 22

SINGING SCRIPTURE: **Psalm 137:3**

For there they that carried us away required of us a song; and they that wasted us required of us mirth, saying, Sing us one of the songs of Zion.

As we read this Psalm, we are confronted with the question, "To sing, or not to sing?"

The perplexing problem of the preacher is likewise the problem that faces a message brought in a beautiful song, sung by a capable soloist.

Music, like preaching, looks for response in the heart. No matter how clear a message is with an excellent delivery, when the heart is cold, the truth has difficulty denting the soul.

The captors of Israel delighted in the melodious songs of their captives. The songs were superbly sung and the accompaniment was flawless.

Most likely, their hearts were cold to the truth of God. An immovable heart is one of the characteristics of the sinner and at times, the wayward saint.

Yet, it is absolutely true that many an heart, tightly closed to preachings, has been made pliable by the singing of significant songs.

Would these people have been more responsive to the singing prophet than they were to the preaching prophet?

Thank God, at times a song may find a way into the soul of a man when preaching has not yet been admitted.

William H. Beeby

September 23

PRAISE PSALM: **Psalm 71:14**

But I will hope continually, and will yet praise thee more and more.

As we praise Him "more and more", we find our doubtings dissolving and a song of assurance taking their place.

I can't — is a quitter.

I don't know — is too lazy.
I wish I could — is a wisher.
I might — is waking up.
I will try — is on his feet.
I can — is on his way.
I will — is at work.
I did — is now the leader.

Happiness is always found on the road to duty. Harry Bollback wrote:

"As I journey along, I sing of one thing,
And the song of my life is Jesus."

Prophecy is said to be God's secret shared with His friends and if we are aware of the marvelous future God has prepared for those, who love Him, our daily activities should be followed with heaven's values in view.

Ed Lyman

September 24

SINGING SCRIPTURE: **Hosea 2:15**

And I will give her her vineyards from thence, and the valley of Achor for a door of hope: and she shall sing there, as in the days of her youth, and as in the day when she came up out of the land of Egypt.

Israel has been an unfaithful wife. She has given up her beauty and youth by willful pursuit of strange gods and she is left despised and desolate. Her lovers have departed and she is forsaken. It is a dismal picture; the direct result of disobedience. Her sin must be judged, but after relating what she must face, God provides reconciliation and comfort. What a marvelous example of the Loving Lord, who cannot look upon disobedience and does not countenance sin. Yet, He provides redemption through His Son and grace greater than all our sin. Barren vines become fruitful. Even the valley of Achor, which meant trouble (Joshua 7:26), becomes a "door of hope". God had promised Israel life, but she chose the way of death. Instead of taking the high road of faithfulness, she walked the low road of faithlessness.

In His love and mercy, God promises Israel that she will once again sing for joy.

Jesus said to His disciples, "Get in the boat and go OVER and I'll meet you on the other side." A storm arose (and storms do come even while we are in His will) and in the midst of it they cried, "We go UNDER."

The whole conflict of life for some people is between two prepositions: OVER and UNDER. God says, "OVER" and we cry, "UNDER."

Let us sing the songs of overcomers through constant attention on the Lord of life.

James T. Johnson
Ed Lyman

September 25

SINGING SCRIPTURE: **Luke 7:32**

They are like children sitting in the market place, and calling one to another, and saying, We have piped unto you, and ye have not danced; we have mourned to you, and ye have not wept.

The Pharisees and their followers in Jesus' day were pious pouters. Neither the prophecies of John nor the preaching of Jesus pleased them and they constantly sought to down-grade the Lord's message and dilute His authority.

Today, similar attitudes of inconstancy are recognizable when people say they accept Jesus Christ as a great spiritual leader, but refuse to acknowledge His Lordship.

The one-time agnostic, C.S. Lewis, was keenly aware of this as he wrote, "I am trying here to prevent anyone saying the really foolish thing that people often say about Him: 'I'm ready to accept Jesus as a great moral teacher, but I don't accept His claim to be God.' That is the one thing we must not say. A man who was merely a man and said the sort of things Jesus said would not be a great moral teacher. He would either be a lunatic — on a level with the man, who says he is a poached egg — or else he would be the Devil of Hell. You must make your choice. Either this man was, and is, the Son of God: or else a madman or something worse. You can shut Him up for a fool, you can spit at Him and kill Him as a demon; or you can fall at His feet and call Him Lord and God. But let us not come up with any patronizing nonsense about His being a great human teacher. He has not left that open to us. He did not intend to."

Let us be done with the melodies of mediocrity, which present no challenge of eternal value, and let us sing of the sovereignty of the Lord, Who is God.

Ed Lyman

September 26

SINGING SCRIPTURE: **Psalm 96:1**

O sing unto the Lord a new song: sing unto the Lord, all the earth.

Notice the vibrancy with which the Psalmist wrote this verse. Too many times we lack enthusiasm and purpose in our ministry of music. If we are not excited about what we are singing or playing, we should examine ourselves and find out what is keeping this enthusiasm from us.

If we do not have real purpose in this ministry, it would be better not to sing or play until we know exactly what our purpose is. Without enthusiasm and purpose, we cannot hope to communicate the message of our music.

The power of music is beyond the comprehension of most people. The foes of Martin Luther said, "Luther's songs are damning more souls than his messages. The people are singing themselves into Lutheranism."

We read many stories that tell of how individuals came to know Christ through a particular song. Fanny Crosby is one such example.

Once we realize the power of music, we should be better able to sing and play with certainty and the enthusiasm necessary to communicate the great message of Jesus Christ.

Larry Mayfield

September 27

PRAISE PSALM: **Psalm 76:10**

Surely the wrath of man shall praise thee: the remainder of wrath shalt thou restrain.

In revealing His majesty and power, God also makes known tha
through His divine providence even man's anger is turned to serve
the Lord's purposes. As we read of the conflict between Pharaoh
and Moses, we find this passage: "And the Lord said unto Moses,
Rise up early in the morning, and stand before Pharaoh, and say
unto him, Thus saith the Lord God of the Hebrews, Let my people
go, that they may serve me. For I will at this time send all my
plagues upon thine heart, and upon thy servants, and upon thy
people; that thou mayest know that there is none like me in all the
earth" (Exodus 9:13, 14). Then, the Lord declares through Moses the
extent of His sovereignty: "And in very deed for this cause have I
raised thee up, for to show in thee my power; and that my name
may be declared throughout all the earth" (Exodus 9:16).

Both of these statements; "there is none like me in all the earth"
and "that my name may be declared throughout all the earth"
result from the positive assurance from the Lord that He does
everything well. The only proper response to such a God is
devotion, adoration, reverence, and praise. Why should we sing of
lesser things? God's pledge to the believer is one of ultimate victory
over the forces of the world, the flesh, and the devil.

Ed Lyman

September 28

SINGING SCRIPTURE: **Deuteronomy 31:19**

*Now therefore write ye this song for you, and teach it the
children of Israel: put it in their mouths, that this song may be
a witness for me against the children of Israel.*

Moses had come to the end of his life. The leadership was to be
passed on to Joshua. God reviews His promises to Moses and to
Israel. This song becomes a witness to the provision, protection, and
purpose of the Lord.

"I sincerely hope father may yet recover his health; but at all
events, tell him to remember to call upon, and confide in, our great
and good merciful Maker, who will not turn away from him in any
extremity.

"He notes the fall of the sparrow, and numbers the hairs of our
heads, and He will not forget the dying man who puts his trust in
Him.

"Say to him that, if we could meet now, it is doubtful whether it
would not be more painful than pleasant, but that if it is his lot to go

have a joyful meeting with loved ones gone
the rest of us, through the mercy of God, hope
em.''
en at the end of a letter to his stepbrother, John
ning his father, Mr. Lincoln, who was somewhat
of a ne   ll and ill at the time, by Abraham Lincoln.
He was putting this same song in his stepbrother's mouth.

Ed Lyman

September 29

SINGING SCRIPTURE: **Psalm 33:2, 3**

*Praise the Lord with harp: sing unto him with the psaltery
and an instrument of ten strings.*

An elderly gentleman at a midweek service offered this prayer:
"Oh, Lord, we will praise Thee; we will praise Thee with an
instrument of ten strings.''

Those in attendance wondered what he meant, but understood as
he continued to talk to the Lord. "We will praise Thee with our two
eyes by looking only unto Thee. We will exalt Thee with our two
ears by listening only to Thy voice. We will honor Thee with our
own two hands by working in Thy service. We will honor Thee with
our own two feet by walking in the way of Thy statutes. We will
magnify Thee with our tongues by bearing testimony to Thy loving
kindness. We will worship Thee with our hearts by loving only
Thee. We thank Thee for this instrument, Lord, keep it in tune. Play
upon it as Thou wilt and ring out the melodies of Thy grace! May its
harmonies always express Thy glory!''

When the Apostle Paul wrote to the Romans, he said, "...Yield
yourselves unto God, as those that are alive from the dead, and your
members as instruments of righteousness unto God'' (Romans
6:13). Then he challenged them to "...present your bodies a living
sacrifice, holy, acceptable unto God.'' He was exhorting each
believer — then and now — to praise God on his "instrument of ten
strings!''

James H. Blackstone, Jr.

September 30

SINGING SCRIPTURE: **Psalm 96:2**

Sing unto the Lord, bless his name; shew forth his salvation from day to day.

Let us make sure that our singing is unto Him and not merely for the sake of the music or to delight the ears of the audience.

The name of God speaks of His nature; His character. To bless God is to praise Him with a personal affection, a wishing well to Him, to desire blessings upon His cause and His children.

The highest ministry in music is to the Lord in worship, prayer, praise, and song. This enables the believer to become a ministering priest unto God. The primary function of a priest was first to minister to God (Exodus 28:1, Deuteronomy 10:8) and then to the people (Numbers 6:23).

Having satisfied the heart of God, our singing will then minister joy, assurance, and encouragement to the saints. Ultimately, the ministry of song will influence sinners and result in their conversion. The Lord has designed singing as a means of saving the lost. Some, who have not responded to the preaching of the Word were won to Christ through the gospel in song.

May the Lord make us channels of blessing as we "shew forth His salvation day by day" in song and in daily living.

Deoram Bholan

October

DAILY PRAISE

October 1

PRAISE PSALM: **Psalm 71:8**

Let my mouth be filled with thy praise and with thy honor all the day.

Not long ago there lived an old bed-ridden saint; a Christian lady who visited her found her always very cheerful. This visitor had a lady friend of wealth who constantly looked on the dark side of things, and was always cast down, although she was a professed Christian. She thought it would do this lady good to see the bed-ridden saint, so she took her down to the house. She lived up in the garret, five stories up, and when they had got to the first story the lady drew up her dress and said: "How dark and filthy it is!" "It's better higher up," said her friend. They got to the next story, and it was no better; the lady complained again, but her friend replied: "It's better higher up." At the third floor it seemed still worse, and the lady kept complaining, but her friend kept saying: "It's better higher up." At last they got to the fifth story, and when they went into the sick room, there was a nice carpet on the floor, there were flowering plants in the window and little birds singing. And there they found this bed-ridden saint — one of those saints whom God is polishing for His own temple — just beaming with joy. The lady said to her: "It must be very hard for you to lie here?" She smiled and said, "It's better higher up." Yes! And if things go against us, my friends, let us remember that "it's better higher up." That's a living praise song!

Dwight L. Moody

October 2

SINGING SCRIPTURE: **Daniel 3:14, 15**

Nebuchadnezzar spoke and said unto them, Is it true, O Shadrach, Meshach, and Abednego do not ye serve my gods, nor worship the golden image which I have set up? Now, if ye be ready that at that time that ye hear the sound of the cornet, flute, harp, sackbut, psaltery, and dulcimer, and all kinds of music, to fall down and worship the image which I have made, well; but if ye worship not, ye shall be cast the same hour into the midst of a burning fiery furnace. And who is that God, that shall deliver you out of my hands?

Just a polite bow. It couldn't hurt — and who could resist the wooing of such music?

The *strategy of the world* is to move the Christian off center, to catch him up in the comfort of conformity to keep him from the will of God. Shadrach, Meshach, and Abednego — as we should — took a *steadfast stand* when others fell prey to the music and magnificence of sensual satisfaction. These men were hearing music from another *Source.*

The king's *decree* was to be *obeyed.* His word was law. Death came to the disobedient. In the midst of these dangerous and hostile circumstances, the *determination* of these men was *observed.* The greatness of the image, the grandeur of the occasion, and the glory of the music had some men asking, "What's wrong with a little knee bending?" Yet, their heads were not turned. Though the king used all the sights and sounds, which impressed the masses, the hearts of these men were not swayed. The *deliverance observed* was miraculous, but something else is more noteworthy. For these three men, GOD WAS ENOUGH! They answered Nebuchadnezzar — "If it be so, our God, whom we serve, is able to deliver us from the burning fiery furnace, and he will deliver us out of thine hand, O king. But if not, be it known unto thee, O king, that we will not serve thy gods, nor worship the golden image which thou hast set up" (Daniel 3:17, 18). Yes, HE IS ENOUGH for us also!

Still, as of old, Man by himself is priced.
For thirty pieces Judas sold Himself, not Christ.

Ed Lyman

October 3

SINGING SCRIPTURE: **Psalm 47:6**

Sing praises to God, sing praises: sing praises unto our King, sing praises.

The invitation arrived and I looked forward with anticipation to being a part of the program as I packed my tux in my suitcase. Then, in a couple of weeks, on Saturday night, September 23, 1978, John Blanchard drove me past Marble Arch and through the streets of London to the auditorium. After asking directions, we found the dressing room where I changed clothes and had a brief time to go over last-minute details about my music with the accompanist.

At 7:00 p.m. the program began and as guest soloist with the Massed Male Voice Chorus of 1,000 Voices in the Royal Albert Hall, London, England, I heard the first sounds of singing by those men, who had been chosen from all over the British Isles to sing in this festival of praise. What an exhilarating spiritual experience it was and, as my turn came and I stepped to that famed stage, a kind of quiet exultation quickened my heart as I gazed upon the splendid auditorium with its golden balconies. I sang of the hiding place we find in the Rock of our Salvation and of the Lamb of God, Who alone was worthy to be slain for our sins and transgressions. There, in that palace-like concert hall, built in honor of an earthly prince, we raised our voices in combined songs of praise to the Heavenly King, Who became sin for us that we might gain a throne in heaven.

From magnificent halls, such as the one I've just described, to makeshift huts in backward areas of the world, we can sing praises unto the Lord and know that we are in the presence of the King of Kings, Who has made us His heirs. "Worthy is the Lamb that was slain to receive power, and riches, and wisdom, and strength, and honor, and glory, and blessing."

Ed Lyman

October 4

PRAISE PSALM: **Psalm 119:164**

Seven times a day do I praise thee, because of thy righteous ordinances.

The key to the understanding of God's Word is not so much scholarship as it is obedience. "Apply thyself wholly to the Scriptures, and apply the Scriptures wholly to thyself." Here is the exhortation to daily encountering the Lord through His Word. We don't just *find* time for God's Word, we *make* time! Meditation daily upon the Scriptures involves the intellect, emotions, and will. It may take place at any time during the day. In this same psalm, verse 97 we read, "Oh, how love I thy law! It is my meditation all the day." It is a comfort at night: "When I remember thee upon my bed, and meditate on thee in the night watches" (Psalm 63:6).

As we digest God's Word, we are spiritually strengthened. Such meditation is the source of fruitfulness: "But his delight is in the law of the Lord; and in his law doth he meditate day and night" (Psalm 1:2). It is the secret of prosperity: "This book of the law shall not depart out of thy mouth, but thou shalt meditate therein day and night, that thou mayest observe to do according to all that is written therein; for then thou shalt make thy way prosperous, and then thou shalt have good success" (Joshua 1:8). It is the stepping-stone to blessedness: "But whosoever looketh into the perfect law of liberty, and continueth in it, he being not a forgetful hearer but a doer of the work, this man shall be blessed in his deed" (James 1:25).

Meditation is the handmaiden to the song of praise!

Ed Lyman

October 5

SINGING SCRIPTURE: **Psalm 104:12**

By them shall the fowls of the heaven have their habitation, which sing among the branches.

The Bible seems to place importance in the order of *birds* among living creatures. People often belittle these species by such expressions as, "Bird-brain," or, "It's for the birds." But Jesus implied that even sparrows are objects of the heavenly Father's concern. What is the value of these creatures? What do they contribute to the planet?

They sing! They add delightful sound to silent, inanimate trees on windless days, or, on breezy, blustery days, birds add harmonious obbligatos of melody to the rustling accompaniment of fluttering leaves. Dull, eventless, mundane existence comes alive with the melodious songs from these tiny creatures!

So, the bare, inanimate branches of our hum-drum existence can experience a real resurrection transformation through the creatures God sends to bring music into our lives. Minor moods of sadness and depression are transposed into major keys of joy and hope and confidence.

Jack Aebersold

October 6

SINGING SCRIPTURE: **Joshua 6:15, 16**

And it came to pass on the seventh day, that they rose early about the dawning of the day, and compassed the city after the same manner seven times; only on that day they compassed the city seven times. And it came to pass at the seventh time, when the priests blew with the trumpets, Joshua said unto the people, Shout; for the Lord hath given you the city.

"Joshua fit the battle o' Jericho ... And the walls come tumblin' down!" We've sung that song from childhood. It is a marvelous story of Israel calling upon the Lord and completely depending upon Him as their enemy was devastatingly defeated.

It was as if the Lord, by means of music, asked, "Are you trusting me?" and by their shout, the people responded, "Yes!" When we respond to the Lord's leading, like Israel, we can watch as He does wondrous things. It is *IN* His name that we engage the enemy, and it is *BY* His name that we see the victory.

On December 11, 1917, General Allenby, commander of the British Forces in Palestine, marched into Jerusalem on foot at the head of his army. He had been contemplating how he could capture the city without marring or destroying the places dear to Christians. To fire upon Jerusalem would certainly mean ruin. He cabled the King of England for advice and the reply simply said, "Pray about it and use your discretion." The general prayed. While this was taking place, the Turks, who held the city, were overcome with fear, because of the similarity of Allenby's name and their words, "Allah-en-ebia" GOD IS AGAINST US. The population of the city thought God was really fighting against them. When the general arrived at the gates, not a shot was fired and Jerusalem was taken with no resistance.

The Lord's name gave him the city!

Ed Lyman

October 7

SINGING SCRIPTURE: **Luke 2:25-32 (This is called "Simeon's Song")**

And, behold, there was a man in Jerusalem, whose name was Simeon; and the same man was just and devout, waiting for the consolation of Israel: and the Holy Ghost was upon him.

And it was revealed unto him by the Holy Ghost, that he should not see death, before he had seen the Lord's Christ.
And he came by the Spirit into the temple: and when the parents brought in the child Jesus, to do for him after the custom of the law,
Then took he him up in his arms, and blessed God and said,
Lord, now lettest thou thy servant depart in peace, according to thy word:
For mine eyes have seen thy salvation,
Which thou hast prepared before the face of all people;
A light to lighten the Gentiles, and the glory of thy people Israel.

Ed Lyman

October 8

SINGING SCRIPTURE: **Deuteronomy 31:30 and Deuteronomy 32:1-4**

And Moses spake in the ears of all the congregation of Israel the words of this song, until they were ended.

"Give ear, O ye heavens, and I will speak; and hear, O earth, the words of my mouth.

"My doctrine shall drop as the rain, my speech shall distil as the dew, as the small rain upon the tender herb, and as the showers upon the grass:

"Because I will publish the name of the Lord: ascribe ye greatness unto our God.

"He is the Rock, his work is perfect: for all his ways are judgment: a God of truth and without iniquity, just and right is he."

Ed Lyman

October 9

PRAISE PSALM: **Psalm 78:4**

We will not hide them from their children, showing the generation to come the praises of the Lord, and his strength, and his wonderful works that he hath done.

This could be called *A Parental Pledge in Song* for it comes as a result of an exhortation to be diligent in the pursuit of the law of the Lord. The purpose of the praise, which is passed from one generation to the next, is to preserve the intimacy and purity of the relationship between the believer and the Lord Jesus Christ.

Moses exhorted the Israelites to obedience, saying, "Only take heed to thyself, and keep thy soul diligently, lest thou forget the things which thine eyes have seen, and lest they depart from thy heart all the days of thy life: but teach them thy sons, and thy sons' sons (Deuteronomy 4:9)."

Solomon, the son of a musical king, certainly heard David sing the songs of salvation and preservation, which belong to all who put their trust in God. Speaking of his father, Solomon said, "He taught me also, and said unto me, Let thine heart retain my words: keep my commandments and live (Proverbs 4:4)."

Solomon repeats the theme often in his writings and makes the pursuit and preservation of the Lord's Word very personal: "My son, let not them depart from thine eyes: keep sound wisdom and discretion: So shall they be life unto thy soul, and grace to thy neck. Then shalt thou walk in thy way safely, and thy foot shall not stumble (Proverbs 3:21-23)."

Ed Lyman

October 10

SINGING SCRIPTURE: **Psalm 51:14**

Deliver me from bloodguiltiness, O God, thou God of my salvation: and my tongue shall sing aloud of thy righteousness.

No place in the Old Testament relates such depth and tenderness of repentance coupled with such child-like faith in the pardoning mercy of God.

If the sin of David had been omitted in the record of his rule, we would surely have been at a loss to explain the meaning of this passage. However, it is readily understood as it comes from David's mouth and it is because his love for Lord and joy in serving Jehovah are so real that his penitence is so profound.

No hypocrite could have written these lines.

It is truly saying, "Have mercy."

David acknowledges God's immeasurable goodness and vows to sing the praises of the Lord and will make special effort to exalt the righteousness of Jehovah. God is just as righteous when He chastises as when He removes punishment.

The gate by which David entered the presence of the Lord is just as wide for anyone, who truly repents of his sin.

With his conscience free from the guilt of his sin, his heart blessed by the Spirit of God, and his soul humbly thankful for God's great mercy, he determines to seek to turn others from their sin and unto God.

After receiving forgiveness and restoration, he cannot keep silent.

"Therefore, my beloved brethren, be ye steadfast, unmovable, always abounding in the work of the Lord."

Ed Lyman

October 11

SINGING SCRIPTURE: **Psalm 108:1, 2**

O God, my heart is fixed; I will sing and give praise, even with my glory. Awake, psaltery and harp: I myself will awake early.

The Psalmist's mind is made up. He will not be turned from singing the praises of the Lord. He makes a strong case for rising early and spending time with the Lord before going about his other activities. There is an implicit encouragement in these verses that a Morning Watch be kept; a time when we talk with the Lord.

Now, how do I observe the Morning Watch? Well, first of all I study the Word, and then I pray. Here is my authority: "As newborn babes, desire the sincere milk of the word, that ye may grow thereby" (1 Peter 2:2).

When you read God's Word, God talks to you. When you pray, you talk to Him. Hence, after I spend some time with the Book, I turn to prayer, and thus I observe the Morning Watch. Now this is my authority for prayer in connection with the Morning Watch: "My voice shalt thou hear in the morning, O Lord; in the morning will I direct my prayer unto thee, and will look up" (Psalm 5:3).

Oswald J. Smith

October 12

PRAISE PSALM: **Psalm 99:2, 3**

> *The Lord is great in Zion, and he is high above all the peoples.*
> *Let them praise thy great and terrible name; for it is holy.*

The word "terrible" which is used in the King James Version of the Bible means "awe-inspiring". God's "great and awe-inspiring name" is to be praised and worshipped because it is "holy".

Once again we are reminded through the words of the song of inspiration that we are a people with a special relationship to the Lord; a chosen people. As such, we cannot help but bring our songs of praise and adoration to Him, Who loves us. Having been redeemed by the blood of the Lord Jesus Christ, we have a song, which even angels cannot sing. As the old Gospel song says, "Angels never felt the joy that our salvation brings."

We are often so staggered by the extraordinary service of angels such as announcing God's Word, delivering His people, and encouraging the saints, that we don't see the forest for the trees. Yes, it is true that angels are special creations. We know there is a tremendous number of angels (Revelation 5) and they are a separate order of created beings (Psalm 148). They are ministering spirits without human bodies (Hebrews 1) and have supernatural intelligence (2 Samuel 14). They never die (Luke 20) and their power is awesome (2 Kings 19). Yet, after considering all of these extra-special things about angels, we are clearly confronted with the fact that their ordinary or regular service is the praise and worship of God.

"Holy, holy, is what the angels sing.

And I expect (and am expected) to help them make the courts of heaven ring."

Ed Lyman

October 13

SINGING SCRIPTURE: Psalm 57:8

> *Awake up, my glory; awake psaltery and harp: I myself will*
> *awake early.*

Reveille!
This is the "Bugle Call" verse of Psalm 57.
Just as a platoon sergeant calls his sleeping troops to wakefulness

and preparation for the day's military maneuvers with his re-sounding, "Attention", this is choral call sung with exultation and expectancy.

"Awake! Awake! Awake!"

The soul awakes to the possibilities of the day.

The instruments are prepared for the purposes of praise.

The believer is poised for the presentation of a sharing, caring testimony.

This verse is a song of preparation. It is a "salt" song.

Jesus said, "Ye are the salt of the earth (Matthew 5:13)."

The characteristics of this seasoning music are found in the grains of salt.

Salt adds flavor to food. Our singing should add a taste to our testimony.

Salt has curative powers for wounds. Our music should help to assuage the hurt of a sin scarred and bruised life.

Salt makes people thirsty. The chorale of Christian witnessing should be savory enough to raise a thirst for the Water of Life, the Savior, Jesus Christ.

Awake! Let's season our songs with salt.

Ed Lyman

October 14

SINGING SCRIPTURE: Ezekiel 26:13

And I will cause the noise of thy songs to cease; and the sound of thy harps shall be no more heard.

What a calamity it is when we have no song to sing! Such was to be the plight prophesied for Tyre because she had scoffed at God, spoken against the Lord's Jerusalem, and sinned continually before Jehovah.

When God withdraws His favor from a nation or an individual, there is no cause for rejoicing. Instead, the music of gladness becomes the silence of sadness and the soothing chords from the melodic strings of the harp turn to soundlessness as if the lovely instrument were strung with strands of cotton twine.

It has been said that nations are destroyed or flourish in proportion as their poetry, painting and music are destroyed or flourish. God, Himself, was putting an end to Tyre's music and, as a place of power and wealth, it was to be no more. If God can do this to a nation that forgets Him, he can also remove the music from the soul of that man or woman, boy or girl, who seeks only to serve himself.

The music goes, because of the SELF
    Sin
       Of
          Neglecting
          God.
We can bring back the MASTER'S MELODY,
when we
    Sing praises to the Lord
       Increase our commitment to Him
          Nurture fellowship with other believers
             Give our talents and abilities to God.

Ed Lyman

October 15

SINGING SCRIPTURE: **Psalm 144:9**

I will sing a new song unto thee, O God: upon a psaltery and an instrument of ten strings will I sing praises unto thee.

There are several sacred songs mentioned in the Scriptures, the first of which is recorded in Exodus 15. There is no record of the Hebrews singing the Lord's praises while they sojourned in Egypt, but only of their sighing and groaning. However, when they were delivered from the house of bondage and their foes were drowned in the Red Sea, a song of praise ascended from their hearts. We also read of Israel singing when the Lord supplied them with water (Numbers 21:17). Moses ended his wilderness wanderings with a song (Deuteronomy 31:22).

The born-again believer, who has been redeemed by the blood of the Lamb, is no longer a part of the old creation and a slave of Satan's kingdom. In Christ, he is a "new creation" and to testify of God's saving grace, he can now sing a new song with musical instruments of "make a joyful noise" by clapping his hands, his ten fingers constituting the instrument with ten strings (Psalm 100:1; 47:1).

David, the Sweet Psalmist of Israel, composed many new songs out of his experiences. The Christian also will sing new songs as he grows in grace and in the knowledge of his Lord. The Lord's mercies to us are "new every morning" (Lamentations 3:22, 23). Let us with grateful hearts acknowledge His daily mercies, then He will put "a new song in our mouth, even praise unto our God" (Psalm 40:3).

Deoram Bholan

October 16

PRAISE PSALM: **Psalm 74:21**

O let not the oppressed return ashamed: let the poor and needy praise thy name.

"Therefore being justified by faith, we have peace with God through our Lord Jesus Christ;

"By whom also we have access by faith into this grace wherein we stand, and rejoice in hope of the glory of God.

"And not only so, but we glory in tribulations also: knowing that tribulation worketh patience;

"And patience, experience; and experience, hope:

"And hope maketh not ashamed; because the love of God is shed abroad in our hearts by the Holy Ghost which is given unto us.

"For when we were yet without strength, in due time Christ died for the ungodly.

"For scarcely for a righteous man will one die: yet peradventure for a good man some would even dare to die.

"But God commendeth his love toward us, in that, while we were yet sinners, Christ died for us.

"Much more then, being now justified by his blood, we shall be saved from wrath through him.

"For if, when we were enemies, we were reconciled to God by the death of his Son, much more, being reconciled, we shall be saved by his life

"And not only so, but we also joy in God through our Lord Jesus Christ."

Ed Lyman
Romans 5:1-11a

October 17

SINGING SCRIPTURE: **2 Chronicles 23:13**

And she looked, and, behold, the king stood at his pillar at the entering in, and the princes and the trumpets by the king: and

*all the people of the land rejoiced, and sounded with trumpets,
also the singers with instruments of music, and such as taught
to sing praise. Then Athaliah rent her clothes and said,
Treason, Treason.*

Athaliah, the mother of Ahaziah, king of Judah, was a selfish,
wicked woman. In the previous chapter, we are told that Ahaziah
walked in Ahab's evil ways "for his mother was his counselor."
When Ahaziah was then killed, she destroyed "all the seed royal of
the house of Judah" and she kept the throne for herself.

However, one of the king's sons, Joash was saved from her
slaughter and was hidden six years in the house of God. Then
Jehoida, the priest, presented the young man to the congregation:
"Behold, the king's son shall reign, as the Lord hath said of the sons
of David." He was anointed, crowned, and made king.

When the people began to praise the king and the singing was
heard with the sound of the trumpets and musical instruments, she
knew her cause was uncovered and her rule was ended.

This is a conspicuous example of the desperate condition of the
person, who has been confronted and convicted by the truth. Songs
of praise to the king brought the imposter into the spotlight of
reality.

It might well be said as you sing in worship that your "song may
find you out."

Ed Lyman

October 18

SINGING SCRIPTURE: **Judges 5:3**

*Hear, O ye kings; give ear, O ye princess; I, even I, will sing
unto the Lord; I will sing praise to the Lord God of Israel.*

"I remember in Philadelphia, years ago when I was a boy, I heard
an old minister stand and read the hymn, 'There Is a Fountain
Filled with Blood.' I have thought many times of that old man with
his gray hair, and the tears streaming down his face as he read that
hymn, though I have have forgotten his sermon and everything
else. Many a man will come to church, and the sermon will pass in
and out of his ears and be forgotten; but the hymn will linger and
will work for good. I would not try to say what is the best singing for
every church. That would vary. Good, earnest, warm singing I

regard as a necessity in every church."

These thoughts were expressed many years ago by Ira Sankey, the noted song leader. Yet, the challenge is pertinent to the musical ministry today, just as it was in 1879 when this talented musician was traveling with D.L. Moody.

When an interviewer asked him what he would do to get people out to hear the gospel preached, he replied, "Get them out to hear it sung."

Ira Sankey
Ed Lyman

October 19

SINGING SCRIPTURE: **Mark 14:26**

And when they had sung an hymn, they went out to the Mount of Olives.

Jesus and His disciples spent the Passover together. It was the last time they would have such fellowship until after His resurrection. The Lord had presented an intimate picture of the proper relationship there should be between believers. He also spoke of their new position within the family of God. Soon he would be crucified. A sign would be affixed to the cross stating, "King of the Jews", but He would become much more. Upon His resurrection, conquering death, He would become King of the lives of believers. Then, one day "the Lord shall be king over all the earth; in that day shall there be one Lord, and his name one (Zechariah 14:9)."

As a seal is placed on an important document, the hymn of praise, which Jesus and His disciples sang at the close of the meal, was a singing seal upon the new covenant the Lord was instituting. It was a musical "Amen" such as found in Psalm 47:6, 7:

Sing praises to God, sing praises;
sing praises unto our King, sing praises.
For God is the King of all the earth;
sing ye praises with understanding.

In Ephesians 5:19, we find the New Testament equivalent of the psalmist's charge:

Speaking to yourselves in psalms and hymns and spiritual songs,
singing and making melody in your heart to the Lord.

Ed Lyman

October 20

PRAISE PSALM: **Psalm 105:45**

That they might observe his statutes, and keep his laws. Praise ye the Lord.

This psalm is a carefully presented picture of the provision of Jehovah for His people, Israel. It is not just a listing of the good things God has done with no other purpose than to remind the people of past blessings, it is actually an exhortation to praise the Lord in sermon and song as a testimony — a missionary outreach — to the whole world. God had blessed His people in miraculous and marvelous ways in order that they might be the vessels by which the salvation of God would be carried to all people. My friend, Roy Gustafson, states that God made only one religion, Judaism, and completed it in Christ.

God chose Israel:

To witness to the world that there is One God: "Hear, O Israel: The Lord our God is one Lord" (Deuteronomy 6:4).

To show the blessing of serving God: happy people. "Happy art thou, O Israel: who is like unto thee, O people saved by the Lord" (Deuteronomy 33:29).

To carry the oracles of God: as writers, preservers, transmitters of the Bible. "What advantage then hath the Jew? or what profit is there of circumcision? Much every way: chiefly, because that unto them were committed the oracles of God" (Romans 3:1, 2).

To be the channel through which the Messiah should come (Matthew 1:1): the genealogy of Christ "But when the fulness of the time was come, God sent forth his Son, made of a woman, made *under the law*" (Galatians 4:4).

The music of praise becomes the closing AMEN to this presentation of the purposes of God as He prepared His people to be missionaries to the whole world.

Ed Lyman

October 21

SINGING SCRIPTURE: **Psalm 57:7**

My heart is fixed, O God, my heart is fixed: I will sing and give praise.

A song is like a smile and it can also be like a frown. It can set the course of action that is to follow. I remember the days of puppy love. Once, when I parted company with a young girl friend, my heart was broken. I began to sing songs of sorrow that were popular back then. I particularly hung onto, "I Walk Alone" and "Lovesick Blues". Those sad songs reminded me of my disappointment and worked on my feelings as salt works on a wound. I was feeling down in the dumps.

David was in the midst of despair as everything seemed to be going against him. King Saul was seeking his life. He felt as he were all alone. David could have sung songs with lyrics that reminded him of his condition, but he didn't do so. Instead, he turned to songs that illustrated the joy of the Lord. David determined to fix his heart with the proper attitude and then give praise to the Lord. As he sang his songs of praise, his heart was turned Godward and he regained strength. In verse 9, he determines to praise God among the people. In verse 10, he recognizes God's great mercy and then in verse 11, David exults in God's sovereignty "Be thou exalter, O God."

If you wallow in despair, don't remain defeated by songs of self-pity. Lift up your heart to the Lord with songs of praise and the joy of the Lord will be your strength.

Bill Salisbury

October 22

SINGING SCRIPTURE: **Psalm 59:17**

Unto thee, O my strength, will I sing: for God is my defense, and the God of my mercy.

President Abraham Lincoln and his cabinet attended a patriotic rally when Julia Ward Howe was called upon to sing her famous hymn, the "Battle Hymn of the Republic". She had not even finished the first line when those attending joined her in the song. At the conclusion, President Lincoln called out to her while tears rolled down his cheeks, "Please sing it again".

Before leaving that night, the Howes were introduced to the President.

"Mrs. Howe, the verses you wrote have inspired the nation and one cannot hear them sung without an intense patriotic fervor coursing through one's heart!"

Mr. Lincoln was not alone in feeling that this hymn was the most stirring song of the war. No other comforted the people with such hope.

It was the last verse that particularly inspired men and women during those trying days of the Civil War. It remains an inspiration today.

In the beauty of the lilies Christ was born across the sea
With a glory in His bosom that transfigures you and me;
As He died to make men holy, let us die to make men free.
While God is marching on.

Ed Lyman

October 23

SINGING SCRIPTURE: **Genesis 4:21**

And his brother's name was Jubal: he was the father of all such as handle the harp and organ.

"How many of us ever stop to think
Of music as a wondrous link
With God?"

King David said, "Thy statutes have been my songs in the house of my pilgrimage." Our lives on earth are like pilgrimages, which can be bright journeys as we sing unto the Lord.

Clarence McCartney wrote, "On a visit to Bergen in Norway I saw in a park a monument to the great Norwegian violinist Ole Bull. The great minstrel stands playing his violin while a savage holding a lyre bows before him. The statue is meant to symbolize the fact that 'music hath charms to soothe a savage breast.' Ever since the days of Jubal, the father of all who handle the harp and the organ, mankind has felt the power of music. Are not the great chapter of man's life opened and closed with music? There is music when he is born, when he is married, and even at this death."

"Music must take rank as the highest of the fine arts, as the one which, more than any other, ministers to human welfare.

Ed Lyman

October 24

PRAISE PSALM: **Psalm 106:48**

Blessed be the Lord God of Israel from everlasting to everlasting: and let all the people say, Amen, Praise ye the Lord.

The Everlasting God has provided everlasting life for all people, but all people will not experience the provision, because they have placed their salvation in their own methods and merits.

Set on a pedestal, Bible in hand, stands a life-size statue of a man, who changed the world. The place is the city park in Worms, Germany. The man is Martin Luther. Gazing at the piercing eyes, people may recall the significance of his life and teachings: the authority of God's Word, salvation by faith, and the priesthood of the believer, but there is no way this replica of a true servant of the Lord can look into the watcher's thoughts and character. However, one day, all people will stand before the Living God. Their hearts and lives will be opened before Him, Who is The Everlasting Lord, for examination. Claims of good moral living, relief of poverty, social accomplishments, church attendance, and other "good-nesses" will be paraded before God as standards by which men will compare themselves with others. Before the Holy God, they'll be worthless — "all our righteousnesses are as filthy rags (Isaiah 64:6)." However, "If thou shalt confess with thy mouth the Lord Jesus, and shalt believe in thine heart that God hath raised him from the dead, thou shalt be saved. For with the heart man believeth unto righteousness; and with the mouth confession is made unto salvation (Romans 10:9, 10)." The song, which is everlasting, is only sung to the Everlasting Son.

Ed Lyman

October 25

SINGING SCRIPTURE: **Psalm 146:2**

While I live will I praise the Lord: I will sing praises unto my God while I have any being.

Today, music is everywhere: at sports events to increase the excitement of the crowds, at shopping centers to put you in the mood to buy, and even in the dentist's office to soothe your anxiety and concern over the drilling about to take place. Its power of influence is well-known.

Thus, we should put much energy, planning, and prayer into our music ministry to utilize this powerful tool in spreading the Gospel message of Jesus Christ in a world very much affected by and concerned with sounds. Our purpose should be to reach people with the Gospel and the deeper teachings of the Word of God. As I consider my musical responsibilities, I use a variety of styles to reach a larger cross section of people, but the message is always in the forefront of the presentation. It is necessary to spend time and effort to do it well. If the world is concerned about such details, we can do no less than to bring care and creativity to our program of singing.

God grant us the wisdom in choosing our music of evangelism and exposition, excellence in its presentation, and impact in its message. With the help of the Lord and our motives molded to His leading, we will rejoice in the results.

"My mouth shall speak the praise of the Lord" (Psalm 145:21).

David E. Williams

October 26

SINGING SCRIPTURE: 2 Chronicles 29:30

Moreover, Hezekiah, the king, and the princes commanded the Levites to sing praise unto the Lord with the words of David, and of Asaph, the seer. And they sang praises with gladness, and they bowed their heads and worshipped.

Hezekiah became king of Judah. The fortunes of the nation had been decimated by decadence. Favor in the sight of God was at a very low level. Was there any way the nation could recover from the damage done by his father and the kings before him, who had forsaken the commandments of the Lord and brought the abominations of idolatry and pagan practices into the Temple? Yes! Hezekiah ordered a spiritual "house cleaning." After the work was finished, the Levites reported, "We have cleansed the house of the Lord." The Temple was reopened, the lamps relit, and worship was renewed with the music of praise, gladness, and rejoicing. Hezekiah's ambition was to once again honor the Lord and restore Judah to its peculiar place of service for God.

In the singing of praise, there was a renewed act of dedication to the Source of their strength and security. Here is encouragement to the Christian to develop his ambition to: *Please the Lord*: "Wherefore, we labor that, whether present or absent, we may be accepted of him" (2 Corinthians 5:9).

Portray Christ: "Always bearing about in the body the dying of the Lord Jesus, that the life also of Jesus might be made manifest in our body" (2 Corinthians 4:10).

Present the Savior: "So, as much as in me is, I am ready to preach the gospel" (Romans 1:15).

Ed Lyman

October 27

PRAISE PSALM: **Psalm 107:8, 15, 21, 31**

O that men would praise the Lord for his goodness, and for his wonderful works to the children of men.

Four times this verse is used in this psalm. It is an exhortation to praise and may be summed up in the declaration, "Let the redeemed of the Lord say so, whom he hath redeemed from the hand of the enemy (Psalm 107:2)." The psalm closed with the observation that "Whoso is wise, and will observe these things, even they shall understand the lovingkindness of the Lord (Palm 107:43)."

This verse is a musical manifestation of the missionary commission: "Now then we are ambassadors for Christ (2 Corinthians 5:20)." Christ, Himself, was our example as He was a

Home Missionary in the house of Lazarus.

Foreign Missionary when the Greeks came to Him.

City Missionary when He taught in Samaria.

Sunday School Missionary when he opened up the Scriptures and set men to studying the Word of God.

Children's Missionary when He took them in His arms and blessed them.

Missionary to the Poor when He opened the eyes of the blind beggar.

Missionary to the Rich when He opened the spiritual eyes of Zaccaeus.

and even on the cross, Christ was a

Missionary to a Robber — and His last commission to His disciples was "Go ye!"

Ed Lyman

October 28

SINGING SCRIPTURE: **Lamentations 3:14**

I was a derision to all my people, and their song all the day.

The prophet shares the sorrow of his fellow citizens as he enumerates the predicaments in which God's people find themselves. He sets forth the case that God sometimes must act in sovereign retribution in order to show His rulership and fulfill His

Word. "If thou wilt not hearken unto the voice of the Lord thy God, to observe to do all his commandments and his statutes which I command thee this day, that all these curses shall come upon thee, and overtake thee" (Deuteronomy 28:15). Songs of derision point to their plight.

However, a new note in a symphony of hope is sounded in verses 22 and 23: "It is because of the Lord's mercies that we are not consumed, because his compassions fail not. They are new every morning; great is thy faithfulness." No calamity can blot out God's

— Faithfulness to His CREATION: "Wherefore, let them that suffer according to the will of God commit the keeping of their souls to him in well-doing, as unto a faithful Creator" (1 Peter 4:19). This is stability under pressure!

— Faithfulness to His COVENANT: "Know, therefore, that the Lord thy God, he is God, the faithful God, who keepeth covenant and mercy with them who love him and keep his commandments to a thousand generations" (Deuteronomy 7:9). This is standing for purpose!

— Faithfulness to His CALLED: "God is faithful, by whom ye are called unto the fellowship of his Son, Jesus Christ our Lord" (1 Corinthians 1:9). This is singing in His presence!

Ed Lyman

October 29

SINGING SCRIPTURE: **1 Chronicles 15:22**

And Chenaniah, chief of the Levites, was for song; he instructed about the song, because he was skillful.

'Twas battered and scarred, and the auctioneer thought it scarcely worth his while
To waste much time on the old violin but held it up with a smile.
"What am I bidden, good folks?" he cried "Who'll start the bidding for me?
A dollar — now two, only two — two dollars and who'll make it three?
Three dollars once, three dollars twice. Going for three" — but no!
From the room far back a grey-haired man came forward and picked up the bow;
Then wiping the dust from the old violin and tightening up all the strings

He played a melody rare and sweet; as sweet as an angel sings.
The music ceased and the auctioneer with a voice that was quiet and low
Said "What Am I bid for the old violin?" and he held it up with the bow.
"A thousand dollars — and who'll make it two? Two thousand — and who'll make it three?
Three thousand once, and three thousand twice and going and gone," said he.
The people cheered but some of them cried, "We do not quite understand —
What changed its worth?" The man replied: "The touch of the Master's Hand!"
And many a man with life out of tune, and battered and torn with sin,
Is auctioned cheap to a thoughtless crowd much like the old violin...
But the Master comes and the foolish crowd never can quite understand
The worth of a soul and the change that's wrought by the touch of the Master's Hand.

Anonymous

October 30

SINGING SCRIPTURE: **Psalm 61:8**

So will I sing praise unto thy name for ever, that I may daily perform my vows.

Some time ago, I found the following prayer as I was going through some materials I had collected in my travels across the country. Several times I had taken it from a box of news items, clippings, and notes I'd been saving. I placed it on my desk and then, as my desk became cluttered, I once again removed it and filed it with "Things to Think on." As I read this verse about singing praise and performing my daily vows before the Lord, I remembered it.

"This is the beginning of a new day.

"God has given me this day to use as I will. I can waste it — or use it for good, but what I do today is important because I am exchanging a day of my life for it.

"When tomorrow comes, this day will be gone forever, leaving in its place something that I have traded for it.

"I want it to be gain, and not loss; good, and not evil; success and not failure; for the high price I have paid for it."

This kind of vow involves the analyzing of alternatives, balancing of benefits, and calculating the contingencies in our speech, our singing, our service.

"Singing I go along life's road
Praising the Lord, Praising the Lord."

Ed Lyman

October 31

SINGING SCRIPTURE: **Matthew 26:30**

And when they had sung an hymn, they went out into the mount of Olives.

The singing of an hymn after their supper was not a spontaneous gesture or afterthought by the Lord and His disciples. It was part of the prescribed Hillel Psalms used at all Passover Services.

Psalm 113 through Psalm 118 were and still are sung by Israel at the Paschal Supper. There are four cups of wine, which were then and are now drunk. The first three Psalms of this group are sung after the fourth cup.

The Greek text of this verse states: "And having sung (the last Hillel Psalm), they went forth to the Mount of Olives."

There is no doubt that these Psalms are the ones referred to in this text. They were and are sung by all faithful Israelites at the Passover.

When they are read in the atmosphere of that Last Supper of the Lord, they have a greater preciousness to the believer.

Ed Lyman

November

DAILY PRAISE

November 1

PRAISE PSALM: **Psalm 109:1**

Hold not thy peace, O God of my praise.

Although Psalm 109 is included in what are called the Imprecatory Psalms, which are cries unto the Lord for Him to call down his wrath and judgment in vengeance upon His enemies, this verse conveys a desire for peace and praise in the midst of disorder.

Increasing contentions, bitter factions, and multiplied misunderstandings plagued the Corinthians church. Difficulties in deportment and doctrine riddled and rocked the church. Paul wrote to them: "What? know ye not that he which is joined to an harlot is one body? for two, saith he, shall be one flesh. But he that is joined unto the Lord is one spirit (1 Corinthians 6:16-17)." He knew the effect the wrongs and wrangling would have upon the members and others outside the congregation. So, he reminds them of their union with Christ and the peace that should prevail. The glorious salvation, which forgives sin, pardons, and preserves, also puts us into the very Person of Christ Jesus, Himself. It is essential that we present our bodies "a living sacrifice, holy, acceptable unto God" for this is our "reasonable service". Christ is in the believer and the believer is in Christ. Joined with the Lord, we are "one spirit". Vows of praise echo within each member of the body of Christ as we understand this unity, which brings peace: peace *with* God, the peace *of* God, and eventually peace *on* earth.

Ed Lyman

November 2

SINGING SCRIPTURE: **Ruth 1:16, 17 (The Song of Ruth)**

And Ruth said, Entreat me not to leave thee, or to return from following after thee; for whither thou goest, I will go; and where thou lodgest, I will lodge: thy people shall be my people, and thy God, my God.

These lovely words of Ruth, expressing her devotion to her mother-in-law, wind their way into our hearts as the melody of a beautiful song. They go far beyond the sentimental setting in which Ruth finds herself deciding between her country, kin, and culture and the unknown society of a strange land. However, having come to know the God of Israel through the testimony of her husband, who has died, and Naomi, she no longer wishes to serve the god, Chemosh. So, with absolutely no ulterior, self-serving motivation, she faced the onslaught of racial and religious prejudice. Her physical beauty was overshadowed by her unselfish spirit and purity of love. With sweetness and sensitivity, she overcame the animosity, which often alienated the "foreigner" from the Israelite.

Her song becomes her way of living as, back in Bethlehem, she treats her mother-in-law with kindness and respect. Her sublime spirit and inspiring personality have formed a woman of priceless character. Even as she gleaned grain in the hot and dusty fields of Boaz, kinsman of Naomi, she commanded the admiration and regard of everyone who saw her.

Ruth is the epitome of "kindness" — a word, which in Hebrew has a much deeper meaning, and is a characteristic of the Lord Himself. It is the same word used in the song of rejoicing found in Exodus 15:13: "Thou hast led in thy steadfast love (kindness) the people whom thou hast redeemed."

The song of Ruth is a song of steadfast love. Harry E. Fosdick wrote, "We have improved on Ruth's sickle as an agricultural implement, but have we improved on Ruth?"

Ed Lyman

November 3

SINGING SCRIPTURE: Psalm 150:4

Praise him with the timbrel and dance: praise him with the stringed instruments and organs.

How often we are encouraged and cheered by the whistled tune of a passer-by or the hum of a neighbor at work! In turn, we can share gladness by altering our role from *audience* to performer, and replay for others the stirring music which brought lift or serenity to our own lives. As we responsibly listen and tune our hearts to the symphony God's Word performs for our benefit, we can begin to share in the orchestration of the Lord's praise in the world around us.

Listening to the sonatas of others adds inspiring depth and direction to life, but performing symphonies and oratorios for others adds thrilling purpose and dimension to life.

"Sing (what Christ taught) to each other" (Colossians 3:16).

Jack Aebersold

November 4

PRAISE PSALM: **Psalm 79:13**

So we thy people and sheep of thy pasture will give thee thanks for ever: we will shew forth thy praise to all generations.

Summer can be a drag, a sleeper, a time to goof off. Or, summertime can be profitable and purposeful — a time of spiritual growth. The summer can be fruitful in the Gospel's work and witness. What will your summer be: Dullsville or delight?

Christian, we are God's people and sheep of His pasture. As summer approaches, we can tune up on our song of praise that with the *sunshine*, we may present the *Sonshine* of God, the Lord Jesus Christ.

Plan for spiritual growth by studying a Bible book. Read Christian literature. Spend quality time with the Lord in prayer and meditation. Think of those to whom you may present the Good News. Then, communicate.

Anticipate a vacation time as you are able. Our Lord said to His own, "Come apart and rest awhile." Make your vacation Christ centered. Attend a Bible-believing church on Sundays.

Be faithful in your giving to the Lord's work.

Find a ministry, where you can serve Him by serving others. How about Vacation Bible School, summer choir, visitation outreach, caring for some who have special needs?

Maintain fellowship with believers. Learn to share the Word and pray with those of "like precious faith." We must edify and exhort one another. Let's be alive for Christ.

Ernest L. Laycock

November 5

SINGING SCRIPTURE: **Psalm 66:2**

Sing forth the honor of his name: make his praise glorious.

After leading the troops of King Saul in victory after victory, David rode triumphantly through the cities of Israel.

"And it came to pass as they came, when David was returned from the slaughter of the Philistine, that the women came out of all cities of Israel, singing and dancing, to meet King Saul, with tabrets, with joy, and with instruments of music."

"And the women answered one another as they played and said, Saul hath slain his thousands, and David his ten thousands."

They sang forth the honor of his name for all to hear. The praise was so great that Saul became jealous. Such adulation might have made a lesser man swell with conceit, but David gave God the glory.

He entreats us to sing with exuberance and fervor to honor the name of the Lord and to make his praise glorious.

Christ has conquered sin! He has triumphed over death! A victor's praise belongs to the Lord.

Ed Lyman

November 6

SINGING SCRIPTURE: **Isaiah 5:1**

Now will I sing to my wellbeloved a song of my beloved touching his vineyard.

God is speaking to his people and he does so in the following song:

"My well beloved hath a vineyard in a very fruitful hill: And he fenced it, and gathered out the stones thereof, and planted it with the choicest vine, and built a tower in the midst of it, and also made a winepress therein: and he looked that it should bring forth grapes, and it brought forth wild grapes.

And now, O inhabitants of Jerusalem, and men of Judah, judge I pray you, betwixt me and my vineyard.

What could have been done more to my vineyard, that I have not done in it? wherefore, when I looked that it should bring forth grapes, brought it forth wild grapes?

And now go to: I will tell you what I will do to my vineyard: I will take away the hedge thereof, and it shall be eaten up; and break down the wall thereof, and it shall be trodden down:''

The Apostle Paul puts an "Amen" after this song in 1 Corinthians 9:27, "But I keep under my body, and bring it into subjection; lest that by any means, when I have preached to others, I myself should be a castaway."

Ed Lyman

November 7

PRAISE PSALM: Psalm 109:30

I will greatly praise the Lord with my mouth; yea, I will praise him among the multitude.

The mouths of his enemies are open against him, but in the midst of this, David opens his mouth in musical praise, prayer, and preaching. In Psalm 81:10 we read, "I am the Lord thy God, who brought thee out of the land of Egypt; open thy mouth wide, and I will fill it." This promise of God is a mandate for witnessing to the world around us. Jesus said (Matthew 10:18-20), "And ye shall be brought before governors and kings for my sake, for a testimony against them and the Gentiles. But when they deliver you up, take no thought (be not anxious) how or what ye shall speak; for it shall be given you in that same hour what ye shall speak. For it is not ye that speak; but the Spirit of your Father who speaketh in you." This promise is also contingent upon the faithfulness of the believer in studying and knowing God's Word.

We should open our mouths in prayer (John 15:7): "If ye abide in me, and my words abide in you, ye shall ask what ye will, and it shall be done unto you."

We should open our mouths in praise (Hebrews 13:15): "Let us offer the sacrifice of praise to God, continually, that is, the fruit of our lips giving thanks to his name."

We should open our mouths in proclamation (Acts 13:38): "Be it known unto you, therefore, men and brethren, that through this man is preached unto you the forgiveness of sins."

We should open our mouths in presentation (Romans 12:1): "I beseech you therefore, brethren, by the mercies of God, that ye present your bodies a living sacrifice.

Ed Lyman

November 8

SINGING SCRIPTURE: **1 Chronicles 16:7**

Then on that day David delivered first this psalm to thank the Lord into the hand of Asaph and his brethren.

Give thanks unto the Lord, call upon his name,
make known his deeds among the people.
Sing unto him,
sing psalms unto him,
talk ye of all his wondrous works.
Glory ye in his holy name:
Let the heart of them rejoice that seek the Lord.
Seek the Lord and his strength,
seek his face continually.
Remember his marvelous works that he hath done,
his wonders, and the judgments of his mouth:

David

❊

November 9

SINGING SCRIPTURE: **1 Samuel 10:5, 6**

After that thou shalt come to the hill of God, where is the garrison of the Philistines; and it shall come to pass, when thou art come thither to the city, that thou shalt meet a company of prophets coming down from the high place with a psaltery, and a tabret, and a pipe, and a harp before them; and they shall prophesy. And the Spirit of the Lord will come unto thee, and thou shalt prophesy with them, and shalt be turned into another man.

There is, in this unique scene, the essence of the harmony of mind and soul in which the Holy Spirit carries on His ministry as He controls the life of the believer and works through him to touch the lives of others. His presence makes up for those inadequacies, which might lead us into a perplexing plunge down the path to discord. Down the mountain came some prophets, playing their music as the newly anointed king of Israel, Saul, watched and listened. One miscue could have caused bashed-in teeth, bruised bodies, and broken horns and harps — to say nothing of an absolutely atrocious sound. Yet, there was cooperation in making music under difficult circumstances.

F.B. Meyer told of a Christian gentleman who was staying in a fine hotel, where a little child practiced the piano each day in the room, where other guests also assembled. The beginning piano student soon drove everyone from the room until the day a noted pianist registered. That day, as the girl began to pick out the notes, the famous pianist stayed when the other guests left. He sat down next to the child and began to fill in a lovely accompaniment to the feeble efforts of the beginner. The guests returned to listen to the beautiful music and the pianist showed the little girl around the room to receive the thanks of the audience.

"Likewise, the Spirit also helpeth our infirmity" (Romans 8:26). The presence of God's Spirit turned Saul "into another man" and this Heavenly Conductor can bring the scattered nervous notes of our lives into beautiful harmony.

Ed Lyman

November 10

SINGING SCRIPTURE: **II Chronicles 29:28**

And all the congregation worshipped, and the singers sang, and the trumpeters sounded: and all this continued until the burnt offering was finished.

The good king Hezekiah of Judah knew the value of worship in song. He recognized the worth of praising God with the instruments of that day. As we make a practical application of this passage, we are reminded of several basic concepts in making melody to God's glory.

The first concept is that of every individual participating with his God-given human voice. Nothing is more pleasant sounding and, I am sure, pleasing to God than the voice of every individual in corporate worship singing unto our Lord; affirming our faith in melody.

I like telling the world, "On Christ the solid rock I stand! All other ground is sinking sand." An entire congregation voicing this great truth in harmony is true worship.

A congregation singing out of hearts free from all bondage is also a basic in praising God. There was no praise in the Hebrew heart as we read in Psalm 137. It was a forced song. "By the rivers of Babylon they sat, the oppressor required of them a song.'' Don't ever sing a required song. Sing from the overflow or don't sing at all.

Lastly, I point out the glad song of Psalm 126. "When the Lord turned again the captivity of Zion, we were like them that dream. Then was our mouth filled with laughter and our tongue with singing; then said they among the heathen, the Lord hath done great things for us whereof we are glad.'' It is this love of gladness that perhaps caused Nehemiah to affirm, "The joy of the Lord is your strength.''

Homer Martinez

November 11

PRAISE PSALM: **Psalm 111:1**

Praise ye the Lord. I will praise the Lord with my whole heart, in the assembly of the upright, and in the congregation.

Holding back nothing, but "with my whole heart" I shall endeavor to honor the name of the Lord. The heart of man becomes the inspiration for his song of praise: "For as he thinketh in his heart, so he is" (Proverbs 23:7a).

Peter presents a particularly poignant characterization of the heart in his epistles. In order to properly praise the Lord, we must have *God in our hearts*. "But sanctify the Lord in your hearts, and be ready always to give an answer to every man that asketh you a reason of the hope that is in you, with meekness and fear" (1 Peter 3:15). Those King James terms appear to mean something, which causes us distress, but they are better translated "gentleness and respect."

Our praise is purposeful when we have *love in our hearts*. "Seeing that ye have purified your souls in obeying the truth through the Spirit unto unfeigned love of the brethren, see that ye love one another with a pure heart fervently" (I Peter 1:22).

Praise songs afford comfort when we have *Hope in our hearts*. "We have also a more sure word of prophecy, unto which ye do well that ye take heed, as unto a light that shineth in a dark place, until the day dawn, and the day star arise in your hearts" (2 Peter 1:19).

With our whole hearts let us love the Lord and the music of His Word shall become the hope of eternal fellowship with our Savior.

Ed Lyman

November 12

SINGING SCRIPTURE: **Matthew 24:31**

And he shall send his angels with a great sound of a trumpet, and they shall gather together his elect from all the four winds, from one end of the heaven to the other.

"But I would not have you to be ignorant, brethren, concerning them who are asleep, that ye sorrow not, even as others who have no hope.

"For if we believe that Jesus died and rose again, even so them also who sleep in Jesus will God bring with him.

For this we say unto you by the word of the Lord, that we who are alive and remain unto the coming of the Lord shall not precede them who are asleep.

"For the Lord himself shall descend from heaven with a shout, with the voice of the archangel, and with the trump of God; and the dead in Christ shall rise first;

"Then we who are alive and remain shall be caught up together with them in the clouds, to meet the Lord in the air; and so shall we ever be with the Lord.

"Wherefore, comfort one another with these words."

Paul, the Apostle
1 Thessalonians 4:13-18

November 13

SINGING SCRIPTURE: **Psalm 68:4**

Sing unto God, sing praises to his name: extol him that rideth upon the heavens by his name JAH and rejoice before him.

How true it is that until we have actually experienced the power of the resurrection of the Lord Jesus Christ in our own lives and caught a glimpse of His holiness, majesty, and glory, we cannot truly know the inspiration and the comfort of singing His praises. Until the Savior infuses us with His presence, His peace, His provision, our love for Him and for others comes forth "as sounding brass" and "tinkling cymbal".

We are but organs mute, till the master touches the keys;
Very vessels of earth into which God pours the wine;

Harps are we, silent harps, that have hung on the willow
trees;
Dumb till our heartstrings swell and break with a pulse
divine.

How happily then we raise our song of rejoicing as we find our
place in the family of God.

Praise Him! Praise Him! Join the loud acclaim;
Praise Him! Praise Him! Bless His holy name;
Ever kind and merciful in all His ways,
He alone is worthy to receive our praise.

Well, I've already filled the thought for today with quotes, so I'll
make it complete with a final one:

If singing His praises on earth is so sweet,
What will it be when around Him we meet?

Ed Lyman

November 14

SINGING SCRIPTURE: **1 Chronicles 15:28**

Thus all Israel brought up the ark of the covenant of the Lord
with shouting, and with sound of the cornet, and with
trumpets, and with cymbals, making noise with psalteries
and harps.

In this, another description of the bringing of the Ark into
Jerusalem, we are reminded of David's own concern for musical
excellence in praising the Lord. He chose men, who were skilled in
their various talents. Perhaps Christian musicians today would
find a more effective ministry if they would spend more time
developing their skills and less time concentrating on peripheral
aspects. A fancy suit, a bag of anecdotes, and a quick prayer for "the
Lord's blessing on your ministry" will never substitute for long
hours of energetic, solid practicing and effort to develop the talents
the Lord has given you. Once that practicing has been done and
preparation has been made, then go ahead and add the suit, speech,
and sincere prayer — all of which will be the icing on the cake. Just
be sure there is cake to start with!

At another time (Psalm 81), one of David's chief musicians and
singers, Asaph, exhorts believers to sing "aloud," I'm sure his basic

reason is to be sure the Lord's praise song is heard clearly and distinctly, but when you keep in mind that Asaph accompanied his singing (and that of his fellow musicians) with cymbal-playing (verse 19), the command to "sing aloud" becomes an obvious necessity!

David made use of every musical instrument available — voices, strings, percussion — and probably was very imaginative in his use of them. Not bound by tradition, David and his men praised the Lord with all their might and with all of their creative musicianship.

Douglas E. Schoen

November 15

PRAISE PSALM: **Psalm 84:4**

> *Blessed are they that dwell in thy house: they will be still praising thee. Selah.*

Rejoicing is the result of having joy. When we have joy, we cannot help but rejoice. This joy comes from Christ being proclaimed or announced. In Philippians 1:18, we read, "What then? notwithstanding, every way, whether in pretense, or in truth, Christ is preached; and I therein do rejoice, yea, and will rejoice."

The wise men rejoiced when they saw the star for it proclaimed the birth of Christ.

Joy produces singing. We sing joyously because of what Christ has done, is doing, and will do. "O Come, let us sing unto the Lord: let us make a joyful noise unto the rock of salvation" (Psalm 95:1). "We will be glad and rejoice in thee" (Song of Solomon 1:4).

The world's music reflects the desires, attitudes, morality, emotions, and philosophy of those, who know not Christ. It clearly portrays the hopelessness of a Christless heart, but the song of the redeemed reflects the joy and fullness and positive assurance of those, who know Christ and are free from the bondage of sin. Spurgeon said, "We are ordained to be minstrels of the skies; let us rehearse our everlasting anthem before we sing it in the halls of the New Jerusalem."

Let the lost lament in their music over their troubles, but "let the redeemed of the Lord 'sing' so."

Paul Crosson

November 16

SINGING SCRIPTURE: 1 Kings 1:39, 40

And Zadok, the priest, took an horn of oil out of the tabernacle, and anointed Solomon. And they blew the trumpets; and all the people said, God save King Solomon. And all the people came up after him, and the people piped with pipes, and rejoiced with great joy, so that the earth split with the sound of them.

As we read these verses, we become caught up in the rejoicing and festivities of such an exciting occasion. Such times make marvelous memories.

David had declared that Solomon should succeed him. His mother knew he was one day to sit upon his father's throne. The people of Israel were aware of this succession. Yet, until he was publicly anointed and presented to all Israel, Solomon could not claim his kingship. The trumpets sounded in testimony that the son had become the Sovereign.

We turned into the parking lot of the Lutheran church in Clarksville on Thanksgiving morning and the engagement ring seemed to bore a hole in my pocket as I turned off the engine and looked at Julie. I asked if she had everything and she said she did.

"There is something missing and I'd be proud if you'd wear it this morning — and always," I whispered. I reached into my pocket, took out the ring, and slipped it on her finger.

There were no trumpets there that morning, but as far as I was concerned, there was a band of buglers lining the way into the church playing a testimony that Julie and I were engaged. Only when I took the ring out of my pocket and put it on her finger would our engagement be official and known to others.

The music of the trumpet sounds the call to service.

Ed Lyman

November 17

SINGING SCRIPTURE: Isaiah 16:10

And gladness is taken away, and joy out of the plentiful field; and in the vineyards there shall be no singing, neither shall there be shouting: the treaders shall tread out no wine in their presses; I have made their vintage shouting to cease.

This is the picture of "pride going before a fall." Moab, once proud and haughty, is judged by God in truth and all pretenses are uncovered. Sin is revealed and, as a result, the joy and singing and shouting, which usually accompany a plenteous harvest, is not to be heard. The fields, which were once ripe with produce, are to be empty. The vines, once laden with fruit, are bare. Moab, a land once proud of her position and plenty, displaying her idolatry in the face of God, loses everything.

Safety, security, and confidence are not found in the wealth and self-satisfaction brought about by human endeavor or the "good feeling" property and pride encourages.

It is the security of the Word of God we need, if there is to be reality in our lives. The crux of the matter is based upon what we really want. Do we want to please God or are we more desirous of pleasing ourselves. Is God's will preeminent in our lives or are we satisfied to devise and follow our own plans?

When our priorities get settled properly, we are then on the road to blessing and there is singing because the Lord is present.

Ed Lyman

November 18

SINGING SCRIPTURE: **1 Chronicles 16:9**

Sing unto him, sing praises unto him, talk ye of all his wondrous works.

Here is inspired exhortation for God's people to employ what is perhaps the loveliest means of praising God: singing. Only the redeemed really sing. The world wails; the heathen howl; the sinner sighs, but the saved sing. We are to sing psalms. The New Testament extends this to include hymns and spiritual songs.

We are to sing unto Him, who is our deliverance and this song of praise begun on earth will be continued in His presence for eternity.

Because of His mercies, which are new every day, new songs are given to express our gratitude in praise, but our constant theme will ever be His wondrous work of salvation wrought in the believing heart. There is much in this life of great interest about which we can talk, but it is most essential and appropriate that we talk of all His wondrous works.

Do you have a voice? Is there a song in your heart? If so, then open your mouth and let Him fill it with praise to His name.

Norman Clayton

November 19

PRAISE PSALM: **Psalm 115:17**

The dead praise not the Lord neither any that go down into silence.

Some have incorrectly presumed that the Old Testament view of death was that everything ended with the grave; nothing followed. Such an interpretation is in direct conflict with Psalm 16:9-11: "Therefore my heart is glad, and my glory rejoiceth; my flesh also shall rest in hope. For thou wilt not leave my soul in sheol, neither wilt thou permit thine Holy One to see corruption. Thou wilt show me the path of life. In thy presence is fullness of joy; at thy right hand there are pleasures for evermore." "The dead praise not the Lord" emphasizes the fact that earthly praise will end when death takes place and the opportunity to worship and honor the Lord in the circumstances of our present life style. The verse is to be understood in the sense spoken of by William Cowper as he sings,
"Then in a nobler, sweeter song, I'll sing Thy pow'r to save.
When this poor lisping, stamm'ring tongue Lies silent in the grave."
No other conclusion can be drawn than the inescapable truth that the believer has only this life in which to make his praise for the Lord's salvation, presence, love, and peace known to the world around him. It is a motto of vital import: "Only one life, 'twill soon be past. Only what's done for Christ will last."
"Nevertheless, I am continually with thee; thou hast held me by my right hand. Thou shalt guide me with thy counsel, and afterward receive me to glory" (Psalm 73:23, 24).

Ed Lyman

November 20

SINGING SCRIPTURE: **Psalm 68:25**

The singers went before, the players on instruments followed after; among them were the damsels playing with timbrels.

The importance of color in photography and painting is obvious to even the casual observer. Very different impressions are created by the use of colors. Color in the visual arts becomes a means by which an artist can affect the moods and even the thoughts of the onlooker.

Tone color is just as important in music. The sound of a trumpet, an oboe, a violin, or a cymbal is different with each instrument even though they may be playing the same note. Each instrument has a distinctive tone color. However, when the instruments are tuned properly and played together, the various tone colors blend to produce beautiful sounds.

As the Ark was brought up to Mount Zion, the music of rejoicing could be heard all along the way. It was a blend of vocal and instrumental music in praise to the Lord God of Israel. Tone colors of voices and instruments produced this psalm of triumph and glory — in harmony with each other —unity of sound and spirit.

Paul puts us in mind of this as he writes, "For ye are all the children of God by faith in Christ Jesus. There is neither Jew nor Greek, there is neither bond nor free, there is neither male nor female; for ye are all one in Christ Jesus" (Galatians 3:26, 28).

> "People and realms of every tongue
> Dwell on His love with sweetest song."

Ed Lyman

November 21

SINGING SCRIPTURE: **Song of Solomon 1:1**

The song of songs, which is Solomon's.

"Song of Songs" is the literal name for this book, which in Hebrew is *Shir hashirim*. It is read annually on the eighth day of the Passover and the repetition of the noun in the genitive plural brings out the special character of the song; the best of songs.

It is a poem of love without doubt. However, the interpretation of it is varied. From ancient times, the Jews regarded it as expressing God's love relationship with His chosen people and this idea has also passed over into the Christian interpretation of Christ and His Church. This is called the "allegorical view". The "dramatic view" presents the idea that Solomon has fallen in love with a Shulamite girl, whom he brings to his palace. Some also believe a third party, a shepherd, to whom the Shulamite girl remains faithful in spite of Solomon's wooing, is a third party in the song. Next, the "typical view" holds that Solomon is considered to be a type of Christ and the bride represents the Church. It is similar to the allegorical view, but it does not try to put special meaning to every passage. The fourth is the "natural or literal view" and it regards the song as a presentation of the virtues of human love.

It could easily be said of this "Song of Songs" that the clear message being sung is: "Married to the right person, nothing like it; Married to the wrong person; nothing like it." No matter which interpretation is chosen, it behooves us to think on the truth that a relationship with Christ is The Song of Songs.

Ed Lyman

November 22

PRAISE PSALM: **Psalm 100:4**

> *Enter into his gates with thanksgiving, and into his courts with praise: be thankful unto him, and bless his name.*

I remember when Dr. Arnott, who has gone to God, was delivering a sermon, he used this illustration. The sermon and text have all gone, but that illustration is fresh upon my mind tonight and brings home the truth. He said: "You have been sometimes out at dinner with a friend, and you have seen the faithful household dog standing watching every mouthful his master takes. All the crumbs that fall on the floor he picks up, and seems eager for them, but when his master takes a plate of beef and puts it on the floor and says: 'Rover, here's something for you,' he comes up and smells of it, looks at his master, and goes away to a corner of the room. He was willing to eat the crumbs, but he wouldn't touch the roast beef — thought it was too good for him." That is the way with a good many Christians. They are willing to eat the crumbs, but not willing to take all God wants. Come boldly to the throne of grace and get the help we need: there is an abundance for every man, woman and child.

He that overcometh shall inherit all things. God has no poor children.

The praise we bring into His courts can be a prayer song of thanksgiving and blessing.

Dwight L. Moody

November 23

SINGING SCRIPTURE: **1 Chronicles 16:23**

Sing unto the Lord, all the earth; shew forth from day to day his salvation.

This could be called "Music from the Dust of History" and yet it is just as timely for our day and age. Notice that the singing comes as a glory to the Lord and it comes after God has protected His people. It describes God's preserving character in His dealings with His own people and those nations, which surround them. The people were willing to sing to the Lord and to declare each day that He was the One which saves, to show His glory globally, and to tell everyone throughout the entire earth about His miracles. A good outline for your own heart today would be:

1. Begin singing
2. Begin declaring that He is the Savior
3. Begin to show His glory to the globe
4. Begin to stretch your faith to adopt the entire world and believe God's amazing miracles

With such a song, all the world will hold in awe our Lord and Savior Jesus Christ and honor His majesty with singing.

Merv Rosell

November 24

SINGING SCRIPTURE: **Joshua 6:4, 5**

And seven priests shall bear before the ark seven trumpets of ram's horns; and the seventh day ye shall compass the city seven times, and the priests shall blow with the trumpets. And it shall come to pass that, when they make a long blast with the ram's horn, and when ye hear the sound of the trumpet, all the people shall shout with a great shout; and the wall of the city shall fall down flat, and the people shall ascend up, every man straight before him.

Such an order and attack plan cannot be found in any military manual. To as much as even suggest something of this nature would bring about a round of rousing laughter amongst army men. Most likely, as this plan was implemented by Joshua and the people of

God, the soldiers on the walls of Jericho, who were watching this daily parade, mocked the marchers for such military madness. Israel was the laughing-stock of her enemy.

Then, with the blast of the trumpet, the walls trembled and fell, and the ram's horn sound became the music of total victory.

To actually accept such a program from God and put it into operation, Joshua had first to acknowledge the absolute sovereignty of God. Having done this, what seems ridiculous in the eyes of the world becomes rewarding in the heart of the believer.

Often, the spiritual victories of the Christian are also won by ways and means that are foolish according to the wisdom of the world. As Joshua had to make God's will his will before he could see victory, we must understand that the Lord's sovereignty extends into every aspect of life, companionships, careers, and ministry.

"Teach me to do thy will; for thou art my God. Thy Spirit is good; lead me into the land of uprightness" (Psalm 143:10). If we are to know God's will in our lives, we must be willing to do it. For, only the seeking mind and the willing heart can truly know what God's will really is. In His will — even as did Joshua of old — we'll hear the music of victory.

Ed Lyman

November 25

SINGING SCRIPTURE: Matthew 9:23-25

And when Jesus came into the ruler's house, and saw the minstrels and the people making a noise, He said unto them, Give place: for the maid is not dead, but sleepeth. And they laughed him to scorn. But when the people were put forth, he went in, and took her by the hand, and the maid arose.

Matthew calls the music of the instruments and the singing "noise". They had been mourning in lamentations of death until Jesus stopped them. In the presence of the Lord Jesus Christ there is no place for mourning. He stops the downhearted dirge and replaces it with psalms of praise.

These mourners had no idea that in Christ there is no death and the grave has no dominion. To them, the young girl was dead, but in Christ there is life. To Jesus, she was merely asleep.

Sometimes the noise of self-pity must be hushed before we can hear the music of praise.

After telling his patient to put out her tongue, the doctor started writing a prescription. When he finished, he said to her, "That will do."

"But doctor, you didn't even look at my tongue," protested the woman.

"It wasn't necessary," replied the doctor, "I just needed to keep you quiet while I wrote out the prescription.

Ed Lyman

November 26

SINGING SCRIPTURE: **Psalm 69:12**

They that sit in the gate speak against me; and I was the song of the drunkards.

David is aware of the fact that there are those who hate him, and he is afflicted on every hand by his enemies. However, he is also clearly conscious of the fact that the Lord has not forsaken him and later in this Psalm, he prays for deliverance. His faith is unshaken by his adversaries.

This "man after God's own heart" reiterates the trust he has only in the Lord when he uses the phrase in the 13th verse, "But as for me, my prayer is unto thee, O Lord." His hope is not in men, but in the God of his salvation.

So, it becomes clear that being "the song of drunkards" portrays to us the unmindful musical foolishness of those whose minds have been muddled by strong drink. What David tells us is that the songs sung about him by his enemies have no rhyme nor reason, because they haven't taken God into account. The drunkard sings with his mouth, but his mind is in "neutral". This is the significance of Paul's statement in Ephesians 5:17-19 where the apostle tells us "be ye not unwise but understanding" and "not drunk with wine, wherein is excess" because our songs should be sung with understanding. When the world laughs at us for our praise of the Lord, it is because their songs are muddled by the strong drink of ungodliness, irreverence, and misunderstanding about God's plan.

Ed Lyman

November 27

PRAISE PSALM: **Psalm 111:10**

The fear of the Lord is the beginning of wisdom: a good understanding have all they that do his commandments: his praise endureth forever.

With grateful hearts we rejoice in the inheritance we have in Christ and in the light, which we receive by directing our attention to the Word of God. The source of our praise song is the innermost shrine of the Scriptures, where God causes fresh understanding and light to break from His Word. The treasures available go far beyond the literary element and into the spiritual content. What are the steps, which lead us to this song of rejoicing? To unveil these truths, we must:

1. Pray. In Psalm 119:18, we read, "Open thou mine eyes, that I may behold wondrous things out of thy law." Prayerfulness produces a mental mood for the reception of divine truth.

2. Search. In order to properly search the Scriptures, you must know the Author first. Then by study, understanding will come. Two ways, which produce fruitfulness in searching are *daily encounters* (Proverbs 8:34) and *diligent excavation* (1 Peter 1:10, 11).

3. Meditate. "This book of the law shall not depart out of thy mouth; but thou shalt meditate therein day and night, that thou mayest observe to do according to all that is written therein" (Joshua 1:8).

4. Obey. The key to understanding the Scriptures is not scholarship, but obedience. There is a nautical saying, which wraps up our thought: "He that is slave to the compass has the freedom of the seas."

Ed Lyman

November 28

SINGING SCRIPTURE: **1 Samuel 16:23**

And it came to pass, when the evil spirit from God was upon Saul, that David took an harp, and played with his hand; so Saul was refreshed, and was well, and the evil spirit departed from him.

The Lord God of Israel had rejected Saul from reigning over His people and now commanded Samuel to follow His instructions in anointing a new king: one chosen by God. The Lord's Spirit departed from Saul and he became troubled and vexed in his heart and mind. The very same man, whom God had chosen to be king, also became Saul's court musician.

As the music of the harp soothed the restless spirit of the king, so the music of God's word brings comfort and relief to the distraught nature of the sinner. It provides harmony to the discord of muddle thinking. As he played, I can also imagine that David softly sang some of the psalms he had written on the hillsides of Bethlehem and perhaps they brought to remembrance the early relationship Saul had with the Lord.

> *And the night shall be filled with music*
> *And the cares, that infest the day,*
> *Shall fold their tents, like the Arabs*
> *And silently steal away.*

Saul's cares were temporarily concealed by the sounds of the harp, but our worries can be removed by the song of security in Christ.

Ed Lyman

November 29

SINGING SCRIPTURE: **Psalm 47:5**

> *God is gone up with a shout, the Lord with the sound of a trumpet.*

It strikes us that the words "is gone up" — ascended — are the key to the thought we should be aware of as we think on this verse. As children of God, we think of the ascension of the Lord Jesus Christ into heaven when he had completed His earthly ministry. He conquered death and ascended on high. He took His seat on His throne. What better way to praise our Lord, than to not only look upward, because He reigns in glory, but to think "upward" — striving to become the kind of person God intends us to be in order that we might praise Him with our whole heart.

To think "upward" is to praise the Lord. To think "upward" is to acknowledge God's sovereignty. To think "upward" is to realize we are His servants. To think "upward" is to know our weakness makes His strength perfect.

Many years ago, this illustration made a real impact on our hearts and we've never forgotten it. Man is the only creature on earth created by God to look "upward". As you watch animals, you'll notice how they move along with their heads downward, toward the ground, sniffing and searching. However, the Lord intends man to look "upward" — to raise our heads and hearts to Him — to praise Him for loving us so much that He gave us His Son.

Is that alone not enough to make us think "upward"?

Jim and Diane Montgomery

November 30

PRAISE PSALM: **Psalm 86:12**

I will praise thee, O Lord my God, with all my heart: and I will glorify thy name forever.

This Psalm, written by David, certainly is a Psalm of praise. In reading it over and over, one becomes aware that a story or lesson can easily be found in each of the verses of this 86th Psalm without neglecting the context in any way. Each verse is a sermon preached of God's goodness, mercy, faithfulness, righteousness, and everlasting love. David, as all faithful believers should, tells God that he will abundantly proclaim His great goodness and sing of His righteousness.

Recently, I attended the funeral service of a friend. As my wife and I stood talking with his wife, offering our condolences, this radiant woman was full of praise and thanksgiving to God that her loved one had been taken without suffering. She virtually sang of God's righteousness. Regardless of the situation we find ourselves in, we can and should utter the memory of God's goodness and sing of His righteousness.

Jack Schurman

December

DAILY PRAISE

December 1

SINGING SCRIPTURE: **Isaiah 18:3**

All ye inhabitants of the world, and dwellers on the earth, see, when he lifteth up an ensign on the mountains; and when he bloweth a trumpet, hear ye.

"Watch and listen"; the Lord has done marvelous things and has spoken unto us through His Word. His ensign is the miracle of salvation and His message is the music of love.

"He came unto his own, and his own received him not.

But as many as received him, to them gave he power to become the sons of God, even to them that believe on his name" (John 1:11, 12).

This new relationship to the Lord brings with it a new kinship with other believers "Where there is neither Greek nor Jew, circumcision nor uncircumcision, Barbarian, Scythian, bond nor free: but Christ is all, and in all.

"Put on therefore, as the elect of God, holy and beloved, bowels of mercies, kindness, humbleness of mind, meekness, longsuffering;

"Forebearing one another, and forgiving one another, if any man have a quarrel against any: even as Christ forgave you, so also do ye.

"And above all these things put on charity, which is the bond of perfectness.

"And let the peace of God rule in your hearts to the which also ye are called in one body; and be ye thankful" (Colossians 3:11-15).

As we "watch and listen" we learn to sing the song of rejoicing together as ONE in Christ. "And again he saith, Rejoice, ye Gentiles, with his people" (Romans 15:10).

Robert Johnson

❀

December 2

SINGING SCRIPTURE: **Ecclesiastes 2:8**

I gathered also silver and gold, and the peculiar treasures of kings and of the provinces; I got men singers and women

*singers, and the delights of the sons of men, as musical
instruments, and that of all sorts.*

This is the last verse of the listing of the accumulated treasures,
accomplishments, and assorted pleasures Solomon presents as
proof of his greatness, wealth, and wisdom. Then, as he looks over
everything he has gained, he pronounces it all unsatisfactory and
lacking in lasting value. The climax of his compilation of pleasures
and riches is a picture of delightful vocal and instrumental music.
Yet, it too fails to meet his real need. Why?

We find the answer in the last two verses of this significant
autobiography.

Let us hear the conclusion of the whole matter: Fear God, and
keep his commandments; for this is the whole duty of man. For God
shall bring every work into judgment, with every secret thing,
whether it be good, or whether it be evil.''

Solomon shows throughout the book that worldly things, whether
they are riches, wisdom, or pleasure, vanish. He concludes that
keeping the commandments brings eternal value. This does not in
any way encourage the life of a hermit. Instead, this mighty king is
stating that a life of faith expressed by works (for the Lord)
prepares man to stand before God. "Fear God" (faith); "keep his
commandments'' (works).

Music is a worthy pursuit, unlifting and edifying, but it fails to
effect a change in man unless it carries a meaningful message. That
message must speak of eternal values and not merely passing
pleasures.

Ed Lyman

December 3

SINGING SCRIPTURE: **Psalm 32:7**

*Thou art my hiding place; thou shalt preserve me from
trouble; thou shalt compass me about with songs of deliverance.*

God is involved in every effort to make Jesus Christ known to a
wandering, wondering world. Music as a method of communication
expresses many of the inner reactions of a person to his external
experiences and impressions. People experience many things such
as love, beauty, sorrow, and loneliness. Music has the capacity to

express these emotions. So, we can say that God has provided music as a means of communicating the experiences of the soul: soul music.

Volume, rhythm, tempo, and tone, by integration and combination, may express a variety of moods and feelings.

In this way, a capable composer or skilled arranger can put together musical patterns that speak to the hearts of listeners and performers alike and encourage a response.

Certain musical forms and sounds are associated with certain experiences. However, the message in the words makes a particular piece a gospel song or Christian hymn. As the music and lyrics of a certain song remind us of spiritual experiences, we lift our thoughts to God, Who is our help and hope for time and eternity.

Ed Lyman

December 4

PRAISE PSALM: **Psalm 112:1**

Praise ye the Lord. Blessed is the man that feareth the Lord, that delighteth greatly in his commandments.

This "fear" is that of reverence rather than dread and it evokes a spirit of praise and thanksgiving. Praising God should be the believer's chief expression of worship. It is the "service of song" of the sanctuary. To hang our harps upon the willows is like saying, "Christ is not Lord."

As we delight in His Word and His worship, we enjoy the delightfulness and refreshment of His commandments. That's why no child of God ever falls suddenly into the morass of sin. All slippage starts in unwatchfulness and neglect of the Word of God. The awareness of God's presence becomes dulled by the incursion of Satanic deception. The mind and heart of the saint turns from the precepts of the Lord, the snare tightens, and sin takes over. The devil often operates like the practiced con-artist. He allows his dupes some brief success along the way in order that he may completely strip them of everything. More and more sin piles up and the captive is held fast in the chains of self-righteousness and deceptive security. If, through confidence in ourselves or in worldly wisdom, we refuse the counsel of God and His Word, the Lord may leave us to ourselves in order that we may prove first-hand that our wisdom is pure folly.

Ed Lyman

December 5

SINGING SCRIPTURE: **1 Chronicles 16:33**

> *Then shall the trees of the wood sing out at the presence of the Lord, because he cometh to judge the earth.*

The Old Testament has many poetic expressions; in fact, the Hebrew language is very picturesque in nature. Rather than speaking literally, the writer is affirming that even nature responds and reflects the presence and glory of God, not only by sight, but by sound.

What would your reaction be if you stood in a forest of towering pines as they swayed in orchestrated choreography and produced diapason tones from the rush of the winds through the leafy branches? Would you not sense they were responding in choral "Alleluias" directed by the Master Conductor? Ah! it demands a committed, sensitive spirit to follow the Master's direction and hear the music He produces in nature.

The writer is implying that the presence of the Lord is so majestic and glorious that any creature encountering His presence cannot refrain from responding with choral "Glorias!"

Any instrument placed in the Master's hand can produce melodious sounds. Experiencing the presence of the Lord releases and energizes a person to respond in a life and actions thought impossible and unexpected. Trees sing? God produce music and harmony through my life? Oh! what God could do with us if we gave these instruments to Him in unqualified obedience. As D.L. Moody was challenged, "The world has yet to see what God can do with a life totally yielded to Him."

What about me? Dare I expose myself to His presence? Shall I let Him tune the strings of my life and make music to touch others?

Jack Aebersold

December 6

SINGING SCRIPTURE: **Psalm 69:30**

> *I will praise the name of God with a song, and will magnify him with thanksgiving.*

When Jenny Lind, the great Swedish nightingale, was crossing the ocean on her way to the United States for her first concert tour, she expressed a desire to watch a sunrise at sea. The captain of the ship was happy to comply with this request and invited her to the bridge the next morning.

She stood silently by his side, not moving at all in the early dawn, and watched the changing hues and shades in the sky and their reflections in the waking waters.

Then, the golden rays of the sun burst from the horizon and she filled the calm with rapturous song. It seemed that she was unconscious of the presence of the captain and the seamen, who stood nearby, as she expressed her deep inner feelings and lifted her voice as if to an unseen hearer.

She was paying a musical tribute to the majesty and glory of the Creator, whom she seemed to know personally.

It is not difficult to understand why Captain West, as he described this stirring scene, exclaimed, "No one will ever hear 'I Know That My Redeemer Liveth' sung as I heard it that morning."

Ed Lyman

December 7

SINGING SCRIPTURE: **Matthew 6:2**

Therefore, when thou doest thine alms, do not sound a trumpet before thee, as the hypocrites do in the synagogues and in the streets, that they may have glory from men. Verily I say unto you, They have their reward.

This is the meaning of "blowing your own horn." These hypocrites — actors wearing masks — had the wrong idea about giving. Their acts of religious observance did not correspond with an inward spiritual depth. Human praise was their goal and that's exactly what they received — and *all* they received. Jesus said there would be no further reward, they were *paid in full*.

Many had the idea that the giving of alms would atone for their sins and it could be said that they went about making money music for all to hear as a means of showing their outward conformity to the demands of their religious tradition. However, the louder the "money music" sounded, the less spiritual was the act of giving. Jesus said, "Take heed that ye do not your alms before men, to be seen by them; otherwise, ye have no reward of your Father, who is in heaven" (Matthew 6:1). Jesus was not only referring to the giving of tithes and offerings, but to any righteous act. "Lay not up for yourselves treasures upon earth, where moth and rust doth corrupt, and where thieves break through and steal, But lay up for yourselves treasures in heaven ... For where your treasure is, there will your heart be also" (Matthew 6:19-21).

Ed Lyman

December 8

PRAISE PSALM: **Psalm 89:5**

And the heavens shall praise thy wonders, O Lord: thy faithfulness also in the congregation of the saints.

Music is a major factor in bringing people to the church. It is a very powerful medium. Just keep your ears open today and take note of all the places you hear music. First in your home — your clock radio with the disc jockey playing the bright, happy tunes to get you up and going. Then in the kitchen, or the car, listening to the singing commercials. Why are so many of the commercials set to music? Because of the power of music to help you remember the message. Can you quote three, two, or even one poem you memorized in your early school days? Probably not. But think of all the songs you have learned — and can still sing — with all the words. Why? Because music is such a potent vehicle for carrying a message. Look how in recent years the morality of the Western World has been affected more by music and the message it carries than by any other influence. Sadly to say, for the worse. But we can use it for good! For, when music inspires, exalts the Lord, and reaches hearts, people will be blessed. And when people are blessed, they will fill the church and along with other saints will add their voices, hearts, and minds in grateful praise to their Redeemer. "*Let us* sing of *our* Redeemer and His wondrous love to *us!*"

David E. Williams

December 9

SINGING SCRIPTURE: **2 Samuel 22:50**

Therefore, I will give thanks unto thee, O Lord, among the heathen, and I will sing praises unto thy name.

Names and titles are important! I've often had people ask me the name of a song in order to identify it for their own use at a later time. Many of the Psalms have names and these titles indicate the purpose or meaning of the psalm, such as: "A Psalm of David, when he fled from Absalom, his son" (Psalm 3) or "To the chief Musician, A Psalm of David, to bring to remembrance" (Psalm 70). David often directed his songs and music to the NAME of the Lord and this becomes a strong reminder that it is through His name that "we live, and move, and have our being" (Acts 17:28).

Charles Haddon Spurgeon, the English preacher, said, "In these days we call children by names which have no particular meaning. But it was not so in olden times. Then names meant something. Especially is this the case in every name ascribed to the Lord Jesus.

'His name shall be called Wonderful, Counselor, the mighty God, The everlasting Father, the Prince of Peace' (Isaiah 9:6) because He really is all these things.

His name is called Jesus because no other name could fairly describe His great work of saving His people from their sins.

His name is Immanuel — 'God with us' — because there is no pang that rends the heart but what Jesus has been with us in it all. In the fires and in the rivers, in the cold night and under the burning sun, He cries, 'I am with thee: be not dismayed; for I am thy God.' "

Ed Lyman

December 10

SINGING SCRIPTURE: **II Chronicles 23:18**

Also Jehoida appointed the offices of the house of the Lord by the hand of the priests the Levites, whom David had distributed in the house of the Lord, to offer the burnt offerings of the Lord, as it is written in the law of Moses, with rejoicing and with singing, as it was ordained by David.

Queen Athaliah, daughter of Jezebel, thought she had put down all of the potential rulers of the kingdom, but had not reckoned on the brave and daring rescue of the tiny boy, Joash, who later became king. The story of how Athaliah was destroyed is described very clearly in 2 Kings 11 and also repeated in 2 Chronicles 23. However, in this ancient chronicle, something is added: "They sang with joy as they worked" (Living Bible).

This intriguing little phrase regarding music is one of those delightful sidelights in God's Word. Often the cleansing of the kingdom and the freedom from idolatry and the quiet revolution of a nation into a period of renaissance and revival will bring forth such singing as only a troubled people can sing after difficulties have ceased. Upon the destruction of idols in our lives, which hinder us from the relationship we should have with the Lord, we too should rejoice even as the people did in this marvelous little story. As the people found respite from trouble and riot, there was cause for singing. Verse 18 is a quiet little accent regarding the results of faith and prayer and cleansing. The quietness and peacefulness of resting in the Lord includes the music of the singing heart.

Merv Rosell

December 11

SINGING SCRIPTURE: **Proverbs 25:20**

As he that taketh away a garment in cold weather, and as vinegar upon nitre, so is he that singeth songs to an heavy heart.

At first reading, this verse seems to stand in direct contradiction to everything else we understand the Bible to say about the uplift and enlightenment music can be to those, who are sad and lonely. Such a conclusion is absolutely false and we must read the verse in light of the context of this whole passage of Scripture. The Living Bible puts it into proper perspective: "Being happy-go-lucky around a person whose heart is heavy is as bad as stealing his jacket in cold weather, or rubbing salt into his wounds." The singing of songs in this context has to do with light-hearted frivolity; non-sensical ditties. However, this verse also sustains the truth that proper musical understanding can be curative.

Music is like a medicine for many disorders.

It soothes when we are disturbed. It cheers when we are disconsolate. It softens the bitter and hardened heart.

It drives away anger. It calms fears.

We may never know just how much suffering and sorrow has been eased and assuaged by music.

It is a balm to the spirit and a healing for the soul.

Ed Lyman

December 12

SINGING SCRIPTURE: **Isaiah 23:15, 16**

And it shall come to pass in that day, that Tyre shall be forgotten seventy years, according to the days of one king; after the end of seventy years shall Tyre sing as an harlot. Take an harp, go about the city, thou harlot that hast been forgotten; make sweet melody, sing many songs, that thou mayest be remembered.

One of the great themes of the book of Isaiah is the judgment of God upon pride. Tyre — "a rock" — had its ups and downs in the ancient world. She was trampled under foot again and again, yet seemingly always able to rise from her own rubble and resume her role as "merchant of the nations" (Isaiah 23:3). God has declared her doom, because of her sinful pride and corruption. For the seventy-year period of the Babylonian captivity of God's people, "the days of one king," a lifetime, Judah was in exile and Tyre was a desolation. By means of music to attract her lost lovers — those merchants and men of wealth — she seeks to restore her once dominant and distinctive trade business. Material gain and financial satisfaction, like a clinging seductress, make the music of merchandising echo through the chart rooms of commerce. This is the technique of the modern singing commercial — appealing to the senses.

Tyre's failure is the direct result of her misplaced faith and perennial pride — trusting in her energy and ability. Tyre had periods of success in between the times of destruction and decline, but her spiritual instability eventually brought the judgment of God upon her pride — the plague of man's selfishness — and she, "the rock city," was pulverized.

Instead of the seeking song of sensuality, which leads to despair and disillusionment, under the power of conversion to the Lord Jesus Christ, a chorale of commitment can become the expression of consecrated involvement in the service of the Savior.

Ed Lyman

December 13

PRAISE PSALM: **Psalm 113:3**

From the rising of the sun unto the going down of the same, the Lord's name is to be praised.

Wouldn't it be great if we would live so as to allow God to bless us one day at a time? None of us knows what will happen on any given day and if we allow ourselves to be distressed or even overly concerned about this, we won't do anything. The Bible tells us that if a farmer doesn't plant his crops because he is afraid of a possible drought, he'll not produce a harvest. He must have faith to go ahead with his activity.

Events in this life can change from day to day. Yet, we do know that being busy about our calling and attempting to do our work well develops assurance, satisfaction, a sense of well-being no matter what comes our way, and hope.

For those, who believe, God's blessings are renewed one day at a time and yesterday's storms and clouds can enhance today's sunshine.

"Consider the lilies how they grow. They toil not, they spin not; and yet I say unto you that Solomon, in all his glory, was not arrayed like one of these. If, then, God so clothed the grass, which is today in the field, and tomorrow is cast into the oven, how much will he clothe you, O ye of little faith?" (Luke 12:27, 28).

Songs of praise accompany the marvelous ways the Lord blesses our days!

Ed Lyman

December 14

SINGING SCRIPTURE: **2 Chronicles 20:21**

And when he had consulted with the people, he appointed singers unto the Lord, who should praise the beauty of holiness, as they went out before the army, and to say, Praise the Lord; for his mercy endureth forever.

Jehoshaphat, king of Judah, followed not in the paths of his wicked father, but walked in the way of the Lord. His life of faith was blessed by God in a marvelous and miraculous reign. Jehoshaphat's prayer to his sovereign God, as the host of the enemy came to attack, is eloquent in its simplicity and humble in its plea: O our God, wilt thou not judge them? For we have no might against this great company that cometh against us, neither know we what to do; but our eyes are upon thee" (2 Chronicles 20:12).

He wasn't testing God, he was trusting fully — totally depending upon the Lord for his life and that of his people.

The result of putting himself in the hand of God was that God lifted him up and made this promise: "Be not afraid nor dismayed by reason of this great multitude; for the battle is not yours, but God's" (2 Chronicles 20:15b).

With absolute confidence in the Word of the Lord, Jehoshaphat assured his people, "Believe in the Lord your God, so shall ye be established; believe in his prophets, so shall ye prosper" (2 Chronicles 20:20b).

Before an arrow was strung or a spear flung in the battle to take place, Jehoshaphat called a practice session for his musicians, gave them a new song of praise to prepare, and then signalled the downbeat for the Lord's song of victory — a paean of praise to God, Who allows no enemy weapons to touch his children, who live in His will.

Ed Lyman

December 15

SINGING SCRIPTURE: **Exodus 15:1**

Then sang Moses and the children of Israel this song unto the Lord, and spoke, saying, I will sing unto the Lord, for he hath triumphed gloriously: the horse and his rider hath he thrown into the sea.

The Children of Israel stood on the banks of the Red Sea and sang the first song of the Bible. The pursuing host of Pharaoh had been overthrown. The sea that had been a way of life to Israel had become a way of death to Pharaoh's army.

Psalm 77 says: "Thy ways, O Lord are in thy sanctuary" and again: "Thy ways, O Lord are in the sea."

They looked first to the sanctuary and then to the sea and the sea opened. So, they sang.

Hebrews tells us: "By faith, Israel crossed the Red Sea,but the Egyptians, trying to do so, drowned in the sea."

The two groups were from the same section of the Nile, they traveled in the same direction, took the same turns, encountered the same obstacles, but here the similarity ended. One group went over and one went under. What made the difference? One group pursued the promises of God. The other pursued their property. This is the difference between life and death!

The first song of the Bible was a song of redemption and deliverance. The last song of the Bible is of redemption and deliverance.

Revelation tells us that the theme song the redeemed of the ages will sing is, "Glory to the Lamb. This is redemption. We have overcome. This is deliverance." This song goes on and never ends and "he that liveth and believeth shall never die."

James T. Johnson

December 16

PRAISE PSALM: **Psalm 96:4**

For the Lord is great, and greatly to be praised: he is to be feared above all gods.

It is said of Napoleon that while he was reviewing his army one day, his horse became frightened, and the Emperor lost his rein, and the horse went away at full speed, and the Emperor's life was in danger. A private in the ranks saw it, and sprang towards the horse succeeding in getting hold of the horse's head at the peril of his own life.

The Emperor was very much pleased and, touching his hat, he said to him: "I make you Captain of my Guard." The soldier threw his gun away and went up to where the body-guard stood. The captain of the body-guard ordered him back into the ranks, but he said: "No! I won't go!" "Why not?" "Because I am Captain of the Guard." "You Captain of the Guard?" "Yes," replied the soldier. "Who said it?" and the man, pointing to the Emperor, said, "He said it." That was enough. Nothing more could be said. He took the Emperor at his word. My friends, if God says anything, let us take Him at His word. "He that believeth on the Lord Jesus Christ shall not perish, but have everlasting life." Don't you believe it? Don't you believe you have got eternal life? It can be the privilege of every child of God to believe and then know that you have got it.

I believe hundreds of Christian people are being deceived by Satan now on this point, that they have not got the assurance of salvation just because they are not willing to take God at His word. Sing it: "Blessed Assurance, Jesus IS mine."

Dwight L. Moody

December 17

SINGING SCRIPTURE: **1 Samuel 29:5**

Is not this David, of whom they sang one to another in dances, saying, Saul slew his thousands, and David his ten thousands?

The phrase "Saul hath slain his thousands, and David his ten thousands" is found three times in the book of Samuel (1 Samuel 18:7, 1 Samuel 21:11, and 1 Samuel 29:5). This had become a popular song in the land of Israel and had even spread beyond the borders to be known also in other countries. David's fame spread on the wings of song. So significant was the song that its truth carried a very emphatic message of warning and reminder that God's special blessing was upon His servant, David — and His people, Israel.

Upon learning David's identity, that song immediately came to the mind of those present. The song itself came about not because David pursued position and primacy, but because David preferred intimacy with the Lord and God blessed and honored him.

The identify of David was a natural outgrowth of his closeness to the Lord. The result was the enabling of God for affective witness.

The identity of the Christian is directly related to his intimacy with the Lord Jesus Christ.

Ed Lyman

---------------- ❁ ----------------

December 18

SINGING SCRIPTURE: **Luke 1:67-79 (This is called "Zacharias' Song")**

And his father Zacharias was filled with the Holy Ghost, and prophesied, saying,

Blessed be the Lord God of Israel; for he hath visited and redeemed his people,

And hath raised up an horn of salvation for us in the house of his servant David;

As he spake by the mouth of his holy prophets, which have been since the world began:

That we should be saved from our enemies, and from the hand of all that hate us:

To perform the mercy promised to our fathers, and to remember his holy covenant;

The oath which he sware to our father Abraham,

That he would grant unto us, that we being delivered out of the hand of our enemies might serve him without fear,

In holiness and righteousness before him, all the days of our life.

And thou, child, shalt be called the prophet of the Highest: for thou shalt go before the face of the Lord to prepare his ways;

To give knowledge of salvation unto his people by the remission of their sins,

Through the tender mercy of our God; whereby the dayspring from on high hath visited us,

To give light to them that sit in darkness and in the shadow of death, to guide our feet into the way of peace.

Zacharias

December 19

SINGING SCRIPTURE: **Hebrews 10:5-7 (This is known as "The Christmas Carol Jesus Sang")**

Wherefore when he cometh into the world, he saith,

"Sacrifice and offering thou wouldest not,
but a body hast thou prepared me:
In burnt offerings and sacrifices for sin
thou hast had no pleasure.
Then said I,
Lo, I come (in the volume of the book it is written of me.)
to do thy will,
O God."

These words had first been recorded in Psalm 40, but as Jesus came into the world, He placed into this passage a newer, deeper, and greater meaning. This is His Christmas carol stating that He came to do the will of His Father, Who sent Him. He did not come to magnify Himself. He came to be despised and rejected by men, to be acquainted with grief, to be a man of sorrows. He came to declare God's righteousness and to provide God's salvation. At this holiday season, it would do us well to lay aside the tinsel and trappings of commercial Christmas and listen to the words of the Christmas carol Jesus sang!

Ed Lyman

December 20

SINGING SCRIPTURE: **Luke 1:39-45 (This is called "Elizabeth's Song")**

*And Mary arose in those days, and went into the hill country
with haste, into a city of Juda;
And entered into the house of Zacharias, and saluted
Elizabeth.
And it came to pass, that, when Elizabeth heard the salutation
of Mary, the babe leaped in her womb; and Elizabeth was
filled with the Holy Ghost:
And she spake out with a loud voice, and said,*

Blessed art thou among women, and blessed is the fruit of thy womb.
And whence is this to me, that the mother of my Lord should come to me?
For, lo, as soon as the voice of thy salutation sounded in mine ears, the babe leaped in my womb for joy.
And blessed is she that believed: for there shall be a performance of those things which were told her from the Lord.

Elizabeth

December 21

SINGING SCRIPTURE: **Psalm 68:32**

*Sing unto God, ye kingdoms of the earth; oh, sing praises unto
the Lord, Selah.*

"And suddenly there was with the angel a multitude of the heavenly host, praising God, and saying, Glory to God in the highest, and on earth peace, good will toward men" (Luke 2:13, 14).

The very essence of the angelic announcement to the shepherds in the hilly fields near Bethlehem is a musical expression of praise, gladness, and worship. "And the angel said unto them, Fear not; for behold, I bring you good tidings of great joy, which shall be to all people. For unto you is born this day in the city of David, a Savior, who is Christ the Lord" (Luke 2:10, 11).

After seeing the new-born king, "the shepherds returned, glorifying and praising God for all the things they had heard and seen" (Luke 2:20).

Knox translated Isaiah's prophecy concerning the coming of the Messiah as an anthem of adoration: "For our sakes a child is born, to our race a song is given, whose shoulder will bear the scepter of princely power. What name shall be given him? Peerless among counsellors, the mighty God, Father of the world to come, the Prince of peace. Even wider shall his dominion spread, endlessly at peace; he will sit on David's kingly throne, to give it lasting foundations of justice and right; so tenderly he loves us, the Lord of hosts."

This is Christ-music at Christmas!

Ed Lyman

December 22

SINGING SCRIPTURE: **Psalm 150:5**

Praise him upon the loud cymbals; praise him upon the high sounding cymbals.

Here is a majestic proclamation of significant musical proportions. In volume and tonal range, as John R. W. Stott says, it is "the uninhibited exuberance of lives devoted to God." This is praise to the Lord in joyful adoration with loud and high sounding cymbals climaxing the musical exclamation of worship.

At this time of year — Christmas — the Christian has reason to burst forth in exuberant praise at God's demonstration of His love and grace; "Before anything else existed ... THERE WAS CHRIST, WITH GOD. He created everything ... ETERNAL LIFE IS IN HIM ... LIGHT to all mankind. Who, though He was God ... laid aside His mighty power and glory ... becoming like men." Praise Him with the loud cymbals!

Then, as shepherds watched their sheep at night, an angel appeared. "Don't be afraid," he said, "The SAVIOR — yes, the MESSIAH, the Lord — has been born tonight in BETHLEHEM!"

"So JESUS grew both tall and wise, and was loved by God and man. For GOD sent CHRIST JESUS to take the punishment of sins. He used CHRIST'S blood and our faith as the means of saving us. Yes, what JOY there is for anyone whose sins are no longer counted against him, by the LORD." Praise Him with the high-sounding cymbals!

Could anyone possibly say it better? God's unspeakable GIFT! After all, the LIGHT OF THE WORLD is sure to shine brighter than ever when our globe seems so dark. Praise Him with the cymbals of singing certainty — and put CHRIST back in CHRISTmas!

Vi and Merv Rosell

December 23

SINGING SCRIPTURE: **Psalm 66:4**

All the earth shall worship thee, and shall sing unto thee; they shall sing to thy name. Selah.

Amos Wells once wrote a poem entitled, "The Inn that Missed Its Chance." Just think about it! If those people had only known that the name of this Babe of Bethlehem, for Whom there was no room, would one day be that Name placed above every name in the whole world in time or eternity; if they had only known that the story of the birth, life, and death of this One would be the theme of a Book, which would be the best seller of all time, be translated into over a thousand languages and dialects, which would be read by more people, travel down more highways, penetrate more jungles, bring comfort to more hearts than any other book; if they had only known that over four hundred million of this earth's people would one day acknowledge themselves as His followers; if they had only known that He would be history's central Figure, philosophy's greatest Personality, art's greatest Inspiration, music's loveliest Theme, literature's chief Character; if they had only known that in all the world one day there would be found schools, hospitals, institutions, and organizations founded upon His Name; if they had only known that He was God's Son, the promised Messiah, earth's only Hope, the coming King of glory, how quickly and gladly would they have made room for Him!

You know Who He is. You know why He came. Have you made room for Him?

James T. Johnson

December 24

SINGING SCRIPTURE: **Revelation 11:15**

And the seventh angel sounded; and there were great voices in heaven, saying, The kingdoms of this world is become the kingdom of our Lord, and of his Christ, and he shall reign forever and ever.

I don't have any way of knowing whether the wise men from the east had any musical talents or abilities. However, after following this heavenly body over those long, tiring desert trails, coming to Jerusalem for information about a newborn king, and then being disappointed in the apparent lack of information concerning the Child and the event, they must have been overjoyed at again seeing the star. "When they saw the star, they rejoiced with exceeding great joy" (Matthew 2:10). I would like to have been there when they caught the first glimpse after leaving the devious Herod. I'm sure their rejoicing must have resulted in at least an attempt at singing as they headed to Bethlehem.

"And when they were come into the house, they saw the young child with Mary, his mother, and fell down, and worshipped him." Truly, they came before His presence with songs of praise and rejoicing. One day, we shall join the mighty chorus of worshipping believers in that eternal kingdom of God.

Napoleon once soliloquized, "I die before my time. My body will be given back to the earth to be done with as men please and to become the food of worms. Such will be the fate of him who has been called the Great Napoleon. What an abyss between my deep misery and the external Kingdom of Christ, which is proclaimed, loved, and adored, and is extending over the whole earth!"

Ed Lyman

December 25

SINGING SCRIPTURE: **Luke 1:46-55 (This is called "Mary's Song")**

And Mary said,

My soul doth magnify the Lord.
And my spirit hath rejoiced in God my Savior.
For he hath regarded the low estate of his handmaiden: for behold, from henceforth all generations shall call me blessed.
For he that is mighty hath done to me great things; and holy is his name.
And his mercy is on them that fear him from generation to generation.
He hath shewed strength with his arm; he hath scattered the proud in the imagination of their hearts.
He hath put down the mighty from their seats, and exalted them of low degree.

He hath filled the hungry with good things; and the rich he hath sent empty away.
He hath holpen his servant Israel, in remembrance of his mercy;
As he spake to our fathers, to Abraham, and to his seed forever.

Mary

December 26

SINGING SCRIPTURE: **Romans 10:18**

But I say, Have they not heard? Yes, verily, their sound went into all the earth, and their words unto the ends of the world.

When we sing, "Give the winds a mighty voice," I wonder what registers in our minds. Though the apostle Paul was not familiar with the technology of our age, he served the God of technology. Quoting from Psalm 19, he speaks of communication as a "sound...into all the earth." Since this is precisely what radio is all about as sound waves dance and sing from pole to pole, how wonderful it is to know that through modern media we can share "The Sound of Christmas" with those, who have never heard.

The silent night was broken
When Jesus Christ was born;
The heav'nly Voice had spoken
With SOUND like Gabr'el's horn.

That SOUND of jubilation
Announced the holy birth
Of one who brought salvation
To man on Planet Earth.

Today that SOUND reminds us
That He who came that night
Is living, real and precious
To those who walk in light.

But millions sit in darkness
They do not know our Lord;
Let us with joy and gladness
"SOUND out" the saving Word.

All glory in the highest,
Peace and good will to men,
Grace reaches to the lowest —
Praise be to God — Amen!

S.F.O.

Like the angels who broke through from heaven, we can tell the world of "good tidings of great joy, which shall be to all people."

Stephen F. Olford

December 27

SINGING SCRIPTURE: **Luke 2:4-14 (This is called "The Angels' Song")**

And Joseph also went up from Galilee, out of the city of Nazareth, into Judaea, unto the city of David, which is called Bethlehem; (because he was of the house and lineage of David:)
To be taxed with Mary his espoused wife, being great with child.
And so it was, that while they were there, the days were accomplished that she should be delivered.
And she brought forth her firstborn son, and wrapped him in swaddling clothes, and laid him in a manger; because there was no room for them in the inn.
And there were in the same country shepherds abiding in the field, keeping watch over their flock by night.
And lo the angel of the Lord came upon them, and the glory of the Lord shone round about them: and they were sore afraid.
And the angel said unto them, Fear not: for, behold, I bring you good tidings of great joy, which shall be to all people.
For unto you is born this day in the city of David a Savior, which is Christ the Lord.
And This shall be a sign unto you; Ye shall find the babe wrapped in swaddling clothes, lying in a manger.
And suddenly there was with the angel a multitude of the heavenly host praising God, and saying,

"Glory to God in the highest, and on earth peace, good will toward men."

When Jesus was born, night was turned to day as the glory light dispatched the darkness over those hills where the shepherds were watching their flocks. He came to bring new light and life. He took the darkness of our sin upon Himself so we could become the children of light. Now we can walk in His light and become reflectors and dispensers of His light in this dark world. How can we cease praising Him?

Deoram Bholan

December 28

PRAISE PSALM: **Psalm 113:1**

Praise ye the Lord. Praise, O ye servants of the Lord, praise the name of the Lord.

What's in a name?
Is there an adequate answer?
The reminder we've just read, "praise the name of the Lord", cannot help but bring to our lips musical expressions of thanksgiving and adoration, which have become favorites over the years. These particular songs are esteemed by us because of significant circumstances or situations, which have been very meaningful, with which the melodies or lyrics are associated. Perhaps people have contributed to the experiences, which make musical memories. Our praise is directly related to the truth that "there is none other name under heaven given among men, whereby we must be saved" (Acts 4:12).

"His Name is Wonderful," says the song and He is worthy of our praise. "Wherefore God also hath highly exalted him, and given him a name which is above every name: That at the name of Jesus every knee should bow, of things in heaven, and things in earth, and things under the earth; and that every tongue should confess that Jesus Christ is Lord, to the glory of God the Father" (Philippians 2:9-11).

"Praise ye the Lord." Lift your hearts and voices in carols of gratitude for "whosoever shall call on the name of the Lord shall be saved" (Acts 2:21).

Ed Lyman

December 29

SINGING SCRIPTURE: **Revelation 5:11-14 (This is called "The Song of Praise to the Lamb")**

And I beheld, and I heard the voice of many angels round about the throne and the beasts and the elders and the number of them was ten thousand times ten thousand, and thousands and thousands;
Saying with a loud voice,

Worthy is the Lamb that was slain to receive power, and riches, and wisdom, and strength, and honor, and glory, and blessing.

And every creature which is in heaven, and on the earth, and under the earth, and such as are in the sea, and all that are in them, heard I saying,

Blessing, and honor, and glory, and power, be unto him that sitteth upon the throne, and unto the Lamb for ever and ever.

And the four beasts said, Amen. And the four and twenty elders fell down and worshipped him that liveth for ever and ever.

So then, come my Savior, Lord,
I am done with earth and sin.
If the mansions there are finished,
Come and take your children in.
We would join our feeble voices
With the angel host on high;
Singing, "Praise Him, Hallelujah!"
While His glory fills the sky.

Bruce Weber

December 30

SINGING SCRIPTURE: 2 Chronicles 30:21

And the children of Israel that were present at Jerusalem, kept the feast of unleavened bread seven days with great gladness: and the Levites and the priests praised the Lord day by day, singing with loud instruments unto the Lord.

I continue to be amazed and blessed by the fact that whenever singing is mentioned in the Bible, it is usually in connection with a happy occasion. This verse is a perfect illustration. The children of Israel were celebrating a feast, a joyous time, and what were they doing? They were singing. Let's bring it up to date.

Have you listened to the lyrics of today's songs?

Heartbreak, misery, bad times, drugs, "She done me wrong," etc.

As a matter of fact, not only the lyrics, but the music as well, is often a damning statement about the validity and believability of the present world system. How wrenching, how awful, to have created a vacuum with nothing to put in its place! The music of the world is often a wail of despair and loneliness. Contrast that with the music of heaven: music, which was present at creation, present at the birth of Christ, and which will be present at His second coming. Then too, try to imagine the thrill of singing together in the choirs of heaven. Heaven's music: for the Christian, not a hoped-for song "perhaps someday," but available today because of the One, who came to set us free and set our hearts to singing.

Steve Musto

December 31

SINGING SCRIPTURE: **Zechariah 9:14, 15a**

And the Lord shall be seen over them, and his arrow shall go forth like the lightning; and the Lord God shall blow the trumpet, and shall go with the whirlwinds of the south. The Lord of hosts shall defend them.

The old year passes. We are familiar with it. The new year begins. It is an uncharted course. As we sing of the memories of past pleasures and make music of merriment in launching the vessel of life into the waters of the new year, it is well to be reminded that the Lord does have a place, a plan, and a purpose for our lives. Knowing the speed with which time passes, we should tune up the song of service in order to he ready for the call of the Lord in this new year. As the words of the Isaac Watts hymn states, "Time, like an ever rolling stream, Bears all its sons away."

Perhaps, as we begin this new year, we can be inspired by the words of Abraham Lincoln as he left Springfield, Illinois on February 11, 1861 to take up the duties and responsibilities of President!

My friends: No one not in my position can realize the sadness I feel at this parting. To this people I owe all that I am. Here I lived more than a quarter of a century. Here my children were born, and here one of them lies buried. I know not how soon I shall see you again. I go to assume a task more difficult than that which has devolved upon any other man since the days of Washington. He never would have succeeded except for the aid of Divine Providence, upon which he at all times relied. I feel that I cannot succeed without the same divine blessing which sustained him; and on the same Almighty Being I place my reliance for support. And I hope you, my friends, will all pray that I may receive that divine assistance, without which I cannot succeed, but with which success is certain. Again, I bid you an affectionate farewell."

Ed Lyman

INDEX

Judges 5:12	SS	Ed Lyman	May 21
Judges 6:34	SS	Ed Lyman	March 22
Ruth 1:16,17	SS	Ed Lyman	November 2
1 Samuel 2:1-4	SS	John Fletcher	March 11
1 Samuel 10:5,6	SS	Ed Lyman	November 9
1 Samuel 13:3	SS	Winfield F. Ruelke	March 24
1 Samuel 16:16	SS	Robert and RoseMarie Lehmann	April 3
1 Samuel 16:17	SS	Don Wyrtzen	April 9
1 Samuel 16:18	SS	Douglas E. Schoen	April 16
1 Samuel 16:23	SS	Ed Lyman	November 28
1 Samuel 18:6	SS	Mark Moore	April 29
1 Samuel 21:11	SS	Ed Lyman	April 26
1 Samuel 29:5	SS	Ed Lyman	December 17
2 Samuel 6:5	SS	Douglas E. Schoen	May 11
2 Samuel 22:1	SS	Ed Lyman	May 27
2 Samuel 22:50	SS	Ed Lyman	December 9
2 Samuel 23:1-5	SS	Ed Lyman	June 8
1 Kings 1:39,40	SS	Ed Lyman	November 16
1 Kings 4:29,32	SS	Ed Lyman	March 23
1 Kings 10:12	SS	Ed Lyman	April 7
2 Kings 3:15	SS	Ed Lyman	February 7
1 Chronicles 6:31, 32;23:30	SS	Oswald J. Smith	June 23
1 Chronicles 9:33	SS	Ed Lyman	February 9
1 Chronicles 13:8	SS	Mark Moore	July 8
1 Chronicles 15:16	SS	Ed Lyman	March 12
1 Chronicles 15:19	SS	Jack Schurman	August 10
1 Chronicles 15:22	SS	Anonymous	October 29
1 Chronicles 15:24	SS	Ed Lyman	January 31
1 Chronicles 15:27	SS	Ed Lyman	January 24
1 Chronicles 15:28	SS	Douglas E. Schoen	November 14
1 Chronicles 16:7	SS	David	November 8
1 Chronicles 16:9	SS	Norman J. Clayton	November 18
1 Chronicles 16:23	SS	Merv Rosell	November 23
1 Chronicles 16:33	SS	Jack Aebersold	December 5
1 Chronicles 16:37,39,42	SS	Ed Lyman	January 10
1 Chronicles 25:1a,7	SS	Ed Lyman	September 5

Psalm 27:6	SS	Jack Schurman	July 17
Psalm 28:7	SS	Ed Lyman	September 12
Psalm 30:4	SS	Stephen Cushman	June 27
Psalm 30:9	PP	Ed Lyman	April 14
Psalm 30:12	SS	Ed Lyman	September 21
Psalm 32:7	SS	Ed Lyman	December 3
Psalm 33:1	PP	Ed Lyman	April 5
Psalm 33:2	SS	James H. Blackstone, Jr.	September 29
Psalm 33:3	SS	Ed Lyman	July 11
Psalm 34:1	PP	Ed Lyman	April 25
Psalm 35:18	PP	Dwight L. Moody	February 21
Psalm 35:28	PP	Ed Lyman	May 2
Psalm 40:3	SS	Donald J. Jost	July 19
Psalm 42:4	PP	Ed Lyman	May 10
Psalm 42:5	PP	George Whitefield	March 1
Psalm 42:8	SS	Donald J. Jost	August 1
Psalm 42:11	PP	Ed Lyman	May 23
Psalm 43:4	SS	John DeBrine	August 5
Psalm 43:5	PP	Robert P. Evans	March 10
Psalm 44:8	PP	George S. Schuler	April 2
Psalm 45:17	PP	Ed Lyman	May 31
Psalm 47:5	SS	Jim & Diane Montgomery	November 29
Psalm 47:6	SS	Ed Lyman	October 3
Psalm 47:7	SS	Ed Lyman	August 14
Psalm 48:1	PP	George S. Schuler	July 26
Psalm 48:10	PP	Ted and Pat Cowen	April 28
Psalm 49:16-18	PP	Ed Lyman	June 10
Psalm 50:23	PP	Ed Lyman	June 17
Psalm 51:14	SS	Ed Lyman	October 10
Psalm 51:15	PP	Ed Lyman	June 25
Psalm 52:9	PP	Winfield F. Ruelke	August 4
Psalm 54:6	PP	Robert P. Evans	August 23
Psalm 56:4	PP	Ed Lyman	June 29
Psalm 56:10	PP	Ed Lyman	July 7
Psalm 56:12	PP	Ed Lyman	July 14
Psalm 57:7	SS	Bill Salisbury	October 21
Psalm 57:8	SS	Ed Lyman	October 13
Psalm 57:9	SS	J. Allen Blair	August 18
Psalm 59:16	SS	Ron Boud	July 12
Psalm 59:17	SS	Ed Lyman	October 22
Psalm 61:8	SS	Ed Lyman	October 30
Psalm 63:3	PP	Ed Lyman	July 18
Psalm 63:5	PP	Ed Lyman	July 31
Psalm 65:1	PP	Ed Lyman	August 7
Psalm 65:13	SS	Kenneth E. Moon	August 28
Psalm 66:2	SS	Ed Lyman	November 5
Psalm 66:4	SS	James T. Johnson	December 23

Psalm 105:2	SS	Ed Lyman	April 21
Psalm 105:45	PP	Ed Lyman	October 20
Psalm 106:1	PP	Bill Salisbury	April 17
Psalm 106:12	SS	Ed Lyman	April 11
Psalm 106:47	PP	Paul Crosson	April 10
Psalm 106:48	PP	Ed Lyman	October 24
Psalm 107:8,15,21,31	PP	Ed Lyman	October 27
Psalm 108:1,2	SS	Oswald J. Smith	October 11
Psalm 108:3	SS	Ed Lyman	April 4
Psalm 109:1	PP	Ed Lyman	November 1
Psalm 109:30	PP	Ed Lyman	November 7
Psalm 111:1	PP	Ed Lyman	November 11
Psalm 111:10	PP	Ed Lyman	November 27
Psalm 112:1	PP	Ed Lyman	December 4
Psalm 113:1	PP	Ed Lyman	December 28
Psalm 113:3	PP	Ed Lyman	December 13
Psalm 113:9	PP	Ed Lyman	April 8
Psalm 115:17	PP	Ed Lyman	November 19
Psalm 115:18	PP	Ed Lyman	September 19
Psalm 116:18,19	PP	Ed Lyman	August 19
Psalm 117:1,2	PP	Ed Lyman	May 19
Psalm 118:14	SS	Ed Lyman	March 26
Psalm 118:19	PP	Ed Lyman	August 27
Psalm 118:21	PP	Ed Lyman	September 3
Psalm 118:28	PP	David	March 25
Psalm 119:7	PP	Ed Lyman	September 16
Psalm 119:54	SS	Ed Lyman	March 16
Psalm 119:164	PP	Ed Lyman	October 4
Psalm 119:171	PP	Ed Lyman	August 12
Psalm 126:2	SS	Steve Musto	January 20
Psalm 135:1	PP	Ed Lyman	July 22
Psalm 135:3	SS	Ed Lyman	March 3
Psalm 135:21	PP	Ed Lyman	July 10
Psalm 137:2	SS	Ed Lyman	February 24
Psalm 137:3	SS	William H. Beeby	September 22
Psalm 137:4	SS	Ed Lyman	February 16
Psalm 138:1	SS	Ed Lyman	February 11
Psalm 138:2	PP	E. Barry Moore	March 17
Psalm 138:5	SS	Ed Lyman	January 28
Psalm 139:14	PP	Ed Lyman	July 2
Psalm 142:7	PP	Ed Lyman	June 22
Psalm 144:9	SS	Deoram Bholan	October 15
Psalm 145:2	PP	Ed Lyman	June 14
Psalm 145:3	PP	Ed Lyman	June 6
Psalm 145:4	PP	Ed Lyman	June 3
Psalm 145:7	SS	Gordon L. Purdy	January 22
Psalm 145:10	PP	Ed Lyman	May 26

Isaiah 26:19	SS	Ed Lyman	July 6
Isaiah 30:29	SS	Ed Lyman	July 16
Isaiah 35:1,2	SS	Ed Lyman	June 20
Isaiah 35:6	SS	Ed Lyman	June 11
Isaiah 35:10	SS	Ed Lyman	May 24
Isaiah 38:9-17	SS	Hezekiah	July 21
Isaiah 38:20	SS	Ed Lyman	May 4
Isaiah 42:10	SS	Ed Lyman	March 29
Isaiah 42:11	SS	Ron Boud	July 25
Isaiah 44:23	SS	James H. Blackstone, Jr.	June 15
Isaiah 49:13	SS	Ed Lyman	March 9
Isaiah 51:3	SS	John Song	February 1
Isaiah 51:11	SS	John C. Hallett	March 15
Isaiah 52:8	SS	Russell B. Gordon	June 24
Isaiah 52:9	SS	Ev Gourlay	June 30
Isaiah 54:1	SS	Deoram Bholan	April 27
Isaiah 55:12	SS	Don Wyrtzen	May 15
Isaiah 65:14	SS	Merrill Dunlop	September 4
Jeremiah 20:13	SS	John Blanchard	February 8
Jeremiah 31:7	SS	Dave Breese	April 22
Jeremiah 31:12	SS	John A. Beerley	May 18
Jeremiah 33:11	SS	J. Allen Blair	March 27
Lamentations 3:14	SS	Ed Lyman	October 28
Ezekiel 26:13	SS	Ed Lyman	October 14
Ezekiel 27:25	SS	John A. Beerley	April 6
Ezekiel 33:2-5	SS	Ed Lyman	July 4
Ezekiel 33:32	SS	Ed Lyman	February 27
Daniel 3:5,6 (7,10,15)	SS	John Blanchard	March 5
Daniel 3:14,15	SS	Ed Lyman	October 2
Hosea 2:15	SS	Ed Lyman and James T. Johnson	September 24
Hosea 5:8,9	SS	Ed Lyman	April 30
Hosea 8:1	SS	Ed Lyman	April 15
Joel 2:15	SS	Merrill Dunlop	March 20
Amos 5:23	SS	Ed Lyman	September 10
Amos 6:1a,5	SS	Ed Lyman	June 26

Ephesians 5:19	SS	James H. Blackstone, Jr.	March 7
Colossians 3:16	SS	Ed Lyman	February 13
1 Thessalonians 4:16,17	SS	Ed Lyman	January 18
1 Thessalonians 5:16	SS	Ed Lyman	January 12
Hebrews 2:11,12	SS	Roy W. Gustafson	January 7
Hebrews 10:5-7	SS	Ed Lyman	December 19
James 5:13	SS	Ed Lyman	January 3
3 John 3	SS	Ed Lyman	January 25
Revelation 5:9,10	SS	Keith Whiticar	February 2
Revelation 5:11-14	SS	Bruce Weber	December 29
Revelation 11:15	SS	Ed Lyman	December 24
Revelation 14:3	SS	Ed Lyman	July 15
Revelation 15:2	SS	Ed Lyman	August 8
Revelation 15:3	SS	George S. Schuler	June 21
Revelation 18:22	SS	Ed Lyman	September 13

INDEX
of Contributing Writers

Laycock, Ernest L.	Psalm 79:13
Lehmann, Robert and RoseMarie	1 Samuel 13:3
Lyke, Dorothy	Psalm 71:22
Lyman, Talin	Psalm 150:3; Isaiah 5:12
Martinez, Homer	2 Chronicles 29:28
Mary	Luke 1:46-55
Mayfield, Larry	Psalm 96:1
Montgomery, Jim and Diane	Psalm 47:5
Moody, Dwight L.	Psalm 35:18; Psalm 71:8; Psalm 96:4; Psalm 100:4
Moon, Kenneth E.	Psalm 65:13
Moore, E. Barry	Psalm 138:2; Psalm 150:6
Moore, Mark	1 Samuel 18:6; 1 Chronicles 13:8
Musto, Steve	2 Chronicles 30:21; Psalm 126:2
Nader, Fred	Psalm 150
Norwood, Ralph	Psalm 22:22
Olford, Stephen F.	Romans 10:10
Paul	Matthew 24:31; 1 Corinthians 13:1-13
Purdy, Gordon L.	Psalm 145:7
Rosell, Merv	1 Chronicles 16:23; 2 Chronicles 23:18; Psalm 150:5
Ruelke, Winfield F.	1 Samuel 13:3; Psalm 52:9
Salisbury, Bill	Psalm 13:6; Psalm 57:7; Psalm 106:1
Sankey, Ira	Judges 5:3
Schoen, Douglas E.	1 Samuel 16:18; 2 Samuel 6:5; 1 Chronicles 15:28; Psalm 81:1
Schuler, George S.	Psalm 44:8; Psalm 48:1; Revelation 15:3
Schurman, Jack	1 Chronicles 15:19; Psalm 27:6; Psalm 86:12
Smith, Oswald J.	1 Chronicles 6:31, 32; 23:30; Psalm 108:1, 2
Smith, Paul B.	Psalm 22:25; Isaiah 12:2; 1 Corinthians 14:7
Song, John	Isaiah 51:3
TeDeum	Psalm 146:1
Trout, Lynette	Isaiah 14:7
Weber, Bruce	Revelation 5:11-14
Whitefield, George	Psalm 48:5
Whiticar, Keith	Psalm 67:4; Proverbs 29:6; Revelation 5:9, 10
Williams, David E.	Psalm 7:17; Psalm 71:23; Psalm 89:5; Psalm 146:2
Wyrtzen, Don	1 Samuel 16:17; Isaiah 55:12
Zecharias	Luke 1:67-79
Zimmerman, Tim	1 Corinthians 15:52